IMAGES
of America

DeLand

This book is dedicated
to the memory of Henry Addison DeLand and John Batterson Stetson
without whom the town of DeLand would not exist as we know and love it today.
Their vision for DeLand as "The Athens of Florida" caused them energetically to pursue
their dream until it was brought to fruition;
with heartfelt thanks to past entrepreneurs and citizens, lost names, and faded images;
and to present residents and future generations whom we encourage to hold steadfast
to the goals and the dreams of Henry and John.

IMAGES of America

DeLand

Maggi Smith Hall, Michael Justin Holder,
and the West Volusia Historical Society

ARCADIA
PUBLISHING

ISBN 978-0-7385-1575-5

Published by Arcadia Publishing
Charleston, South Carolina

Printed in the United States of America

Library of Congress Catalog Card Number: 2003109645

For all general information contact Arcadia Publishing at:
Telephone 843-853-2070
Fax 843-853-0044
E-mail sales@arcadiapublishing.com
For customer service and orders:
Toll-Free 1-888-313-2665

Visit us on the Internet at www.arcadiapublishing.com

ACKNOWLEDGMENTS

This book became reality because Jackie Kersh, a volunteer for the West Volusia Historical Society, cared. The exhaustive process involved in selecting, securing, and scanning photographs confirmed Kersh's commitment for preserving DeLand's pictorial past. For her unrelenting work ethic, patience, and resolve in getting this book to the publisher on time, these authors humbly bow down to her.

To Bill Dreggors, West Volusia Historical Society's Executive Director, appreciation is extended for his keen memory and proofreading skills. His ability to ferret out false information assured us safe printing.

Sincere gratitude travels across the continent to Jay Mechling, a Stetson University graduate, for sharing his extensive DeLand postcard collection with the historical society.

To DeLand residents Jeanne and Hubert Henderson, whose photographs of Hayden Street inspire us all, a sincere and hearty thank you.

CONTENTS

About the Authors

Maggi Smith Hall is a native Floridian from Jacksonville. She holds a B.A. from Stetson University in DeLand, Florida and an M. Ed. from Francis Marion University in Florence, South Carolina.

During her 30 years as a South Carolina educator, she established two educational institutions, the Marion County Museum and the Fork Retch Environmental Education Center. While a museum director she also directed the South Carolina Rural Arts Program for Marion County. For these endeavors she received local, state, and national recognition including the South Carolina State Archives Award for "Adaptive Restoration of an Historic Facility" (an 1886 schoolhouse listed on the National Register of Historic Places as the longest operating public school in South Carolina), the 1993 National Environmental Women of Action Award for South Carolina, and the 1995 SC Wildlife Federation Education Conservationist Award. Due to her environmental work she was in two national film documentaries, *Conserving America: The Rivers*, for efforts to preserve the Little Pee Dee River, and *When A Tree Falls*, for halting a highway through wetlands. For those activities Hall was interviewed in the July 1995 issue of *Southern Living*.

Since returning to Florida Hall has written for St. Augustine and DeLand newspapers, environmental magazines, and placed second in two national writing contests. In 1999 Tailored Tours Publications published her first book, *Flavors of St. Augustine: An Historic Cookbook*. Her second, *Images of America: St. Augustine*, was published in 2002 by Arcadia Publishing. At present she is writing a book that addresses teachers' rights as citizens.

Hall is a preservationist, having restored over a dozen properties in South Carolina and Florida. While living in St. Augustine and selling real estate, she worked extensively with historic properties. After moving back to DeLand in 1999, she initiated an urban-renewal project in a depressed area of architecturally significant buildings. Hall owns West Volusia Properties, a real estate firm, sits on DeLand's Code Enforcement Board, and chairs MainStreet DeLand's Design Committee. Hall is married to Ronald, chairman of the Philosophy Department at Stetson University. Their family includes two daughters and their husbands, four grandchildren, three dogs, and numerous grand animals.

Michael Justin Holder was born in Georgia, raised in South Carolina, but calls Florida home. He is a graduate of the University of Florida with a major in English and a minor in art. While at UF, Holder wrote for *Student Leader*, a national student magazine. A promising scholar on the Beat Generation, Holder's style of prose can be compared to that of his favorite author, Jack Kerouac.

Holder's preferred art medium is charcoal, which he uses with extreme precision in sketching the images of musicians from Bob Marley to Charlie Parker. Besides art, listening to jazz, reading, writing, and watching baseball, his hobbies also include landscape design and old-house restoration.

Holder is a graduate English major at Stetson University and employed as a realtor for West Volusia Properties. He is married to Maggi Hall's daughter, Erin, a veterinarian. Their family includes one child, two dogs, three cats, and two birds.

At present the Holders and the Halls are restoring three 1930s Craftsman Style Bungalow Cottages for use as a veterinary hospital.

INTRODUCTION

High noon, February 8, 1882, the town of DeLand, originally known as Persimmon Hollow, was incorporated by a unanimous vote of its 23 townspeople. However, human existence had its roots deep in the sandy soil of Central Florida long before DeLand was created or the state of Florida even imagined.

The Timucua Indians were the first inhabitants of this land we now call Volusia County. In "Memoir of Escalante Fontaneda," Fontaneda, a shipwrecked Spaniard who found refuge with the Timucuan, wrote that the area was known to its earliest people as Mayaca, "the fresh water province." And indeed the description fits as the county is bordered to its west and south by the northerly bound St. Johns River. West Volusia, where DeLand, the county seat, is located, is marked with crystal-clear spring-fed streams whose headwaters originate in the Appalachian Mountain range to flow silently and swiftly underground to their destination in the limestone caverns of the vicinity.

During the English occupation of Florida from 1763 to 1783, pioneers north of Florida migrated across the St. Mary's River searching for warmer weather and richer soil. In 1821 when Florida became a United States territory, an even greater influx of settlers moved to the peninsula. They fought the Seminoles for land these Native Americans had been granted by the government. Of course the Indians lost and with their departure into the Everglades of South Florida, the population of Central Florida increased. Cattle cowboys and dirt farmers multiplied and eventually Persimmon Hollow was born.

Lauded for its natural beauty and conservation of its environment, the city of DeLand sits atop a geological formation known as the Volusia Ridge, a worn-down mountain range that predates civilization by millions of years. Its fertile soil nurtures massive live oaks, towering pines, and hearty ferns that sprout without so much as a nutritious act on the part of man. Poinsettias and hibiscus abound, as do non-native camphor trees, noted for their sturdy climbing branches. Of course, though, the favorite tree among DeLand residents is the ubiquitous citrus—orange, grapefruit, lemon, and lime—species by the dozens found growing in cultivated yards throughout the area and originally introduced into Florida in the 1500s by Spanish explorers.

Persimmon Hollow's name change took place after the generous donation of acreage for a school, church, and main thoroughfare by Henry Addison DeLand, a wealthy entrepreneur from Fairport, New York. DeLand first visited the carved-out little hollow of a community with his brother-in-law, O.P. Terry, who had purchased property to raise oranges. Terry, impressed with the favorable agricultural opportunities, encouraged DeLand to accompany him on a trip south.

March 1876 found the men traveling by rail to Jacksonville, then a steamboat up the St. Johns to Enterprise, and finally a rig to the hollow. DeLand was unenthusiastic during his bumpy ride from Enterprise but as the flat terrain transitioned from swamp to rolling acreage, it was reported that DeLand exclaimed, "This looks like the West. Here is snap and push. I am willing to go on." And so he did.

In October 1876 DeLand returned to Persimmon Hollow to assist in the establishment of the town. That same year the settlers voted at their December meeting to name the community "DeLand" in honor of the man whose vision for growth and fervor for citrus production was captured in the hearts of many.

Henry Addison DeLand became the driving force behind education and culture in his fledgling adopted town. In 1884 he contributed $10,000 to build DeLand Academy, forerunner of Stetson University. A hundred years after its construction, the building still bears Mr. DeLand's name and is listed on the National Register of Historic Places as the oldest academic building in continuous use for higher education in the state of Florida.

Henry DeLand proudly boasted that DeLand was the "Athens of Florida" due to its unique cultural and educational attributes. The nomenclature followed the city until the late 1920s when the Florida Land Bust, caused by the Great Depression, hit town.

At present the former hamlet of Persimmon Hollow faces the onslaught of Orlando's voracious growth appetite. It is gratifying though that both Volusia County and the City of DeLand actively pursue the purchase of land for conservation in order to protect their natural resources.

DeLand's downtown was listed on the National Register of Historic Places in 1985. In that same year DeLand was the first community chosen in Florida to receive MainStreet designation, thereby becoming a part of a nationally acclaimed program established to promote the revitalization of America's downtown areas affected by urban sprawl. City officials then created DeLand's Downtown Tax Increment District in order to fund on-going downtown redevelopment.

In 1997 MainStreet DeLand received "The Great American MainStreet" Award from the National Historic Trust. From 1999 to 2002, DeLand was named the "Best Main Street" in Florida. Is it any wonder then that downtown's locally owned outdoor cafes and quaint shops entice residents to shop at home rather than at rambling nondescript malls 20 miles east in Daytona Beach or 35 miles south in Orlando?

DeLand maintains its cultural events and remains home to Stetson University, one of the leading educational institutions in the nation. DeLand has an active art community and museum, a preeminent historical society determined to preserve the city's heritage, and numerous supportive civic organizations. The city government works diligently to offer its residents a quality lifestyle, revering its historical ambiance, while encouraging responsible development.

Stately trees shade the streets, many planted during Henry DeLand's tenure as town leader. There is a tranquility in DeLand that predates the town's founding and continues into the 21st century. DeLand has a sense of place, a sense of community that began decades ago in the heart and mind of Henry Addison DeLand and those who supported his dream for a better life.

Indeed, DeLand as the "Athens of Florida" continues to thrive thanks to those who created it and to those who keep it flourishing.

One

Homesteading the Frontier

Abundant timber, freshwater springs, wildlife, and productive soil brought homesteaders to Central Florida's vast uninhabited terrain. Although small communities sprouted like weeds along the main waterways surrounding present-day DeLand, the area originally known as Persimmon Hollow remained unsettled for decades after the United States purchased Florida in 1821. Legend has it that the little hollow east of the big river was so laden with wild persimmons that it drew an abundance of foraging game, especially quail and deer. In turn such a plentiful source of game provided a popular and productive hunting ground for early Native Americans as well as arriving settlers.

The year 1874 brought the first pioneer to the area, John Rich, a decorated Union captain, who was not afraid of adventure or laborious work. Accompanied by his wife, Clara Wright, Rich filed his homestead, cleared his newly acquired land, built a cabin, and planted crops. Several other spirited pioneers joined the Rich family including Cyrenius Wright, Clara's brother; J.S. Craig; and O.P. Terry.

Life was not easy that first year, but the dauntless few strengthened its numbers with the Hollow's first birth, Clara Belle Rich. Other firsts occurred in 1875: Benjamin Colcord and Anna Kirk were the first married; J.B. Jordan opened the first store; and Dr. Lancaster became the first druggist.

But it was not until O.P. Terry persuaded his brother-in-law, Henry A. DeLand, to come south for a visit in March 1876, that Persimmon Hollow's future was secured. History does not indicate whether DeLand was more impressed with Clara Rich's fried chicken or the verdant orange groves planted by the settlers, but whatever it was, Henry DeLand was hooked. He proclaimed that he could "see for great distances through the tall pine trees." Within hours of rolling into Persimmon Hollow, Henry DeLand was the satisfied owner of 159 acres located between present-day New York Avenue and extending east from present-day Clara to Amelia Avenues.

DeLand, a visionary, returned to Persimmon Hollow in October, purchased additional acreage, called for a town meeting to present his dreams and schemes to the settlers, and set in motion the beginnings of the town we have today.

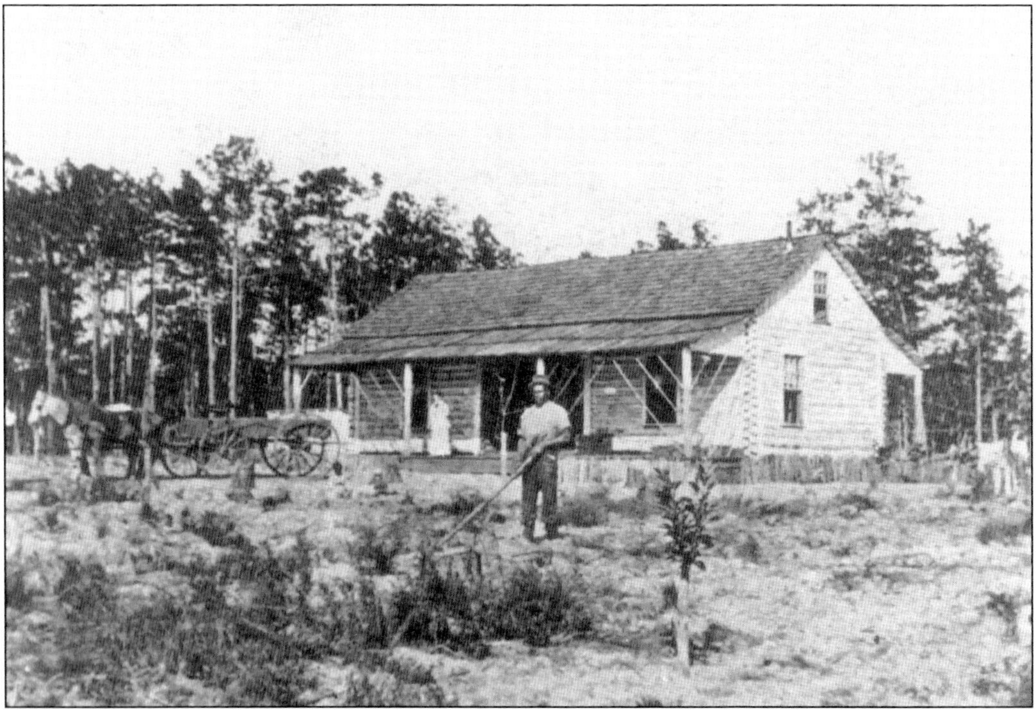

The Rich pole cabin was constructed in 1875 from long-leaf pine, a once plentiful natural commodity along the Volusia Ridge. A plaque now designates the cabin's original location at the corner of Delaware and West New York Avenues.

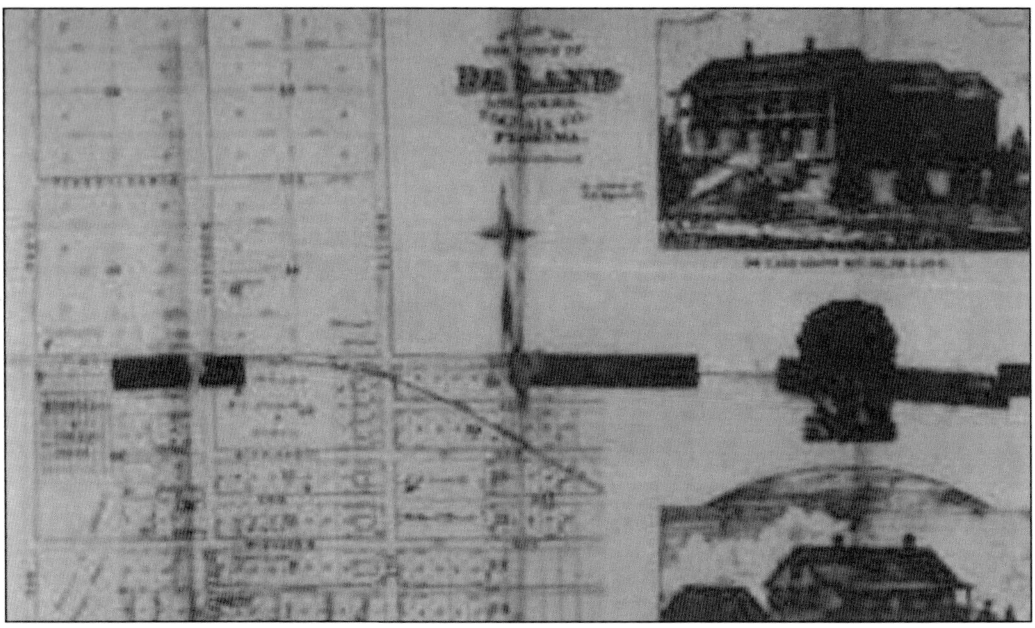

Within two years of Henry DeLand's proposed expansion for the town, an 1878 map indicated how rapidly the community had grown. Mr. DeLand intended for DeLand to become a cultural and educational center, the "Athens of Florida," he promised. This old graphic chart seemed to indicate that his dream was quickly becoming a reality.

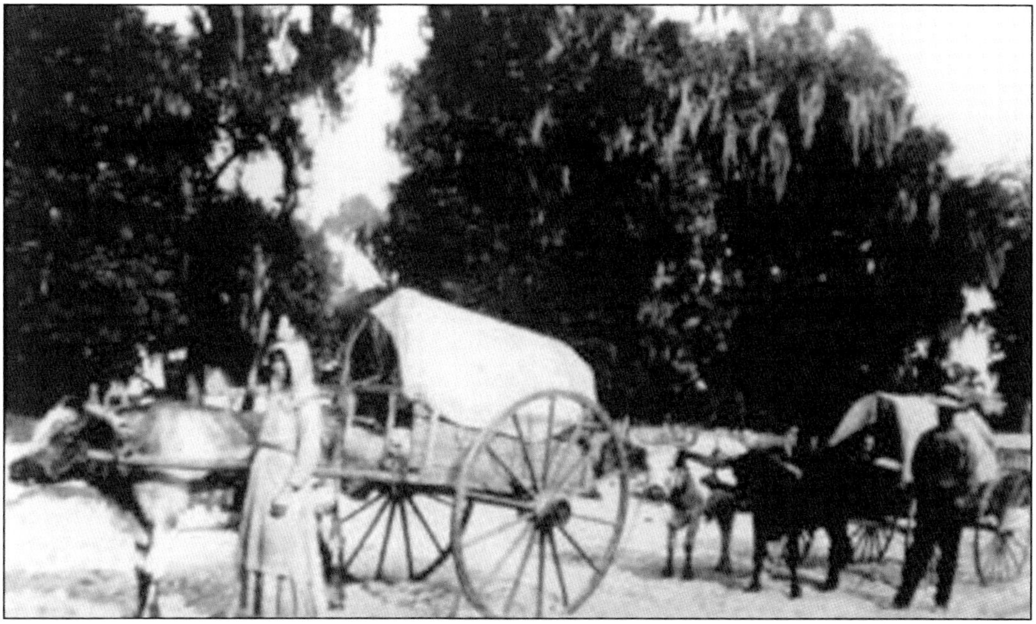

Land was cleared for additional streets while original dirt lanes were renamed for early settlers: Amelia Avenue for Amelia Leete, Henry DeLand's sister; Clara Avenue, for Captain Rich's wife; and Rich Avenue for the first pioneer family. During this exciting time, many more families arrived in town to begin a new life in this new Florida frontier.

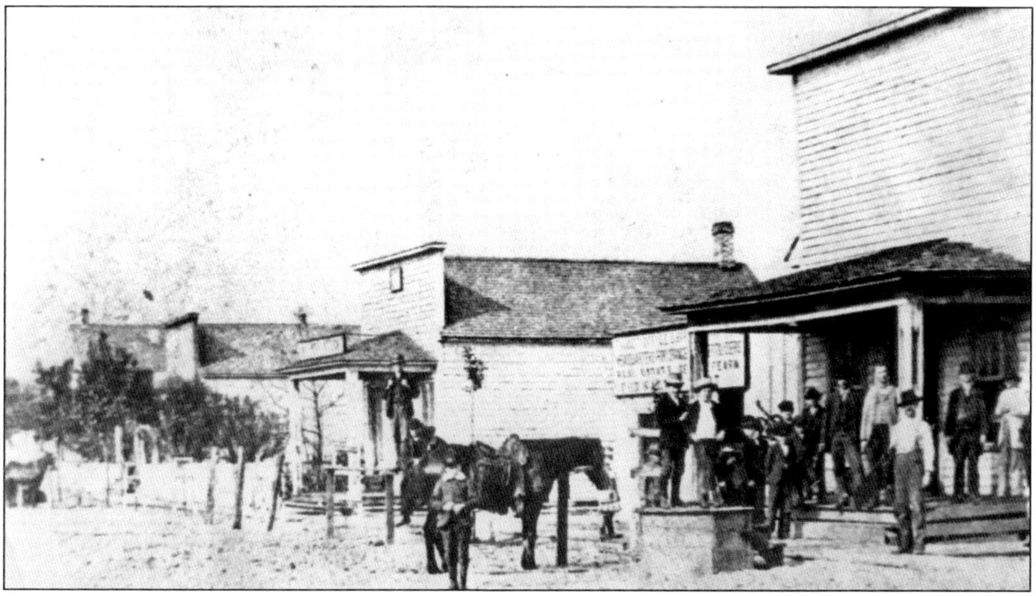

This 1882 photograph shows several newly constructed frame buildings on the southwest corner of Woodland Boulevard (popularly called the Boulevard) and Indiana Avenue. Although the streets were dusty and the mode of transportation sweaty, men dressed for work in long-sleeve cotton shirts and pants, and some wore coats and covered their heads with felt or straw hats. No matter the dress, they took seriously their responsibility to pose for posterity in the shining Florida sun.

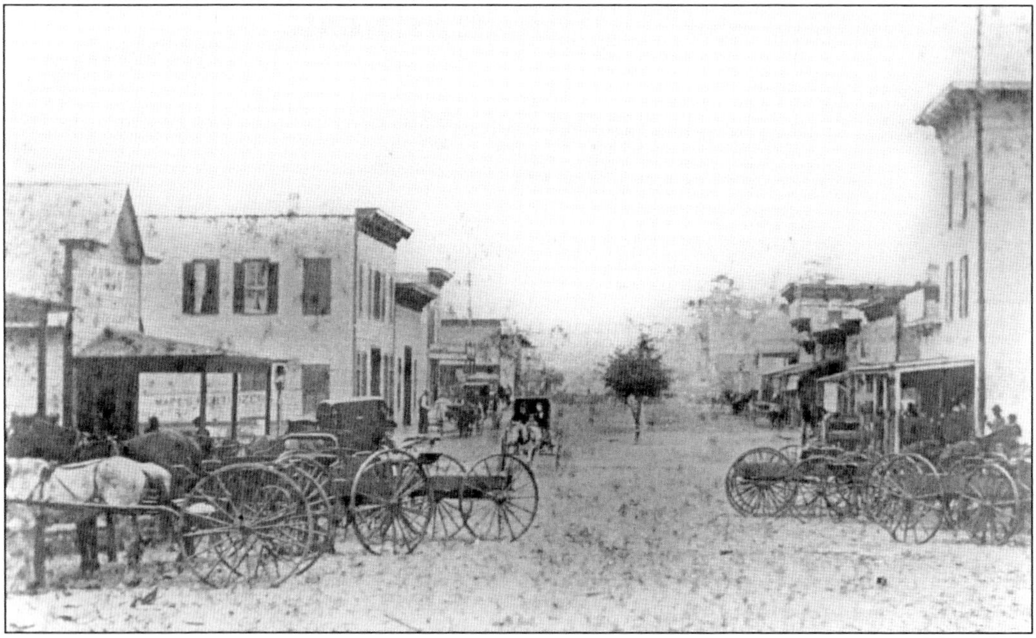

In the late 1880s a Department of Immigration pamphlet listed the following for DeLand: three general stores, a drug store, furniture store, millinery, post office with daily mail, phone service, several boarding houses, a church, school, livery stable, newspaper, two sawmills, a wagon factory, blacksmith shop, two physicians, two dentists, two lawyers, a library, and even a literary society. Indeed, DeLand was moving up. A year later more frame structures were erected on both sides of the Boulevard north from New York. Buggies brought customers to town for shopping and bartering. Per Henry DeLand's request, oak trees were planted in the median down the Boulevard, later to be extensively damaged by horseback riders using the sapling trunks for hitching posts.

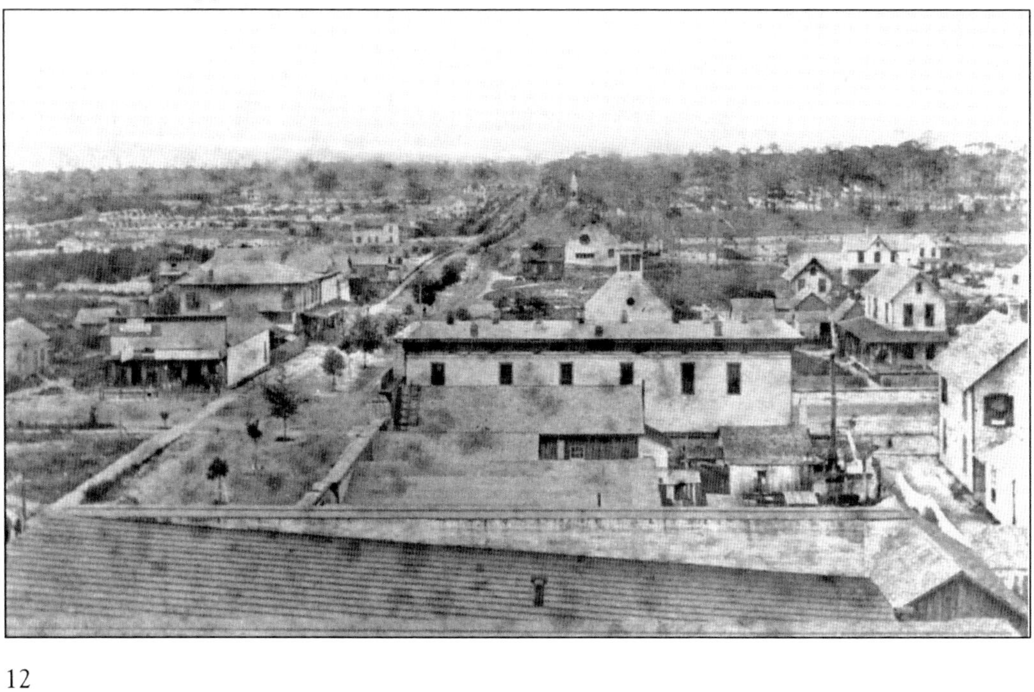

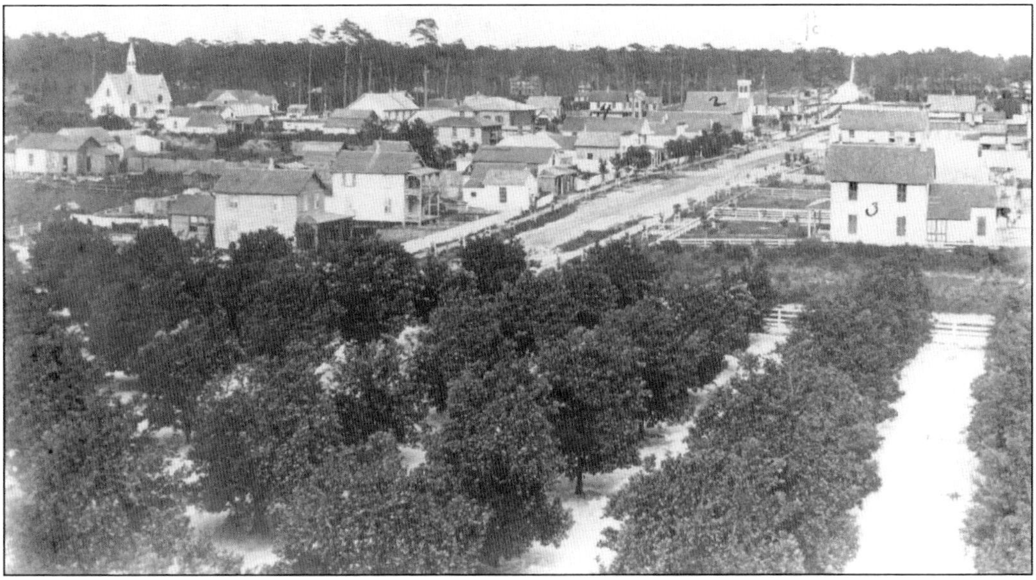

By the end of 1883 the town stretched north, south, east, and west. Both views are from the roof of the newly constructed Putnam Hotel; the top looks east on Indiana; the bottom, east on New York. The Boulevard is seen in the distance (top) with the First Baptist Church in the upper left-hand corner. The lush orange grove surrounding the Putnam offered its guests freshly squeezed juice and lush ambrosia in season. The Athens Theatre is presently located where the grove once existed. Ross Carriage Shop (bottom) was an active supplier of all possible needs for the town's early transportation system.

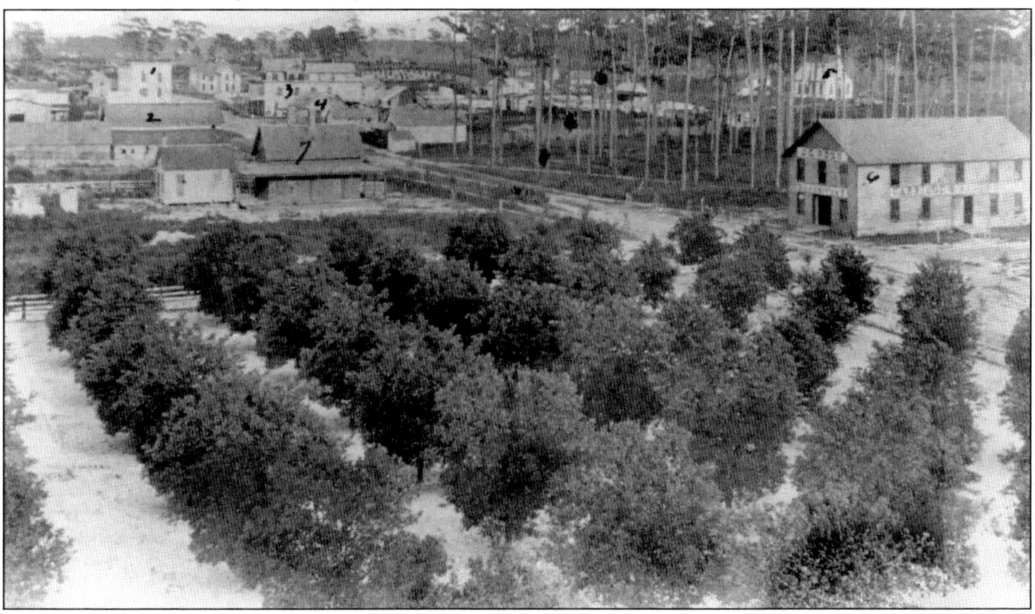

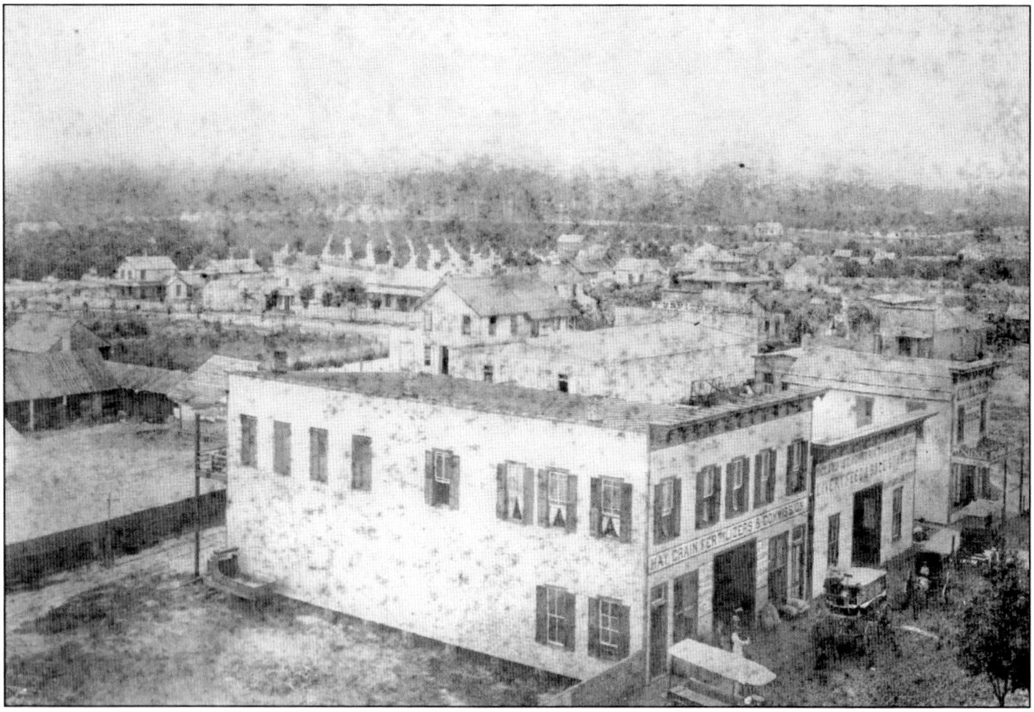

Persimmon Hollow was carved from a pine forest. As the town expanded, Mother Nature's bounty gave way to cultivated orange groves and buildings. The 100 block of North Boulevard, a wide dirt road, became lined with frame businesses. Beyond the commercial area homes were built from the city's dwindling pines. What once had been the lush paradise that brought early settlers to the area became a densely populated community of frame buildings, dirt roads, and alas, bare land.

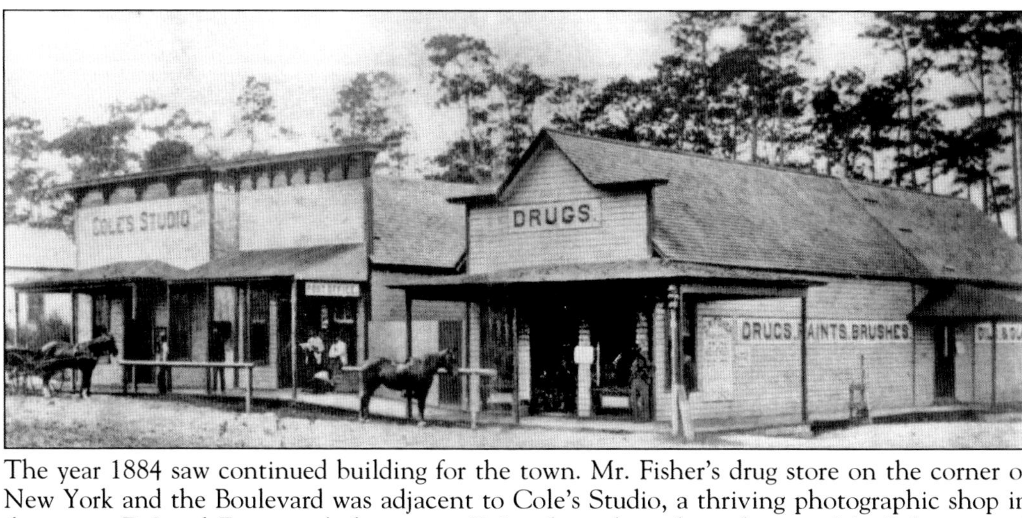

The year 1884 saw continued building for the town. Mr. Fisher's drug store on the corner of New York and the Boulevard was adjacent to Cole's Studio, a thriving photographic shop in downtown DeLand. Fortunately for present DeLandites, throughout the years Mr. Cole captured DeLand's growth spurt on film.

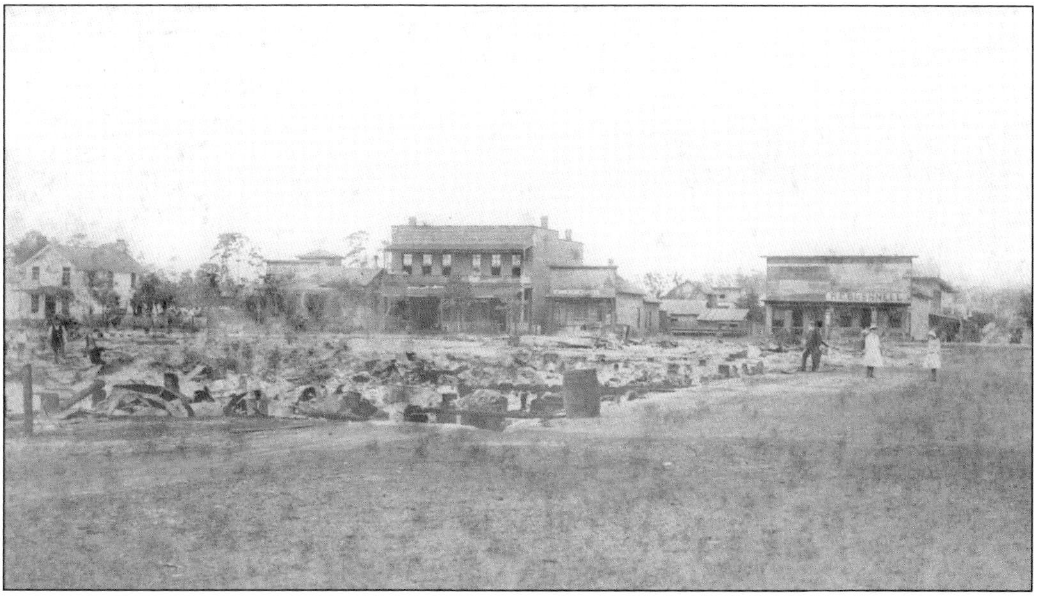

Heart of pine makes for grand buildings; it is also fodder for even grander flames. And so it was in the early hours of September 27, 1886. DeLand's first conflagration, which destroyed an entire city block and dozens of buildings, began at the rear of the Wilcox Saloon on the Boulevard. In the early days many saloons had sawdust floors to accommodate chewing tobacco juices and rowdy, sloppy drinkers. On occasion, an abandoned yet still smoldering cigar butt could easily hide amidst sawdust and spittle to ignite after a group had retired for the evening.

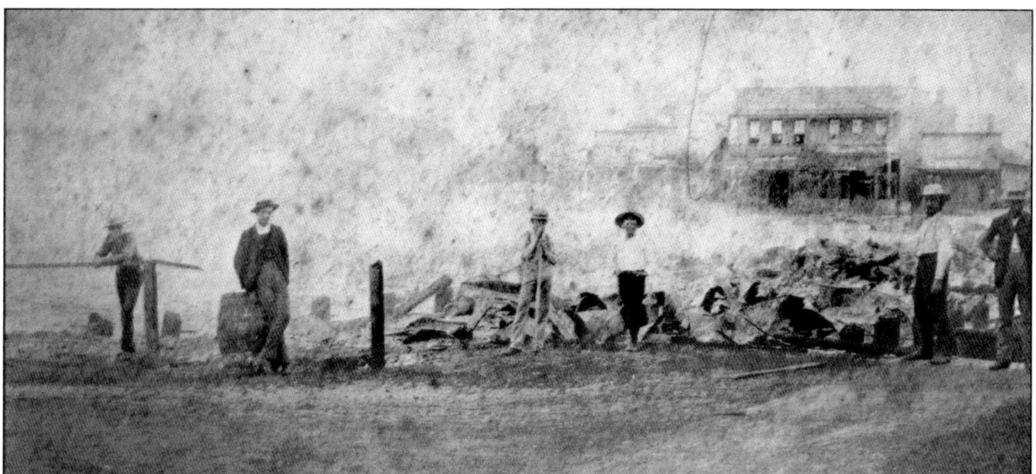

Whatever the cause, the devastation was great as building after building ignited in a burst of fiery energy. Lack of water and inadequate firefighting equipment coupled with closely constructed wooden buildings set the stage for disaster. Fortunately many buildings were saved but nearly 20 commercial businesses suffered a combined loss of $75,000. Good comes from bad, however, and so it did on that occasion. New construction laws prohibited building further frame structures, the fire department was upgraded, and downtown saloons were banned.

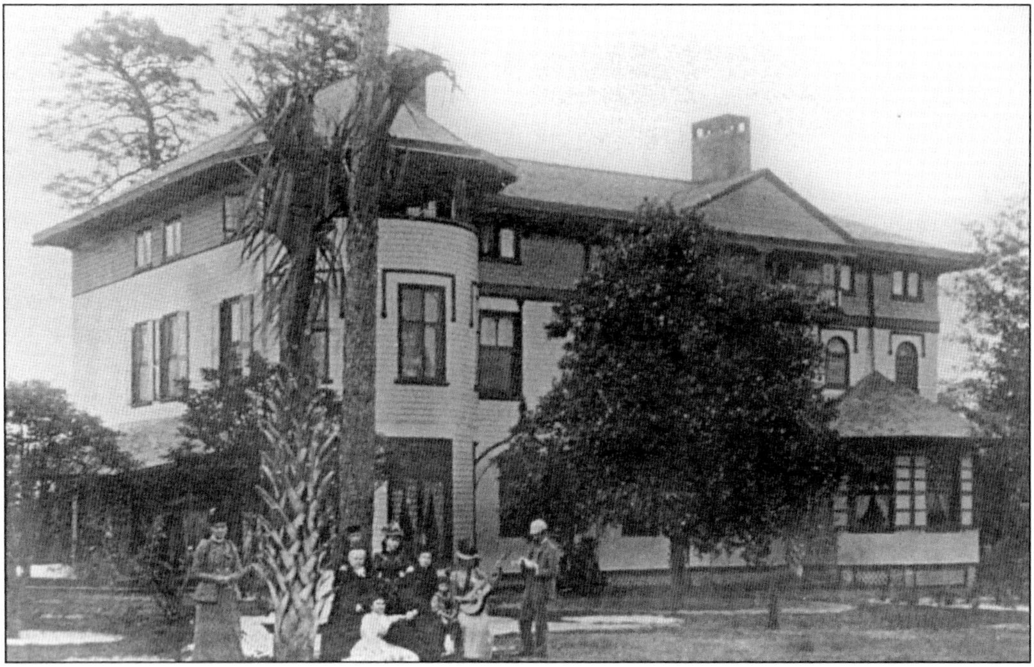

A fortuitous event took place in DeLand in 1886. John B. Stetson, a wealthy hat manufacturer from Philadelphia, finally accepted Henry DeLand's invitation to visit his new town. Stetson was so impressed with what he saw that he immediately purchased 300 acres west of town and ordered workmen to craft him a grand winter residence. Mr. Stetson remained a seasonal resident for almost two decades. Located on Camphor Lane, the 7,500-square-foot Victorian mansion is extant and magnificently restored.

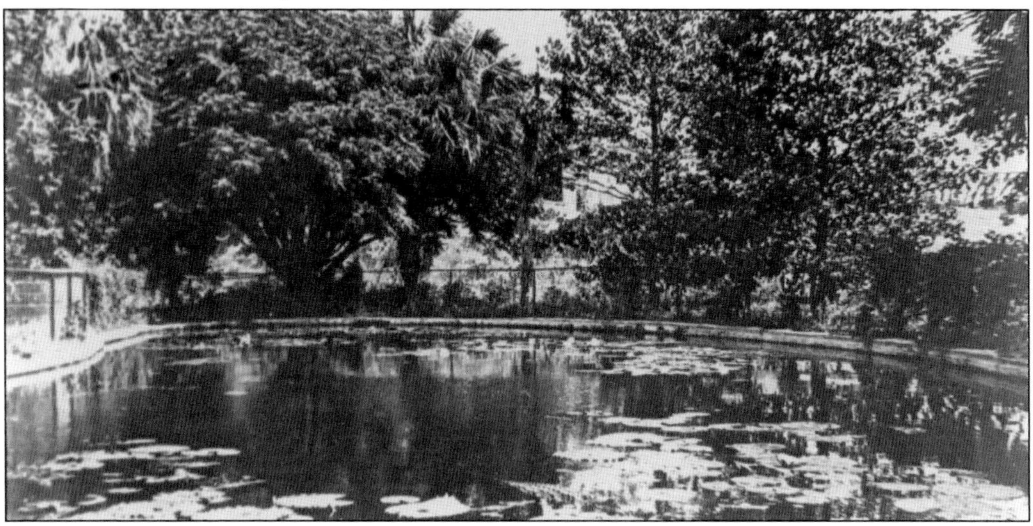

With an obvious sense of humor and also intrigued by one of Florida's most notorious denizens, Mr. Stetson collected an undisclosed number of alligators to stock the fenced-in pond at the back of his property. Frivolous by some standards, Stetson was, however, a serious philanthropist. His numerous financial contributions to the city remain today as proof of his commitment to create a town of excellence and style. Mr. Stetson's 'gator pond also remains, but alas, it is empty of the prehistoric creatures that brought him such pleasure.

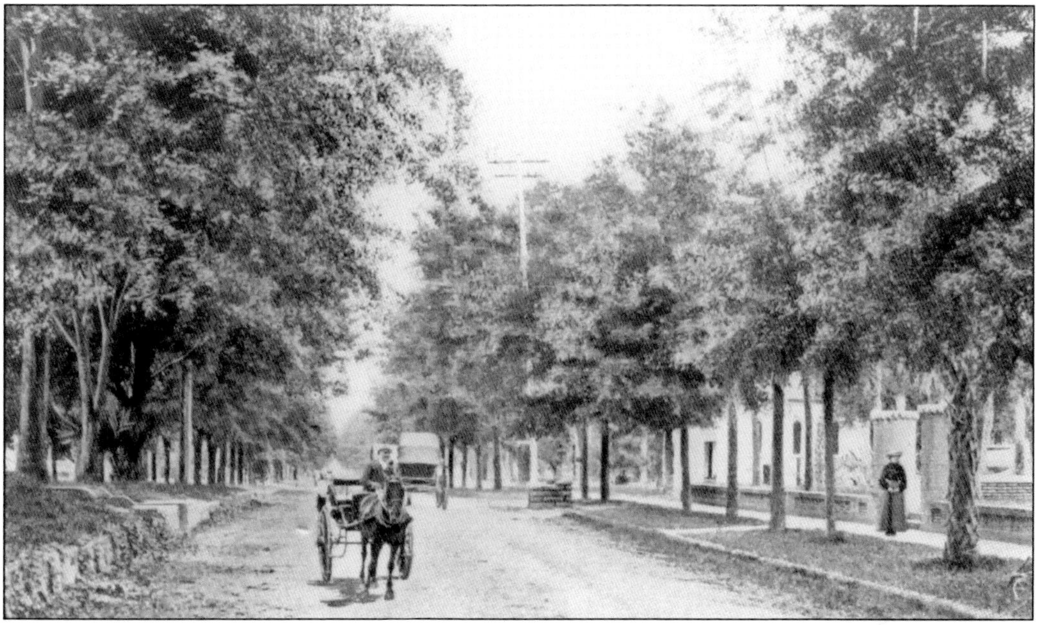

The City of DeLand was an early leader in the environmental movement when in 1886 the town council realized the need for shade trees. It initiated a tax-incentive program to reward property owners for planting oaks on city property in front of their homes. Each tree planted would reduce the owner's tax bill by 50¢. Owners purchased trees for 25¢ each and planted them 15 to 20 feet apart. The beautification project was such a tremendous success that the council found itself in the embarrassing position of having paid out so much money to enthusiastic conservationists that the city coffers were bare.

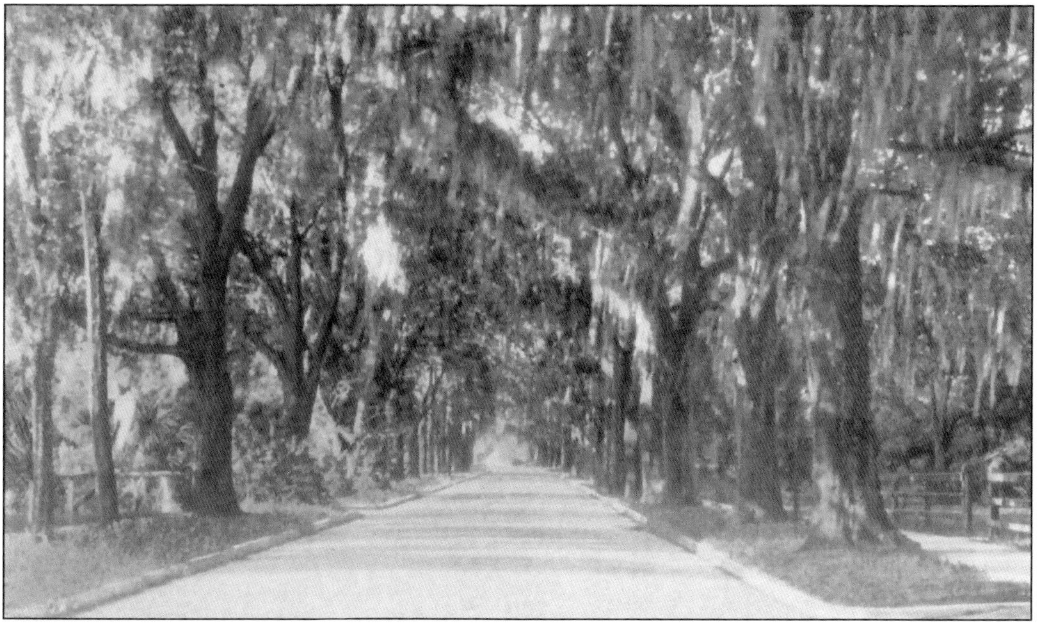

Although the project was repealed after two years it continued to grow and grow and grow, well into the 21st century in fact. Even today, many of those oaks shade city streets, their Spanish moss swaying from gnarled, far-flung limbs.

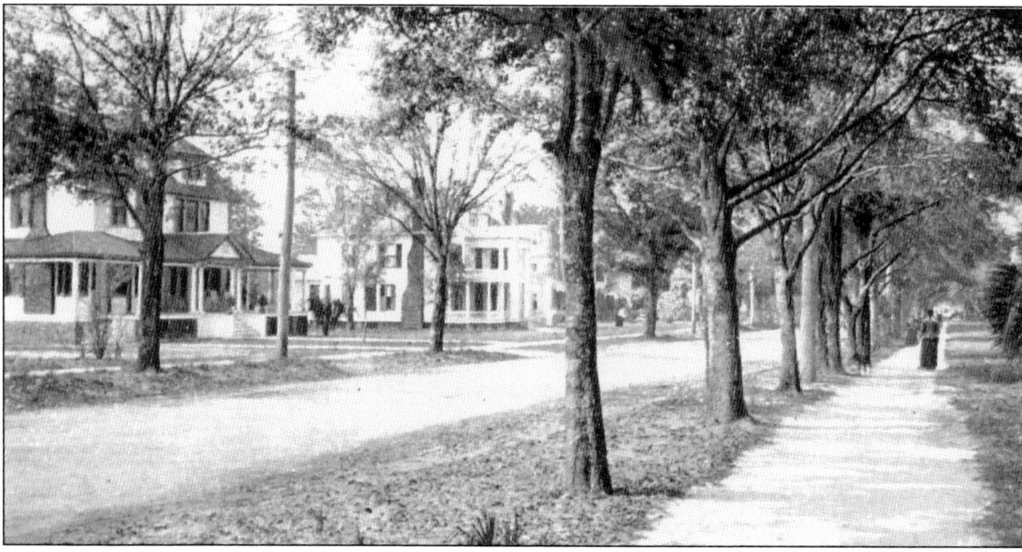

Thanks to that early farsighted town council and its planting project, DeLand became one of the most beautiful towns in Central Florida. With the gracious Victorian homes set on large lots and tree canopies shading the roadways, it must have been a serene delight walking the sandy sidewalks or steering the family carriage or Model T through the neighborhoods. Town council recognized the need to replace Mother Nature's gift. After all, trees create a lush environment, they soften manmade structures, and they ultimately enhance the natural heritage a community bequeaths to its future residents.

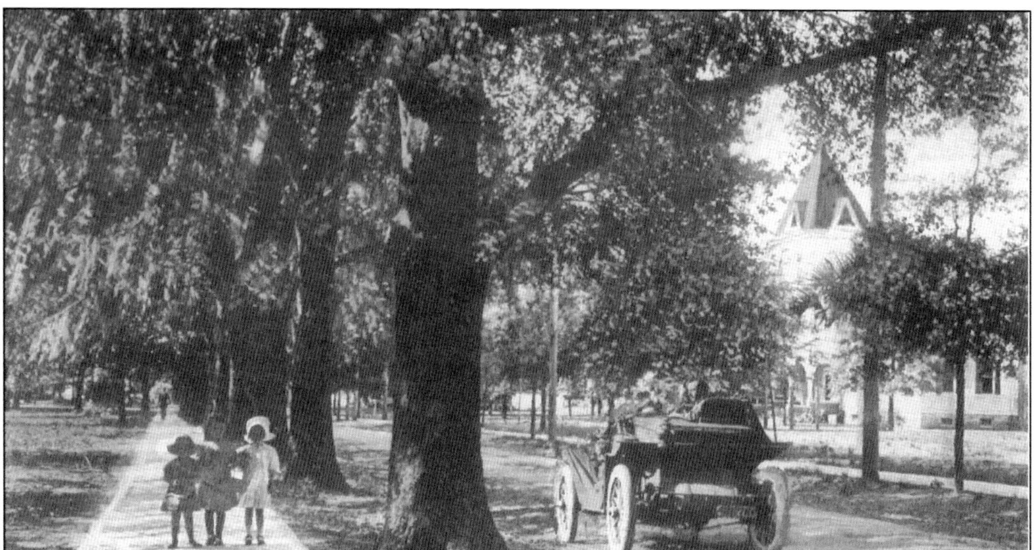

As the years progressed, so did downtown DeLand. From dirt streets to a brick Boulevard in 1916, DeLand was moving forward. This view of the Boulevard looks north from New York. The Boulevard was bricked from the Old Daytona Road to Orange City while New York was bricked all the way to the St. Johns River. By 1917 a shell road was constructed connecting DeLand, Daytona, and New Smyrna. Shells were taken from the remains of ancient Timucua Indian mounds, crushed, and carted away for building material.

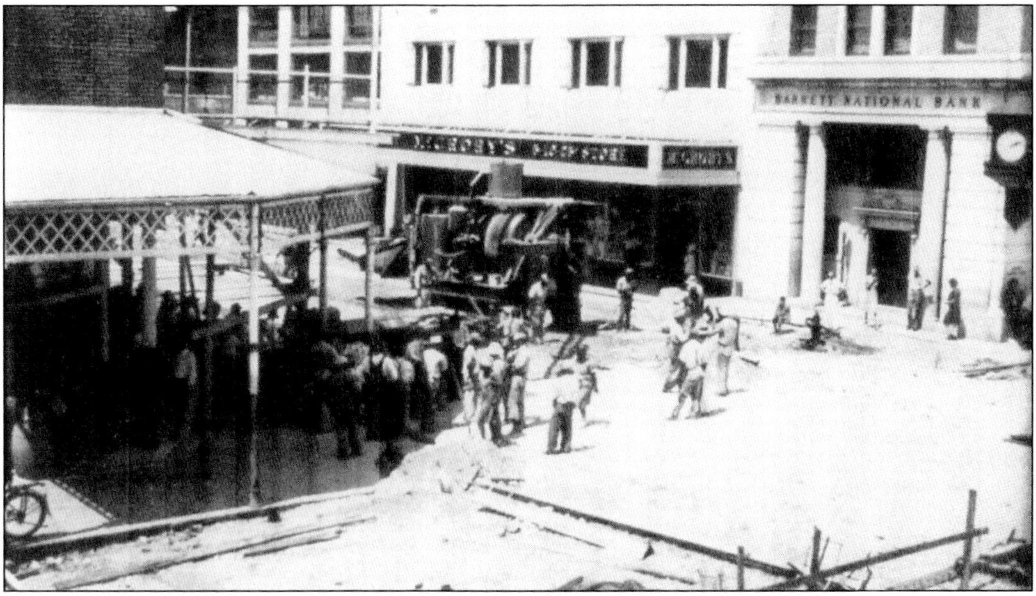

"Progress" sometimes takes strange and often destructive twists and turns as it did with the Boulevard. By the 1940s, amid complaints and thoughtlessness the once-grand brick road was concreted over while majestic oaks were felled to widen the road. Sixty years later the city is once again paving roads with brick and replanting oaks to beautify its streets. Sometimes it takes generations before citizens of a community learn a simple lesson—that quality of life is not necessarily measured by "something new" but by how well the present generation protects its natural and cultural heritage for future generations.

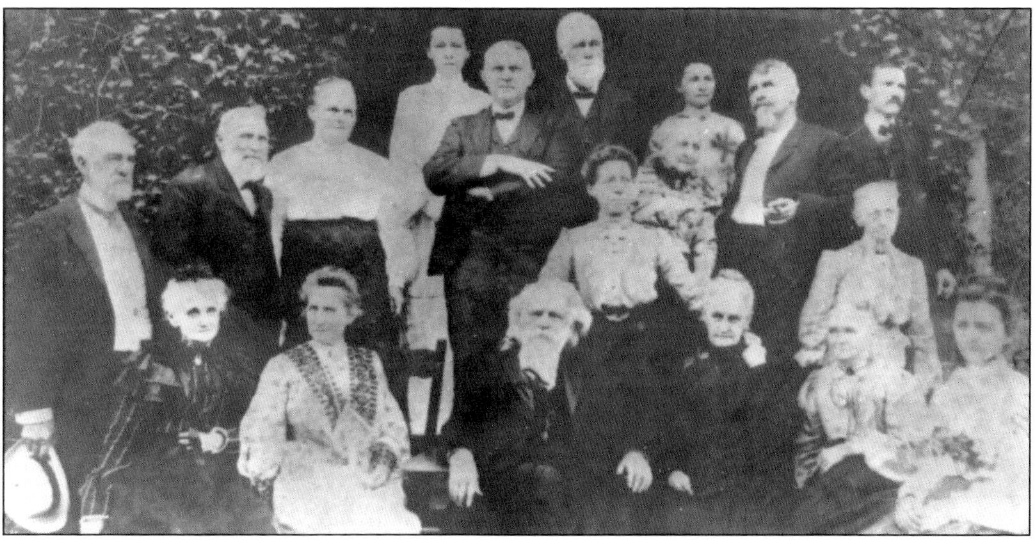

Members of the Old Settler's Society, originally known as "Pioneers of DeLand and Vicinity," stoically posed in February 1904 for a photograph that would last beyond their time. Membership required that they homesteaded in town prior to 1877. Pictured from left to right are the following: (standing) S.W. Walts, J.J. Vinzant, Mrs. J.J. Vinzant, Mrs. G.A. Dreka, G.A. Dreka, E.W. Bond, Mrs. C.O. Codrington, Rudolph Frank, and C.O. Codrington; (seated) Mrs. L.A. Fudger, Mrs. S.W. Walts, Henry A. DeLand, Mrs. C.A. Miller, Mrs. R. Franck, Mrs. Clara F. Rich, Mrs. C.C. Codrington, Mrs. O.J. Hill, and Miss Helen P. DeLand.

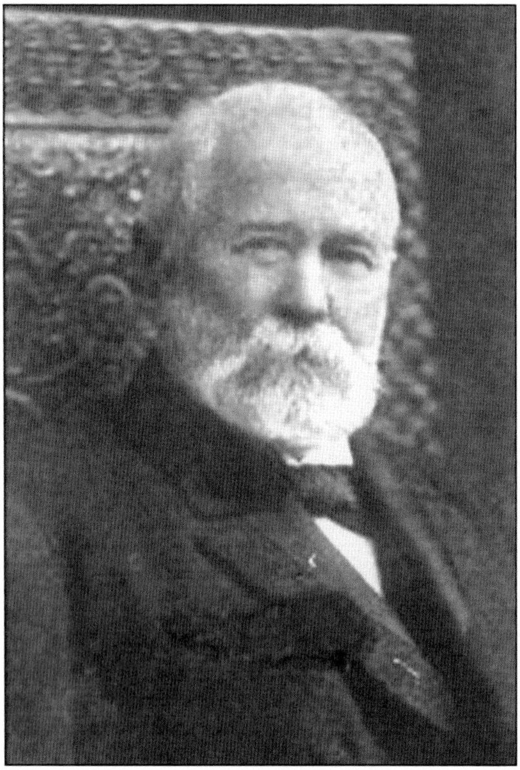

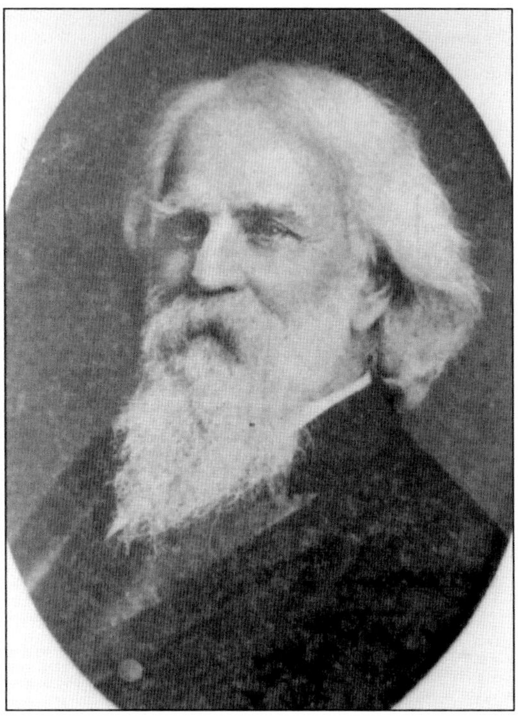

No matter how many pioneers traveled to Central Florida to settle in Persimmon Hollow, it was the goodness, the graciousness, and the genius of Henry A. DeLand and John B. Stetson that forged the beginnings of DeLand, our Athens of Florida. In a letter written February 17, 1906 from his DeLand mansion to his son Henry, working in their Philadelphia hat factory, Stetson, still vastly wealthy, expressed his concern for responsible spending: " . . . I see you would like to bring Butler [Henry's horse]. I have no objections to Butler whatever, but if I was to advise you and under the circumstances, the cost of that trip will be considerable if you look at it. I would sooner have that laid aside for me for the future, which is coming, for something of more moment [that] to spend it just to come to Florida at the present time. Suppose it would cost $300. That laid aside for something that you might need in the future—would not that be better? I would be awfully glad to see you and want to see you, but it's necessary to look these things right in the face some times." But Henry did not make it to DeLand with Butler nor did he ever get the opportunity to face his father again. The following day John B. Stetson died of a massive stroke, his death a deep loss to the residents of DeLand Florida. Two years later, on March 13, 1908, Henry Addison DeLand, the town's founder, passed away at his home in Fairport, New York. During his last visit to DeLand in February of that same year, and accompanied by his grandson, Harlan Page DeLand Jr., Mr. DeLand shared his thoughts with members of the Old Settler's Society at the Aquatic Club. He related that he first came to the area in search of "a delightful home when the blasts of winter were on." Records indicate that he spoke with deep feeling and that "tears filled his eyes." Perhaps he had a premonition that this was to be the last time he would address his stalwart pioneers in the town that he had envisioned so very long ago.

Two

The Seasonal Resident

Tourism came in full force to Florida in 1821 when the United States purchased the territory from Spain. Northern visitors filtered south across the St. Mary's River looking for the tropical paradise described as early as 1791 by the famed naturalist William Bartram. In Travels *Bartram portrayed the land and waters of the St. Johns River near present-day DeLand as having "an almost inexpressible air of grandeur."*

Bartram went on to detail his adventurous sail on the river as seeing "verges and islets of the lagoon . . . elegantly embellished with flowering plants and shrubs . . . laughing coots with wings half spread . . . tripping over the little coves and hiding . . . in the tufts of grass . . . the river . . . one solid bank of fish . . . and the alligators in such incredible numbers, and so close together from shore to shore, that it would have been easy to have walked across on their heads, had the animals been harmless."

Later adventurers and writers embellished the natural beauties of Florida, newspapers wrote of their escapades, and soon hundreds and then thousands eagerly planned a trip to Paradise.

Prior to Henry Flagler's development of the east coast of Florida in the late 1800s with his railroad extension, the northerly flowing St. Johns River was the main thoroughfare for seasonal visitors. Boarding a paddlewheel in the "thriving" metropolis of Jacksonville to float up-river to such exotic destinations as Mandarin, Green Cove Springs, Palatka, Seville, Astor, and ultimately dock at the wharf of DeLand five miles from the village, afforded those curious tourists a glimpse of the wild natural beauty of Florida.

What they experienced caught their breath. The banks of the river were heavy with magnolia, giant cypress, palm, and live oak. Spanish moss hung limp across the boughs of trees to sway above the water as the paddlewheel passed beneath. Limbs were laden with migratory fowl, their splendid plumes coveted for decoration on women's hats. Indeed, one of the sad pastimes of the "gentlemen" aboard those slow-moving water hotels was to stand atop the highest deck, take aim with their shotgun, and blast those innocent creatures from their lofty perch.

And thus, the placid times and lush landscape of early Florida, with its abundance of natural beauty, were rudely interrupted, forever, by the human element.

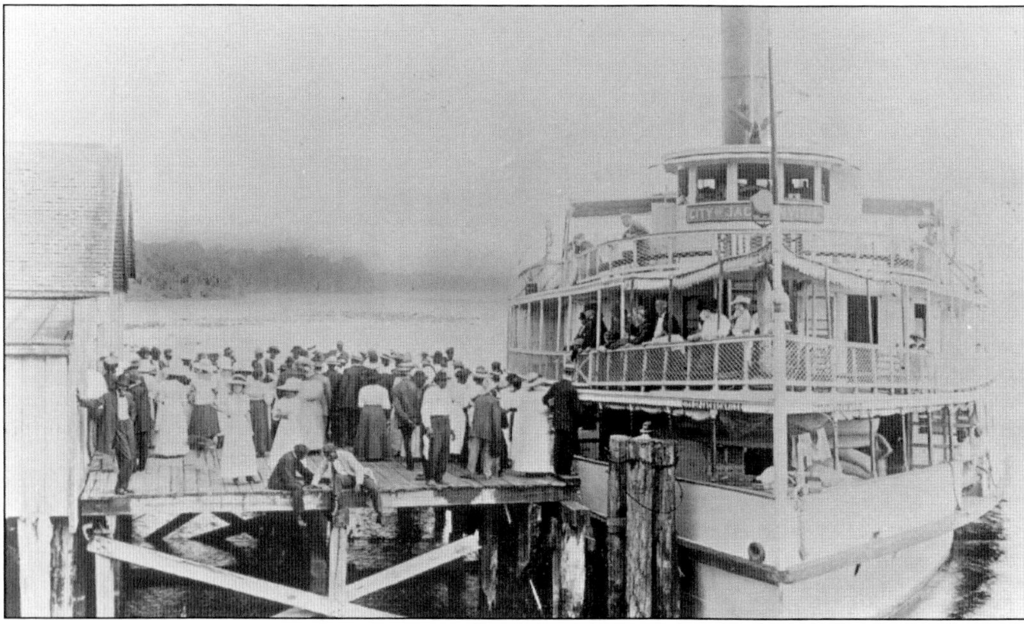

Seasonal visitors to DeLand were enticed to "The Athens of Florida" with illustrations of lakes surrounded by orange groves, an abundance of wildlife, a profusion of flowers, a respite from the harsh winters of the north, and a place to heal a sickly body. By 1885 one of Jacksonville's major steamship companies was advertising that a "through boat leaves Jacksonville at 3:30 p.m. Sundays, Tuesdays and Thursdays; arrives Beresford (DeLand) 4:30 a.m. Mondays, Wednesdays and Fridays." Those taking the "through boat" disembarked from their stately steamship on the St. Johns to board a carriage for one of the numerous hotels or boarding houses that promised to provide adequate, if not often luxurious, facilities amid a bucolic setting.

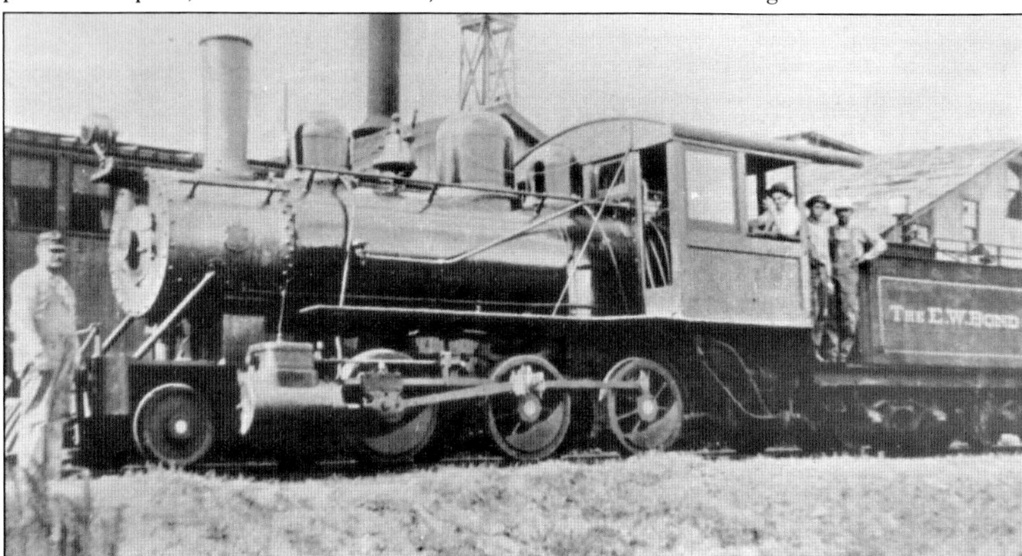

Good news for the weary traveler came in the form of a convenient rail line laid July 1884 from the DeLand Landing on the river. A large contingent of citizens came out to observe such an exciting event. Developed by Eber W. Bond, "the line was a narrow gauge with one engine, two flat cars, three box cars and a passenger coach."

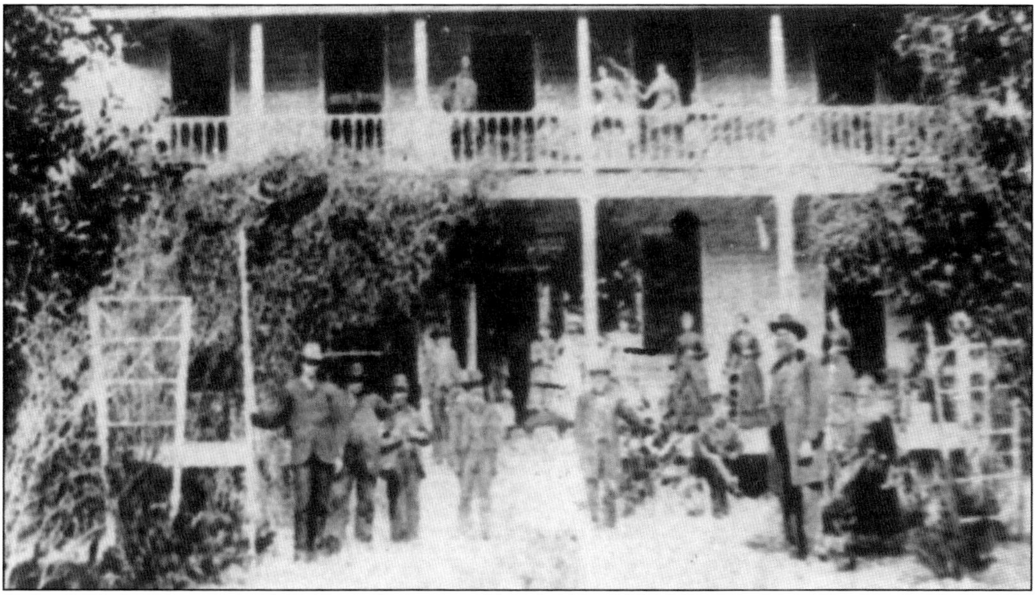

Floral Grove Hotel, built *c.* 1885, afforded its guests a genteel introduction to rural tourism at its best. Located on the northwest corner of West New York and Clara, it was host to numerous visitors from the North. Its double verandas gave ample opportunity to sit and chat, share the day's plans, or watch the goings and comings of the locals. Many tourists traveled to town because family members had settled in the area and they wanted to experience firsthand what the fascination was for this pastoral setting.

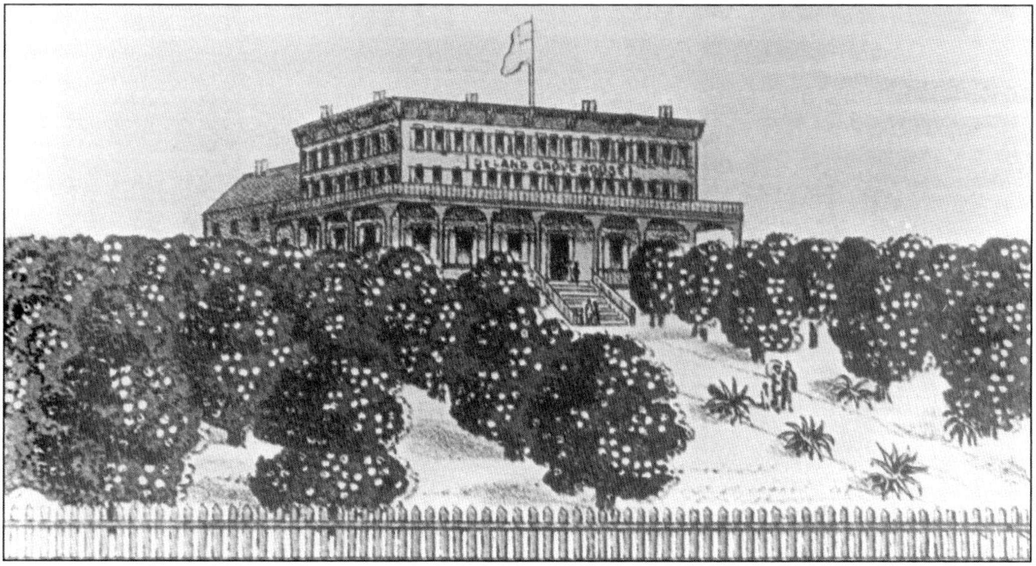

Just down the street from the Floral Grove Hotel was the DeLand Grove House, another frame structure surrounded by lush citrus trees whose winter blossoms filled the air with a sweet scent. Tourists were enthralled with the aroma produced by the orange blossom, possibly attempting to take home a blossom or two as a nostalgic remembrance of their winter holiday. The DeLand Grove House on West New York, built by Henry DeLand *c.* 1880, was eventually renamed the Putnam. It exploded in a blaze and burned to the ground in 1921. Rebuilt in 1923 with the claim of "fireproof," it stands today along a busy thoroughfare minus its famous orange grove.

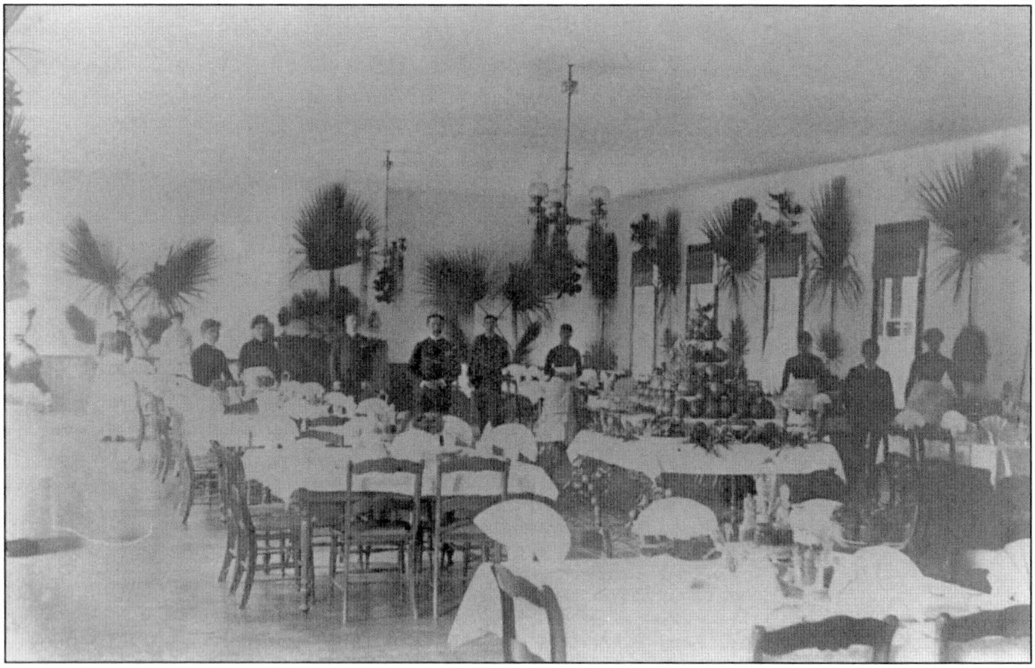

The interior of the Putnam Hotel dazzled its guests with an 1885 Thanksgiving Feast. The dining room was set with starched white linen tablecloths and matching napkins, sparkling crystal, and silver flatware. Walls decorated with cabbage palm fronds and dutiful servers standing at attention gave the hotel an air of sophistication and comfort.

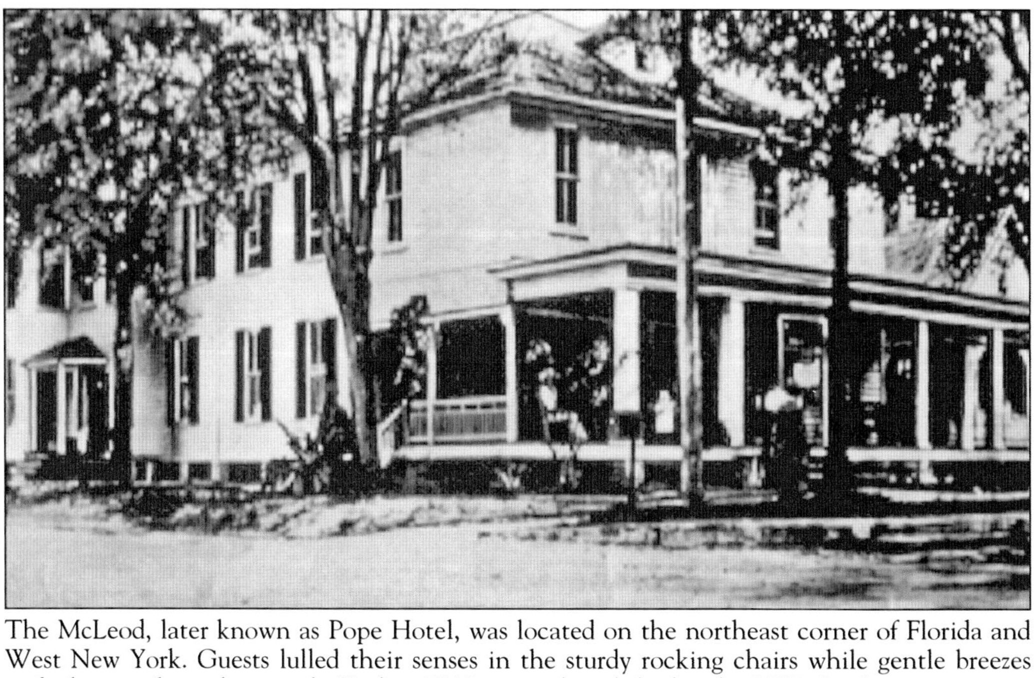

The McLeod, later known as Pope Hotel, was located on the northeast corner of Florida and West New York. Guests lulled their senses in the sturdy rocking chairs while gentle breezes wafted across the wide veranda. Built c. 1910, it was demolished in the 1950s for the construction of a nondescript governmental building.

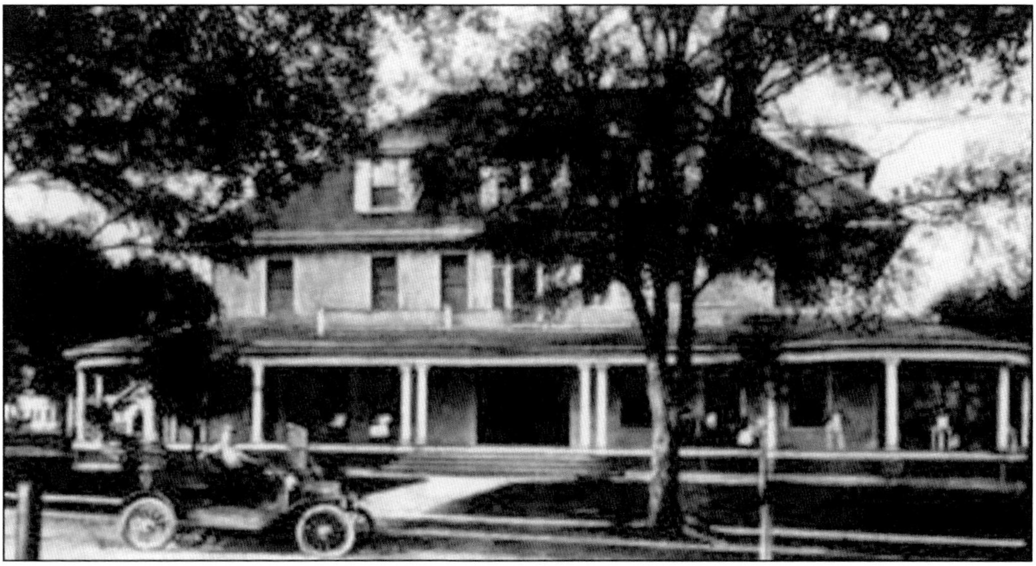

An 1880s pamphlet boasted of updated hotel accommodations in progressive DeLand: "A few years ago our hotel accommodations were limited, and many...who had heard of our climate, and came to it, were compelled to seek quarters in other localities. This...is no longer the case, as other hotels have been built and the old ones enlarged, until today there is no town of our size in Florida with so ample and excellent accommodations.... To say that our hotels are first-class would be saying but little. They are simply models of comfort and excellence, and the reputation they have gained has spread far and wide."

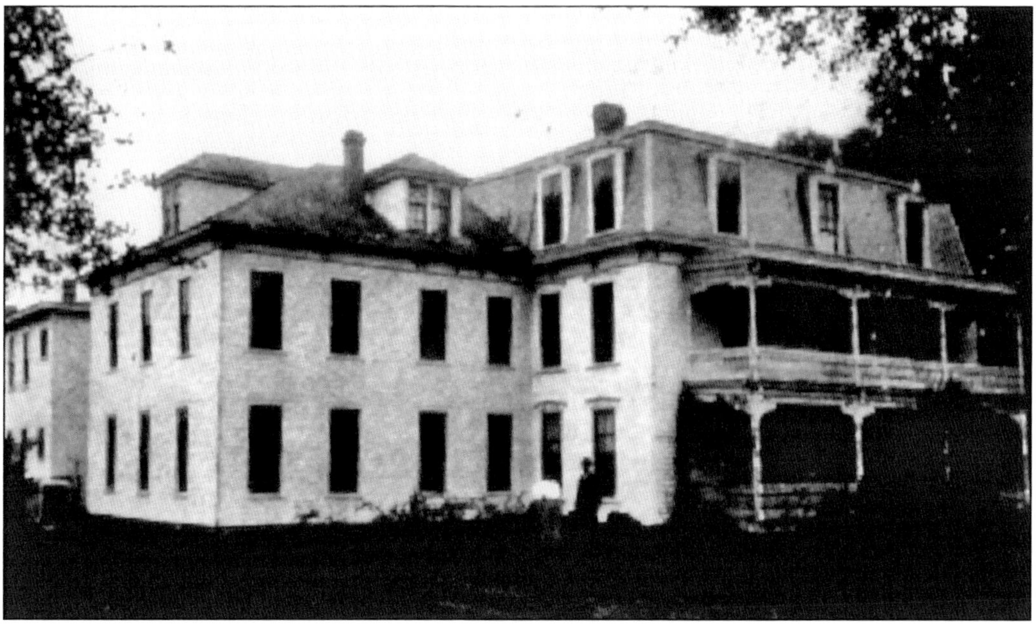

Another classic hotel was the Lexington (top), built *c.* 1915 at 200 West New York. The Melrose (bottom), built that same year, was a three-story gracious frame hotel. Its inviting double veranda and wooden glider swing were well used by winter tourists. Once located at 200 East New York, it was razed in 1980 so the space could accommodate a squat concrete building. Gone too is the Melrose, a victim of thoughtlessness.

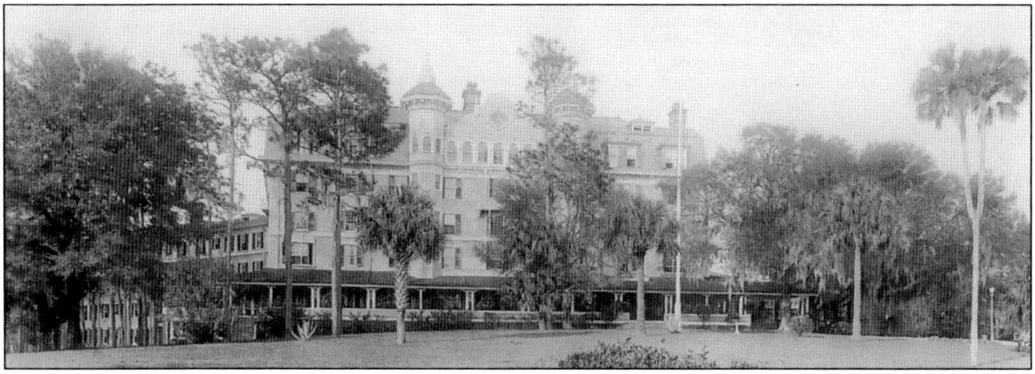

Of all the boarding houses and hotels built for DeLand's wintering clientele, none was more imposing and luxurious than the Hotel College Arms, originally called Parceland. Built in 1877 by Henry DeLand's brother-in-law, Joseph Parce, it was purchased and then extensively remodeled in the 1890s by John B. Stetson. The five-story frame structure eventually boasted an elevator, steam heat, and even a golf course for its more energetic sports-minded guests.

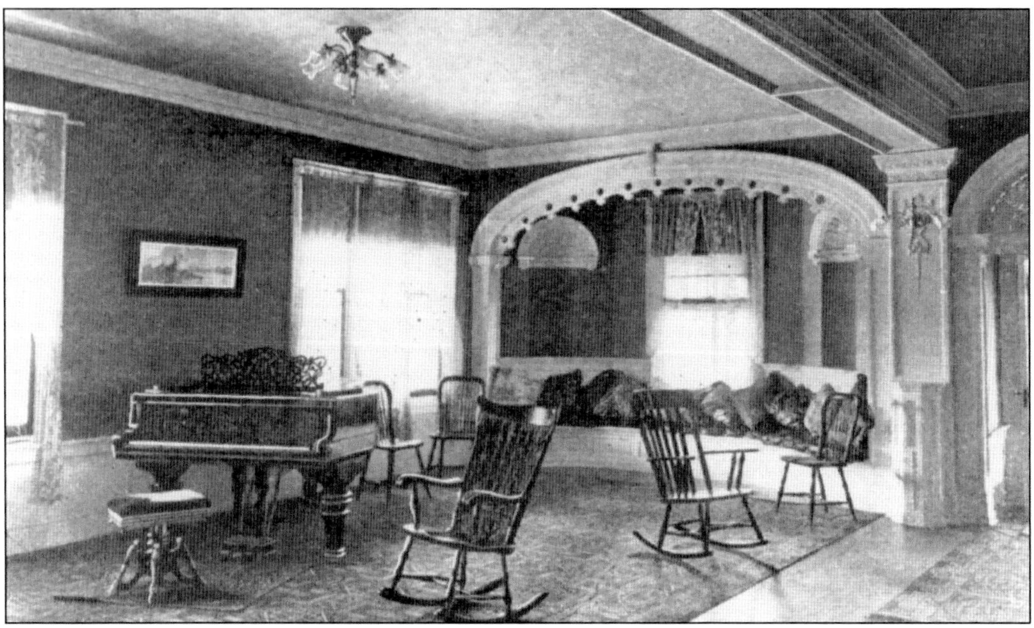

The lobby of the College Arms was elaborately designed with boxed beams, arched inglenooks, gas wall sconces, and area rugs. A parlor grand with swivel seat awaited playing guests while comfortably designed wooden rockers stood ready to relax the weary.

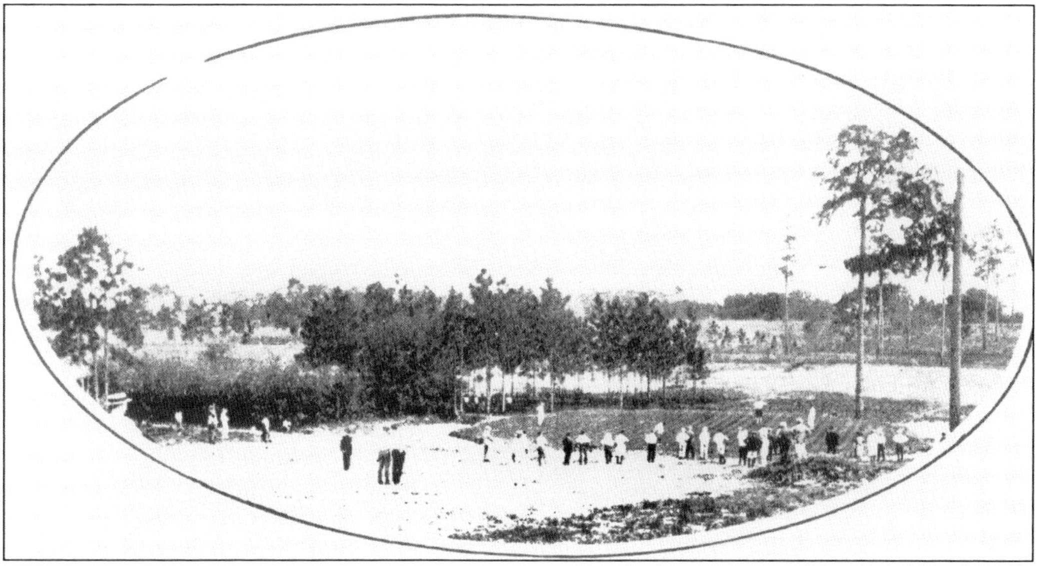

A view from atop Hotel College Arms looked out across a wide expanse of open field. This imposing winter vacation resort stood where today the new Volusia County Courthouse covers the northwest corner of Amelia and East New York. And the once idyllic green field across from the College Arms has been replaced with a strip mall and asphalt parking lot.

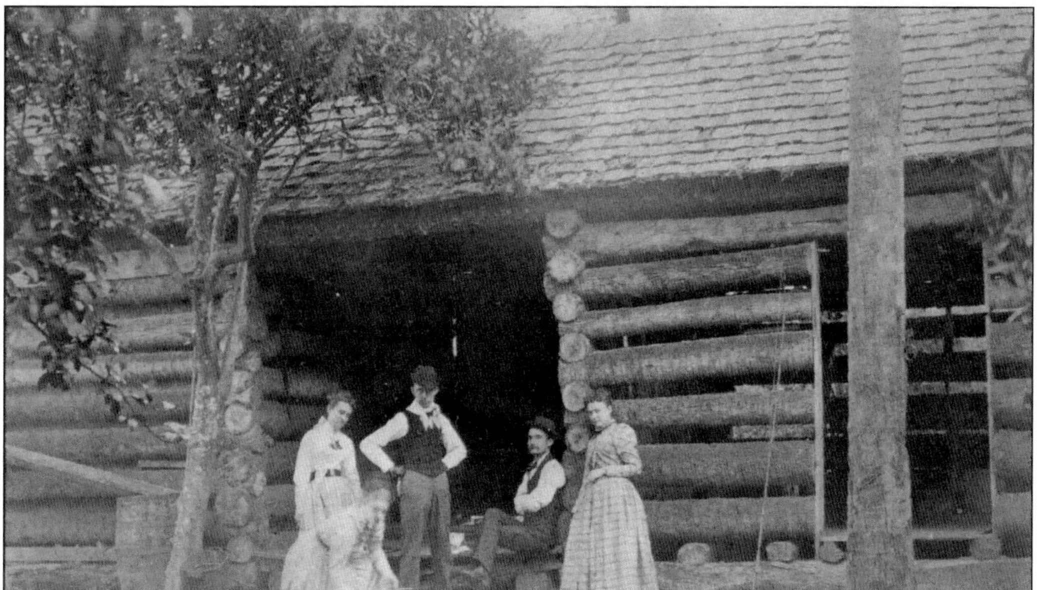

About 1886 Henry Flagler's East Coast Railroad Company extended its line from Jacksonville south while Henry Plant's Jacksonville to Tampa rail was crossing the peninsular. Plant's offer to bring tracks into the growing town of DeLand was declined by city officials who decided the expense was too great; thus, the rail was brought to the small community of Beresford instead. West of DeLand, this rural hamlet still had log houses but grateful residents since travel became easier. As for DeLand residents and tourists, the inconvenience of catching a buggy to the station or the dock still remained—for a while longer, at least.

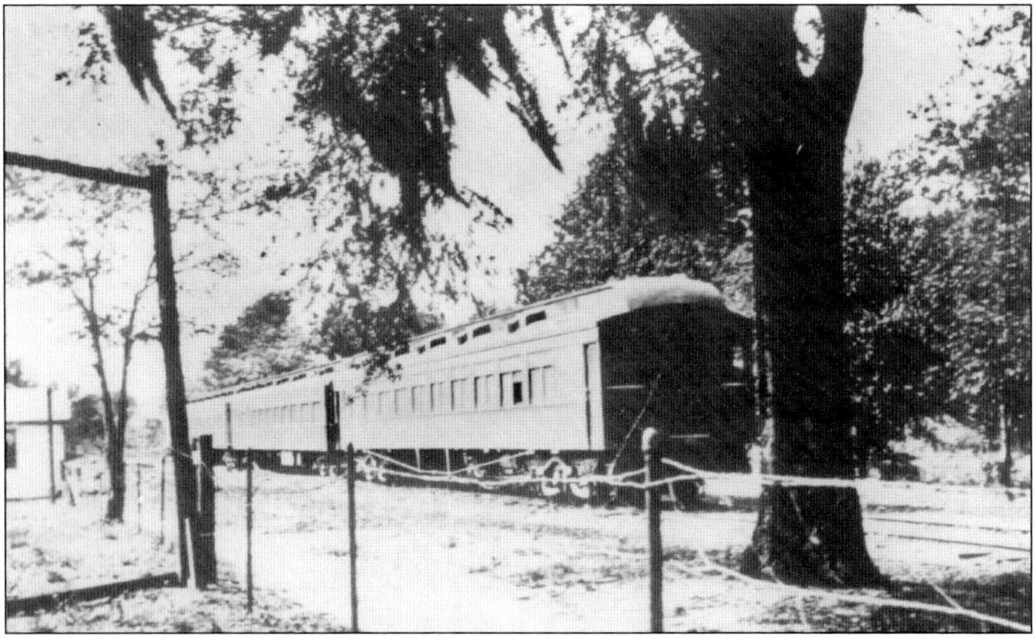

To the relief of all, a broad gauge line was finally extended into town. A depot was constructed on the east side of Amelia Avenue between Rich and East New York and conveniently located across the street from the Hotel College Arms. Private railroad cars carried the wealthy to their ultimate destination.

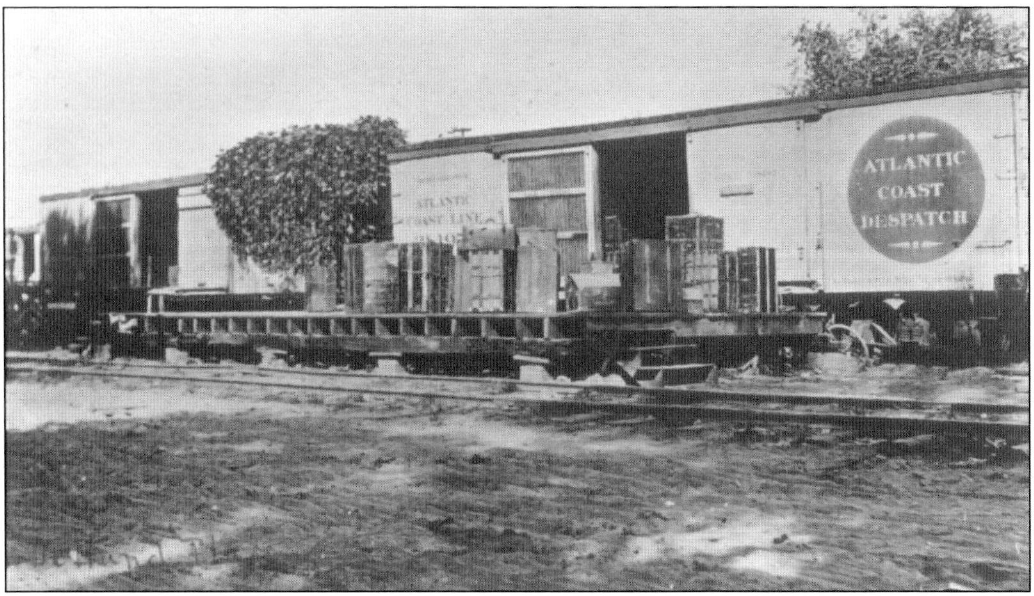

Finally, with the advent of a rail into town, the elite upper class of the north had ample opportunity to travel in style and comfort. Indeed, it was as if they moved the entire contingency of servants and clothing with them for their seasonal visit. Massive trunks stacked on the loading dock attest to the fact that their stay in DeLand was generally quite extended, probably completely contented, and assuredly most stylish.

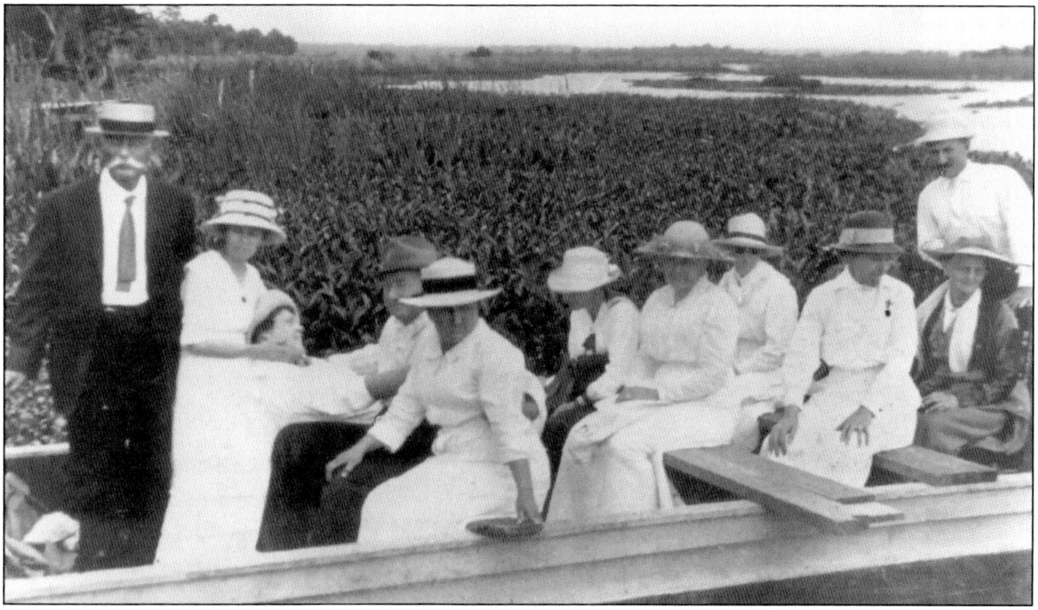

Decorum, published in 1877, was "the" book on dress and etiquette for high American society. For one's trip to Florida, the following advice was given: "The usual costume of gentlemen is white flannel trousers, white rowing jersey, and a straw hat. Peajackets are worn when their owners are not absolutely employed in rowing." Male boaters at DeLeon Springs, north of DeLand, obviously had not bothered to read *Decorum* before traveling to Florida.

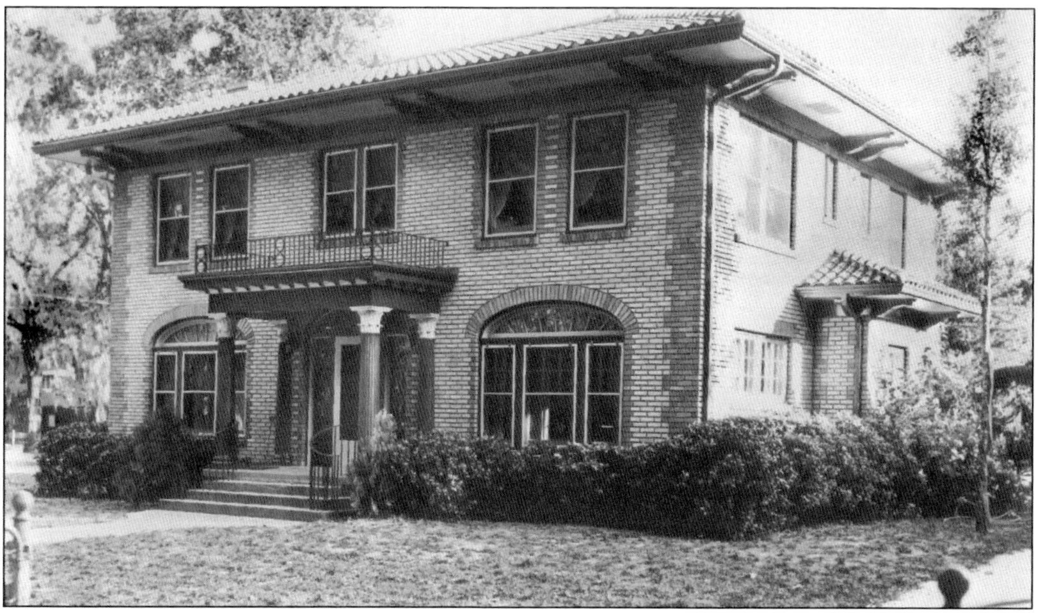

Although most seasonal residents from the late 1880s to the early 1900s wiled away their days in a local hotel or boarding house, many of the more wealthy chose to build personal accommodations they dubbed their "winter cottages." This fine example of an Italian Renaissance style gold-bricked "winter cottage" was constructed in 1926 at 310 West Minnesota for Boston resident William Livingston. Still extant, it remains a private residence on one of the finest residential streets in DeLand.

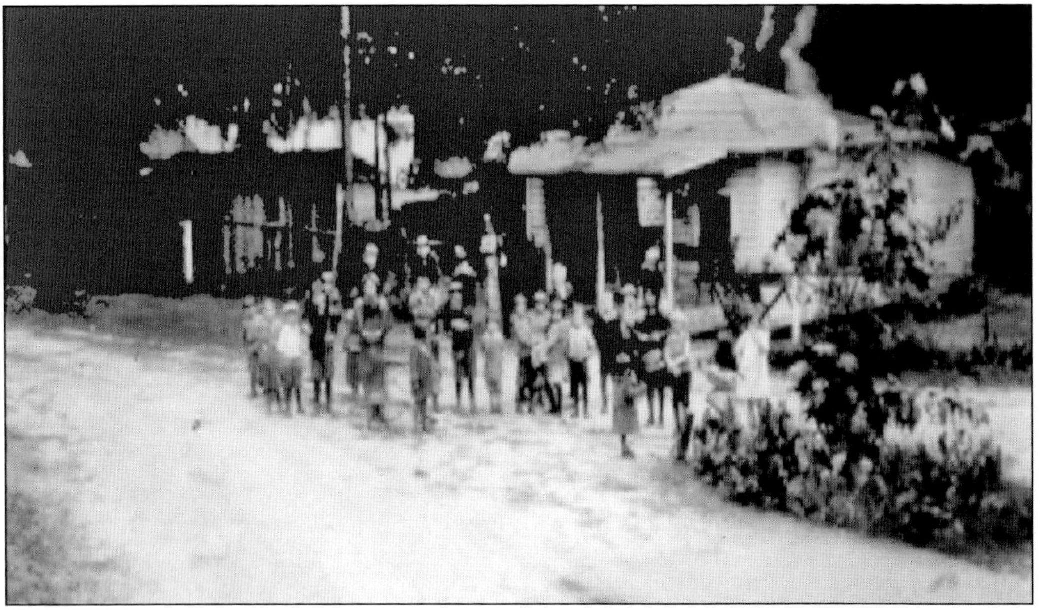

After a few harsh winters in the mid- and late 1890s, many of the Northern "in crowd" moved their vacation destination further south to Palm Beach and Miami. But DeLand's tourist industry regained strength after the completion of the Dixie Highway c. 1915. This newly constructed narrow road of bricks and bumps brought automobiles and their drivers by the thousands to Florida. The new seasonal visitors had less money to spend but their love of the outdoors generated enthusiasm. In the 1920s they even organized a tourist club located on the corner of Walts and Florida.

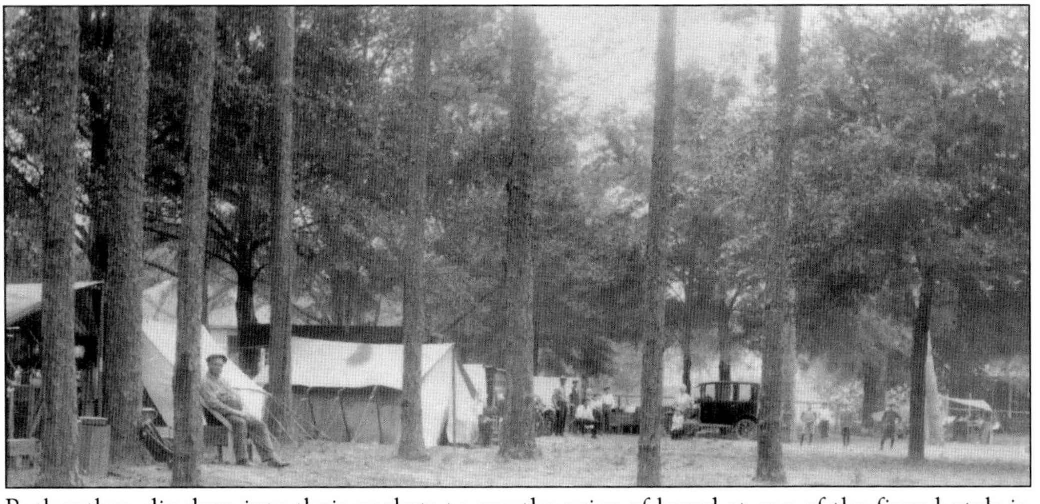

Rather than dig deep into their pockets to pay the price of board at one of the finer hotels in DeLand, Florida's newest breed of tourists bedded down in camps nestled amongst pines and oaks. Canvas tents protected them from rain, open fires kept them warm, and canned food they brought or bought gave these adventurous ragtag vacationers the appropriately descriptive nickname "Tin Can Tourists."

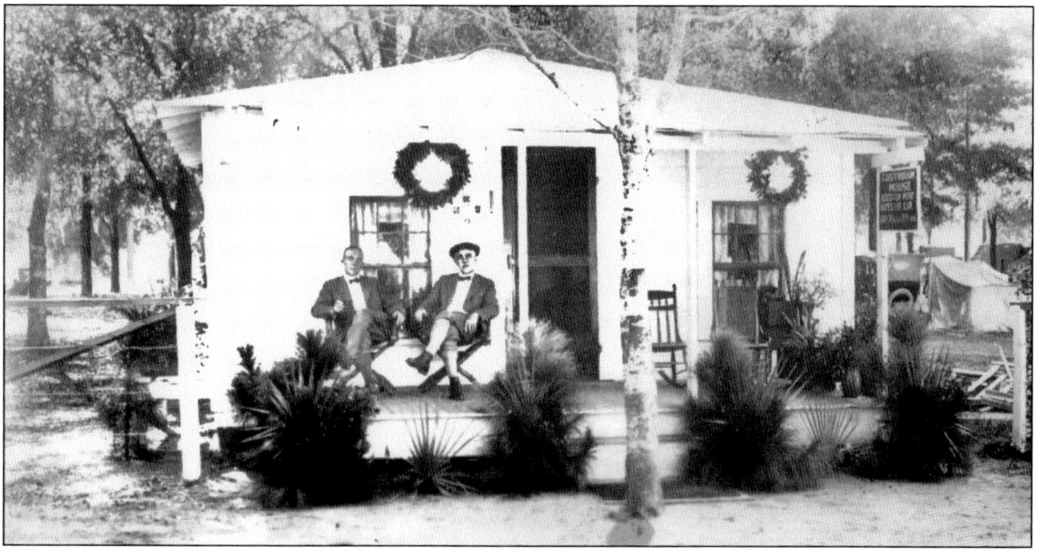

By the early 1920s DeLand City Trailer Park offered reasonable lodgings at only 35¢ per day per car or a bargain rate for only $1.50 per week per car. Many tents were attached to vehicles for camping at its most convenient.

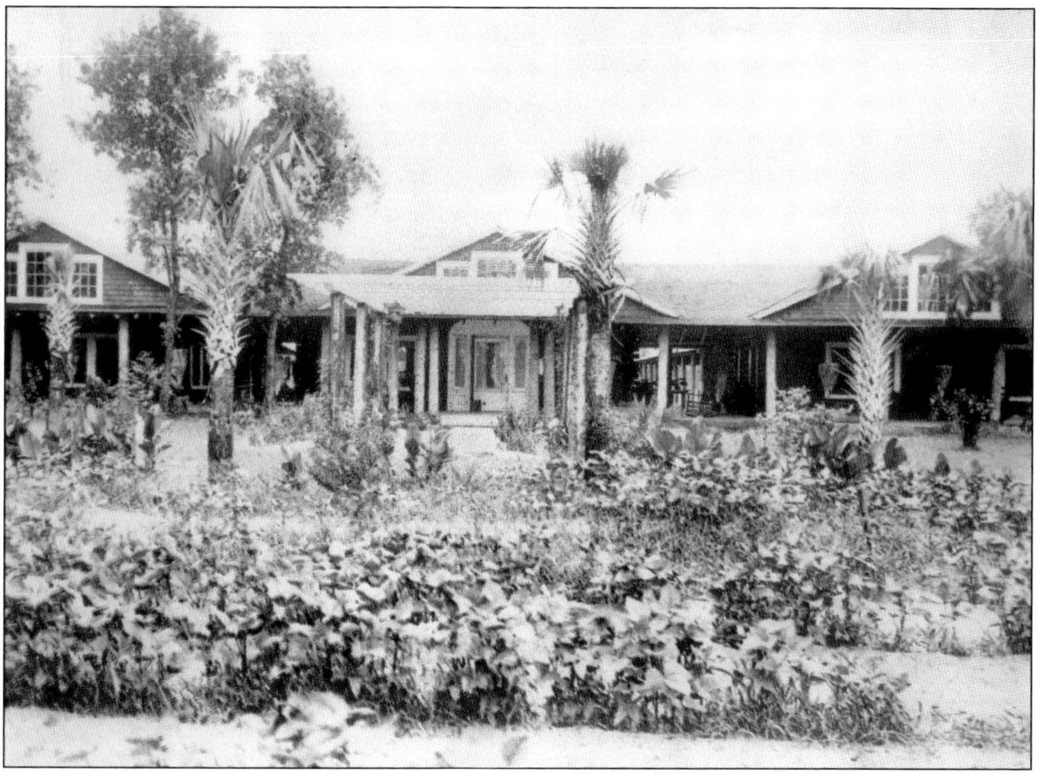

Rustically elegant accommodations also were offered amidst Mother Nature like the Lake Tracey Lodge located on the old DeLand-Umatilla Road. Cabbage palms graced the entrance to this cypress-shingled retreat adjacent to a freshwater lake filled with bass, water hyacinths, and, of course, Florida's ever-present gators.

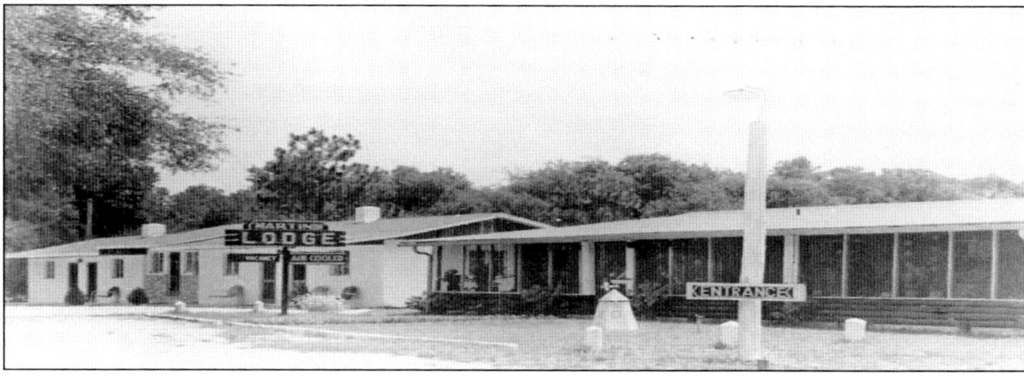

The 20th century moved forward into the 1930s and 1940s. Gone were the glorious days of the elite seasonal residents and their private rail cars to DeLand. Gone were the Tin Can Tourists, their cans, tents, and Model Ts. Enter the "Age of the Middle Class" and their ability to travel great distances with more reliable personal vehicles, cheap gas, and affordable accommodations. Early quaint frame cottages shaded by water oaks gave way to a new Florida building material, the cinderblock, as seen at the Oleander. The use of hotels declined with the increased popularity of motor courts. Tourists simply enjoyed the convenience of parking adjacent to their room.

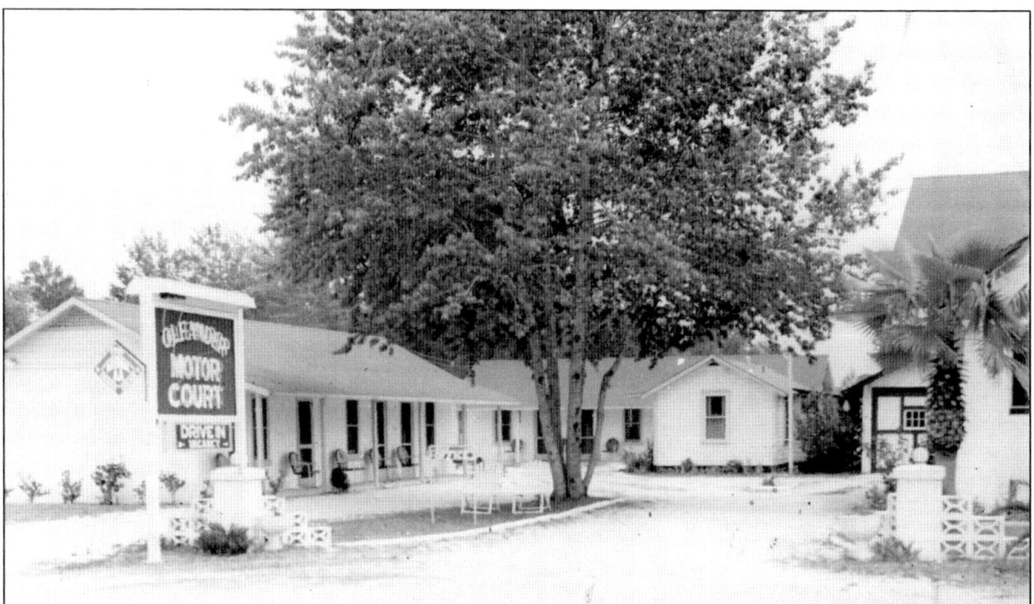

With places to stay from grand hotels to tiny dwellings, what did DeLand's seasonal resident do during his or her stay in town? Same thing the locals did—play.

Three

AT PLAY

In his book The Story of My Heart, *Richard Jefferies wrote, "I hope succeeding generations will be able to be idle. I hope that nine-tenths of their time will be leisure time; that they may enjoy their days, and the earth...that they may rest by the sea and dream; that they may dance and sing, and eat and drink."*

Had the 1876 residents of the little village of Persimmon Hollow read Jefferies's words, they would probably have agreed. But the truth was, they were unable to spend much time in idleness; they were too busy working just to keep a roof over their heads and food in their bellies. But as time passed and the invention of new equipment gave settlers a bit more freedom from grueling chores, they finally found some time to play and dance and sing.

DeLand residents were a creative lot as they chose to blend business with pleasure and make money doing it. They built fine hotels and offered eco-tourism activities before the name was even coined to encourage visitors to spend their money in town. The appeal of the area's rural paradise attracted many with its proximity to the Atlantic Ocean, its warm winter climate, its mysterious and enchanting fresh-water springs, and its abundant native plants and wildlife habitat.

Winter residents came in droves to stretch out under the Spanish moss–laden shade trees or float down the St. John's River aboard a paddlewheel. Visitors came to this wooded retreat to escape the hustle and bustle of their fast-paced Northern life—they came to play, to be leisurely, to enjoy their days, and the earth. And often they enjoyed their stay so much that they never left.

Locals also made great use of their environment. They found time to build clubs and race tracks and clear ponds of tall grasses so swimmers could relax on a sandy beach. They fished and boated and hunted wild game. They played football and baseball and tennis and golf. They rambled down the Boulevard to visit with friends, to see the latest movie, or grab an ice cream at the local hang-out.

As the years passed and the town grew and prospered, after a hard day's work DeLand residents were finally able to admit that they were definitely not against a little play.

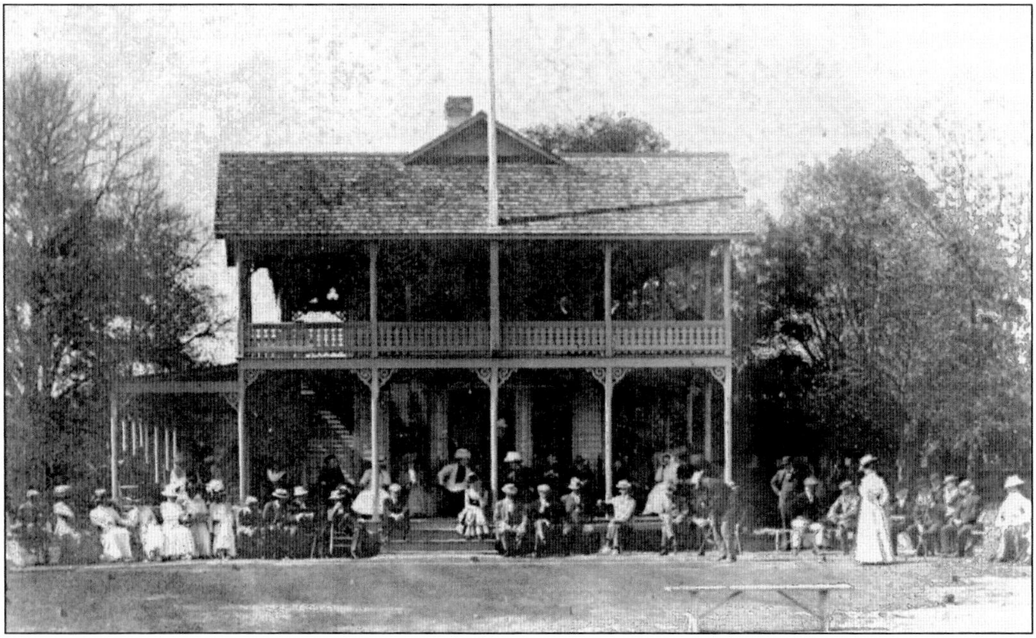

John B. Stetson's Hotel College Arms offered a first-rate golf course and a lavish clubhouse for its guests and members. Both the seasonal resident and the well-to-do DeLandite languished away many a day on a shady veranda of the two-story Victorian's 19th hole.

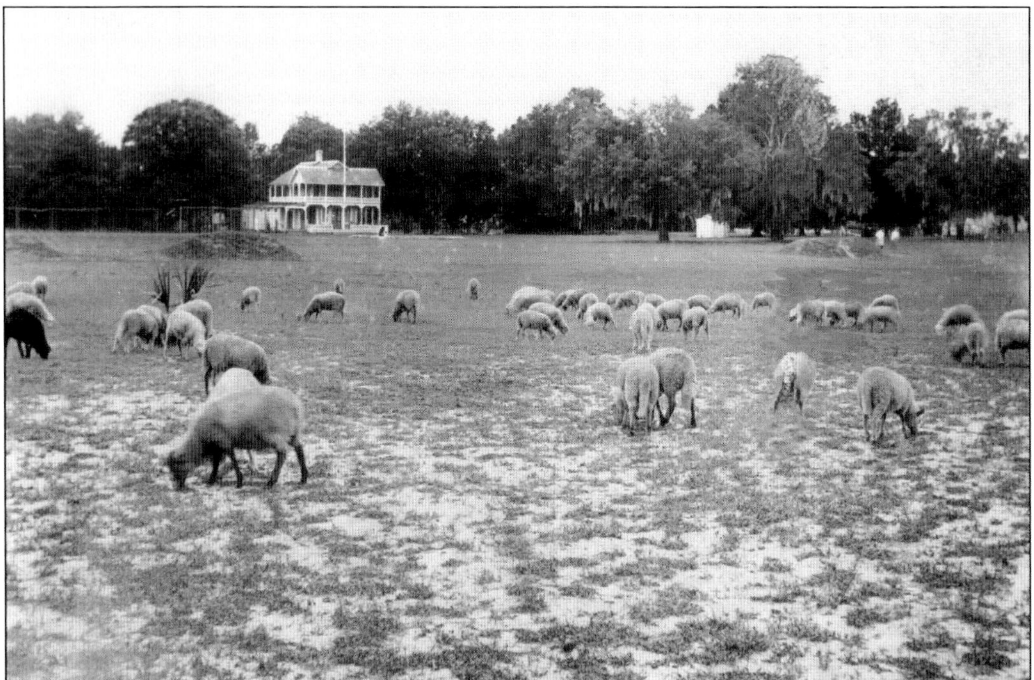

The College Arms Club House was completely surrounded by the golf course and its well-maintained fairways were cared for by some pretty cheap labor—sheep.

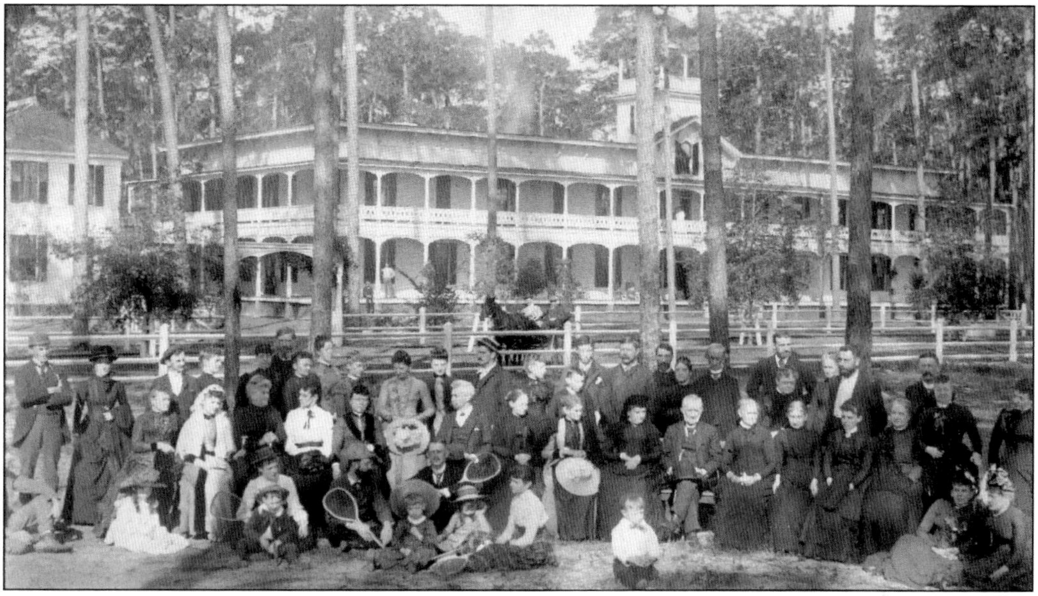

A special retreat from the hectic schedule of loafing tourists and exhausted residents was the 1884 Harlan Hotel in Lake Helen. Henry DeLand named the town after his daughter, then built a hotel and named it after his only son. In front of the hotel and across the street, guests enjoyed water sports in small carpeted and cushioned boats provided free of charge. While also being able to play croquet and lawn tennis on the lush and large grounds surrounded by towering pines, tourists as well as DeLandites wanting a day away from home came in droves, as evidenced by this 1890s photograph.

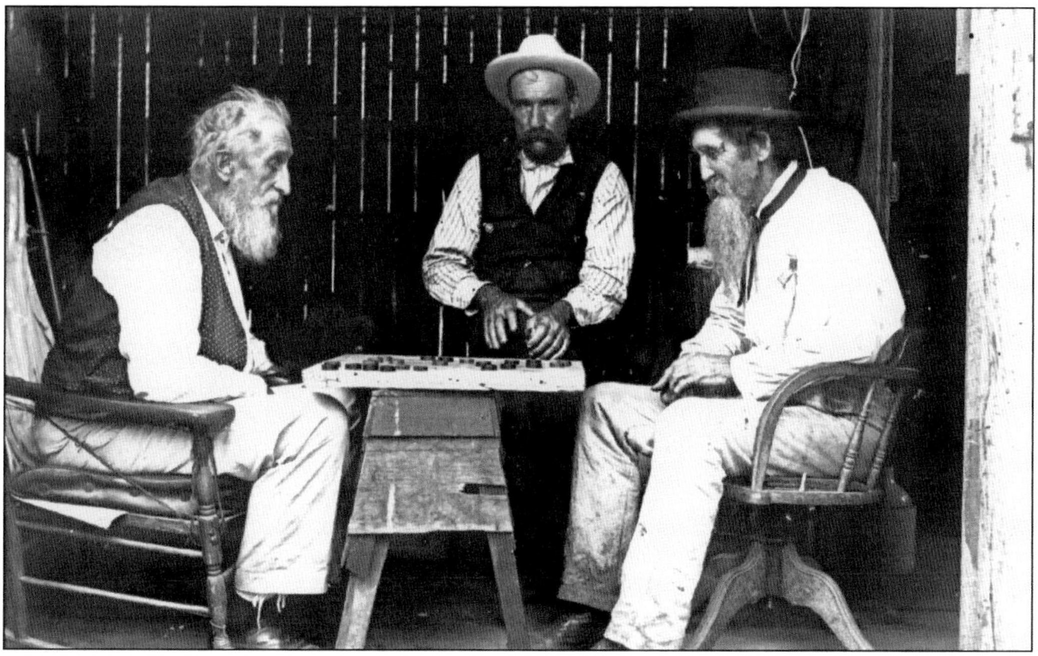

Not all tourists and residents preferred the refined game of golf or the fancy relaxing surroundings of a plush hotel. These serious players found pleasure in a simple game of checkers amidst the heat and sweat of typical Florida weather.

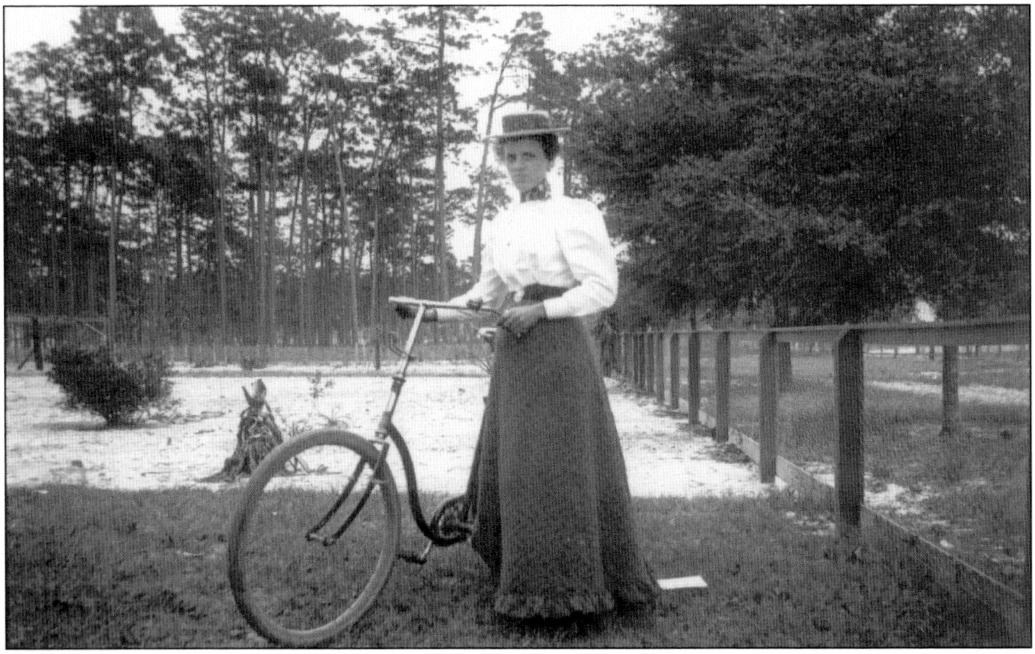

Bicycling was one of the most popular forms of locomotion for residents of DeLand even into the first years of the 20th century. Not only a means of transportation, bicycling also provided a relaxing break from duties indoors and a chance to enjoy the wonders of nature out-of-doors.

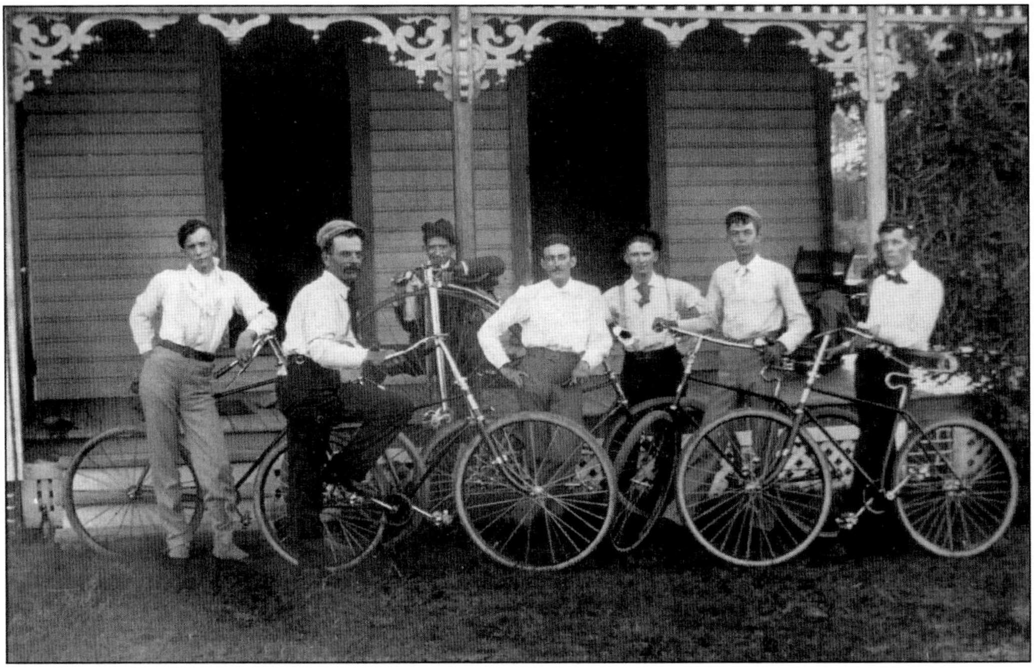

Bicycling was so popular that the town folk formed a bicycling club. DeLand officials supported the club by creating paths that meandered throughout the community and into its idyllic surrounding landscape.

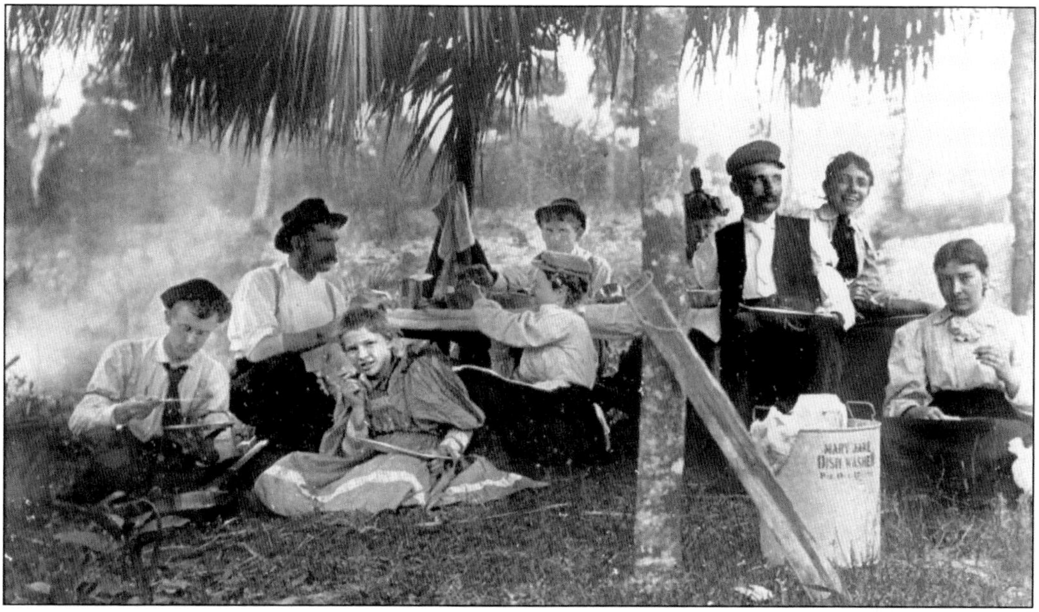

A favorite treat for locals and winter tourists alike was a picnic along the banks of the St. Johns River. Oyster roasts, clam bakes, and Southern fried chicken always tasted extra delicious eaten out-of-doors. Of course the Mary Jane dishwasher accompanied picnickers since paper plates, paper napkins, and plastic eating utensils had yet to be invented. Disposable commodities were still decades away.

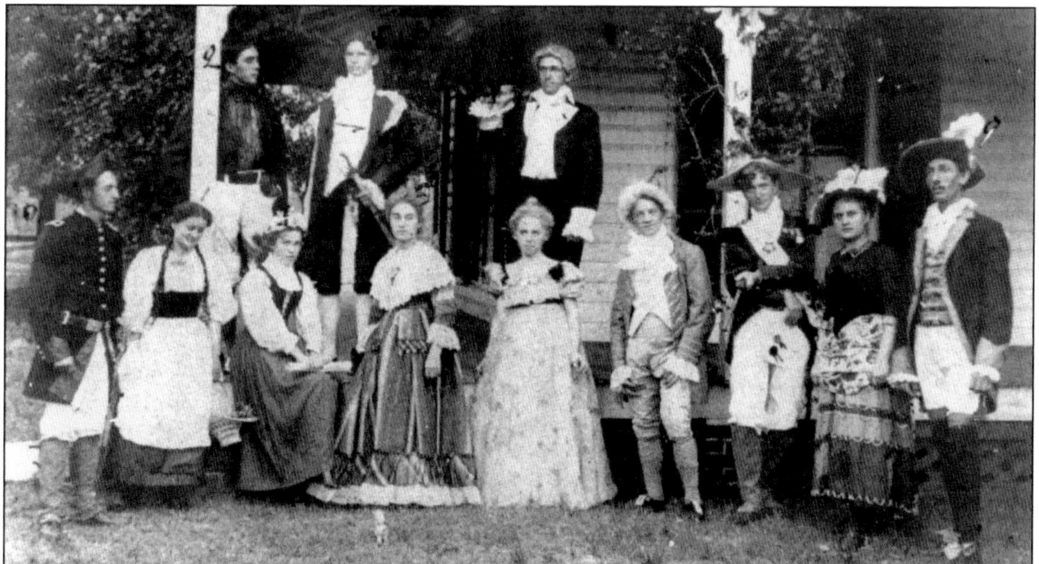

Since 1880, two years before Persimmon Hollow would become DeLand, residents have loved the theater. The first stage show was held in DeLand's first schoolhouse and performed by an all-women cast. One wonders if men in those days had a case of stage fright. However, by 1898 it seemed the men finally came around as evidenced by the cast of *Fantine* standing proudly in full costume. In the front row, from left to right, are John Fudger, Agnes McCoy, Bertha Rogers, Mrs. H.H. Gillen, Ruth Bond, Fred Self, J.F. Alldis, Blanche Bronson, and Andrew Zeigler; in the back row are Sam Walts, Ralph Nix, and R.H. Boyd.

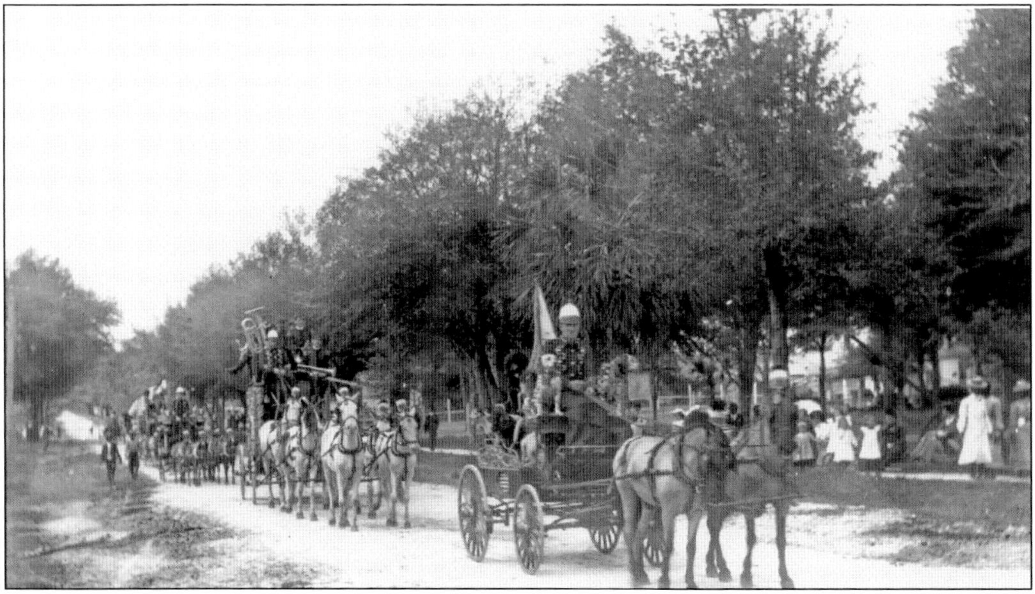

Before the days of radio and television, it was a thrill when the carnival came to town. Its mere mention brought forth imaginations of new and strange attractions witnessed for the first time, special foods to sample, and the novelty of unknown yet anticipated wonders of the world. This 1905 photograph shows a trail of carriages entering DeLand from the railroad station west of town. (Note the still-divided tree-lined Boulevard planned by Henry DeLand decades earlier.)

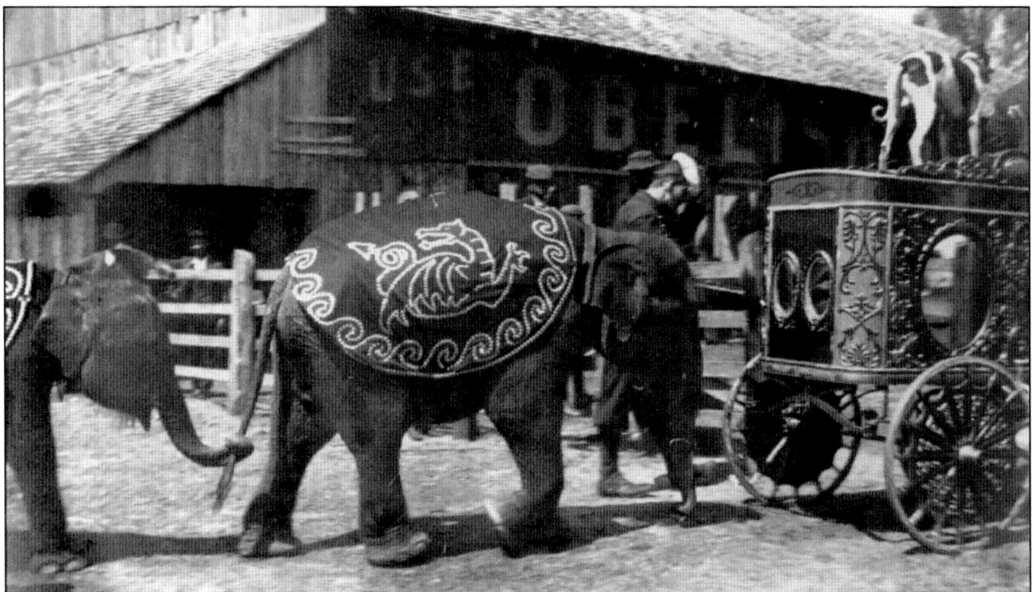

Carnivals were exciting, but it was the circus that held the ultimate thrill for both the young and the old. Beginning around 1914 and for a number of years thereafter, the Johnny Jones Circus wintered at the old fairgrounds west of DeLand and adjacent to the train depot. The circus had almost 400 employees, dozens of lions, tigers, elephants, and other trained animals, and a procession of railroad cars measuring over a mile long. Years later the Clyde Beatty Circus rolled along the tracks into town and resides today in the same location as Jones's earlier circus.

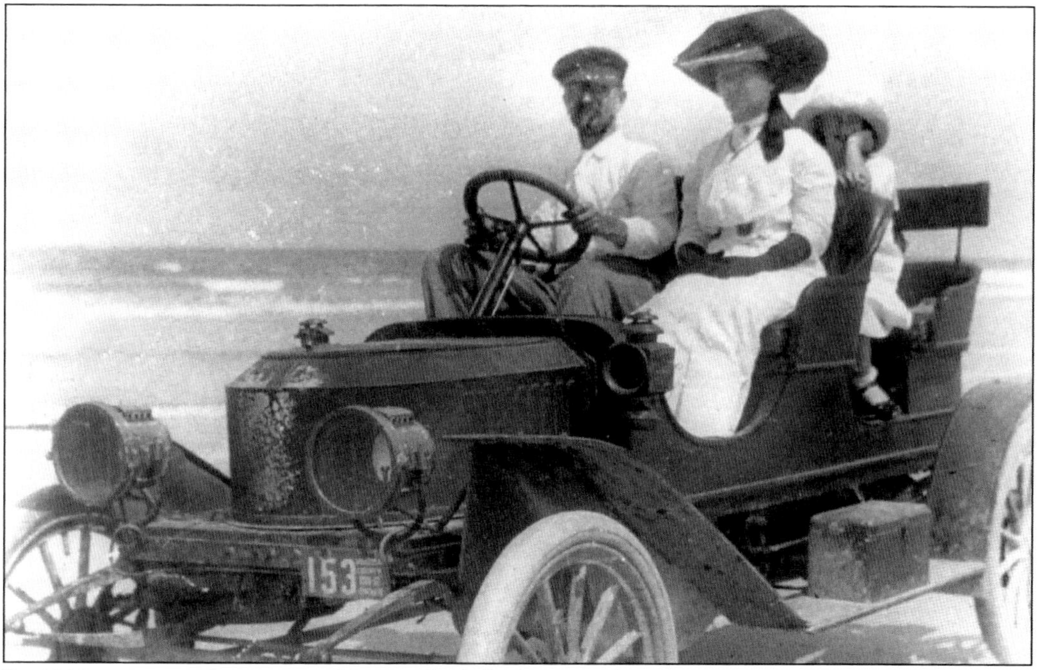

By 1912 many residents were able to afford the luxury of owning an automobile. One fortunate family spent a day at New Smyrna Beach enjoying its newest craze, a fancy "horseless carriage." Averaging approximately 15 to 20 miles per hour, it must have taken these DeLand residents almost two hours to get to the beach and another two hours to return home.

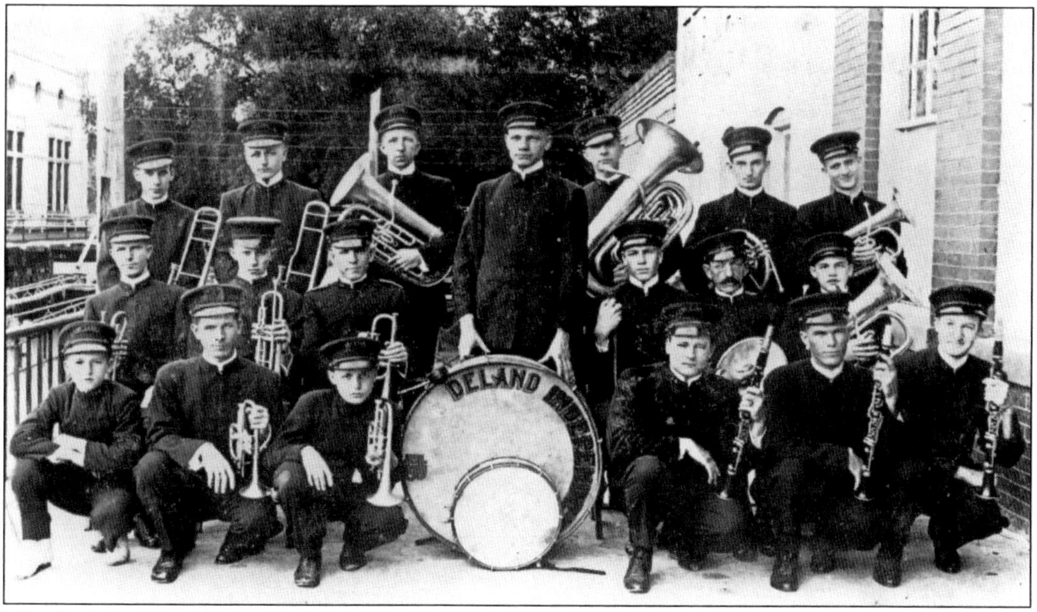

The DeLand Band posed in uniform on a balcony above the Boulevard in 1915. The band offered upbeat and inspiring music for parades and lively tunes for town dances. In the front row from left to right are Wood, Bradley, Peyton, Bushnell, Bradley, and Miller; in the second row are Bradley, Limpus, Bushnell, Brown, Gross, Egbert, and Peyton; the back row are Haynes, Allen, Lindstrom, Messiner, Billis, and Falk.

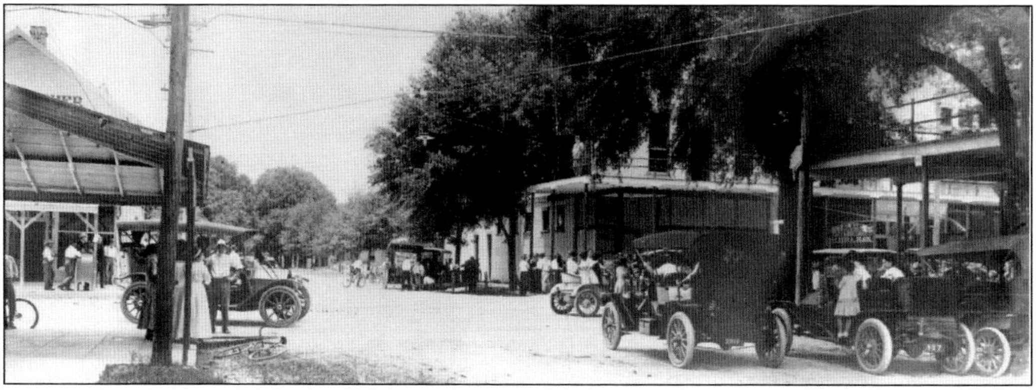

Since DeLand's early days, the Boulevard has been the center of commerce. However, with all of its various businesses, town center has also served as a spot for social activities, as observed in this 1915 photograph. City residents took pleasure in simple activities like visiting together on a street corner.

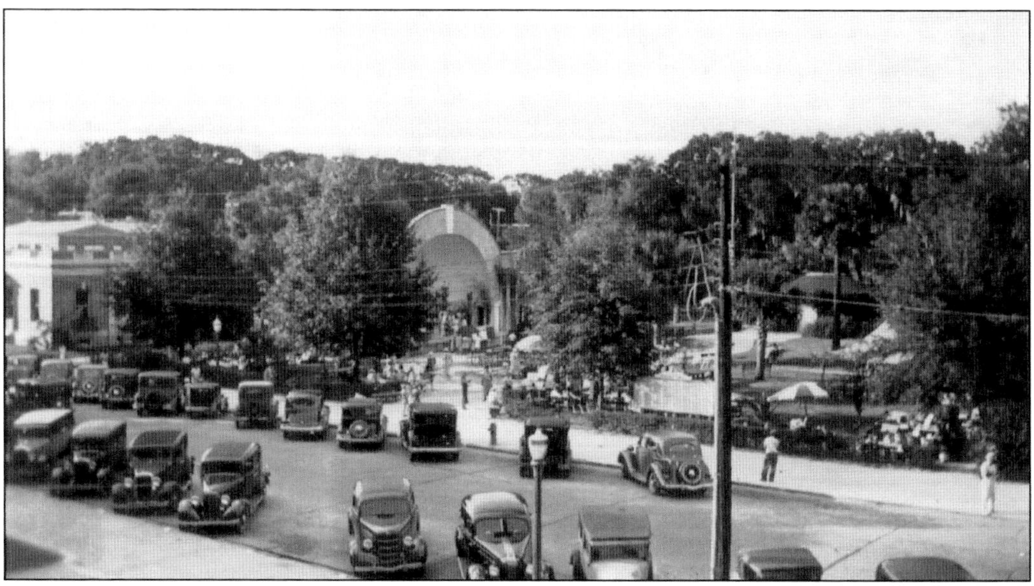

In 1940 Indiana was jammed with cars when residents came to town for a day of music, some tantalizing food, perhaps a little shopping, and of course, a good amount of socializing.

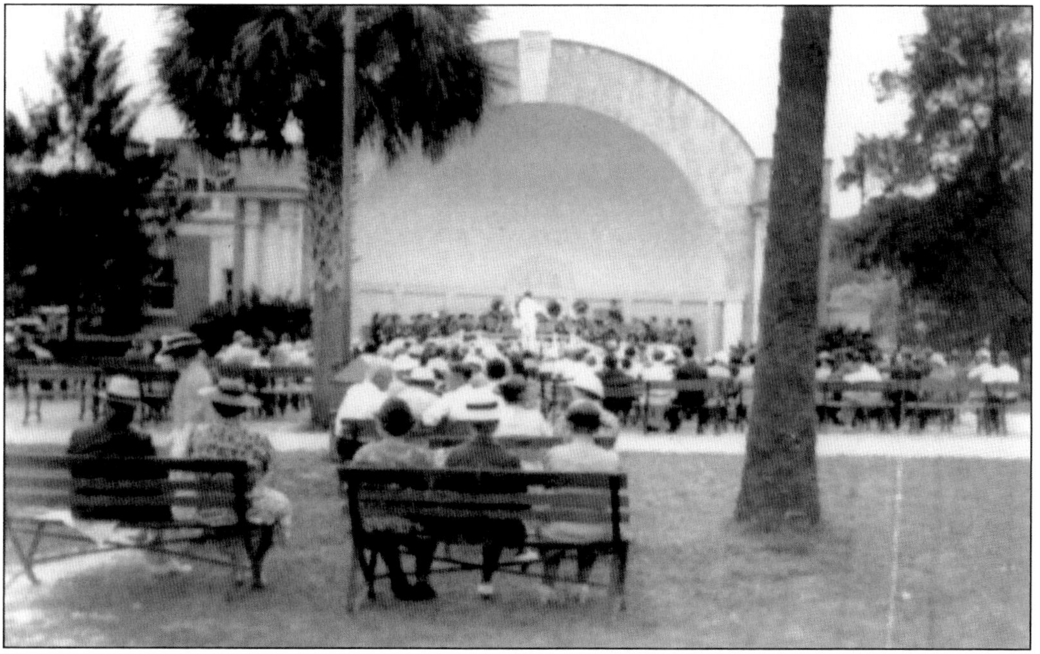

Designed by Medwin Peek in 1929, the DeLand Band Shell at Veterans Park was conveniently located in the heart of downtown DeLand between Rich and Indiana Avenues. Residents took pleasure in Sunday-afternoon concerts under the swaying and majestic palms until this unique outdoor entertainment center was demolished in the 1950s so a multi-storied governmental building could be erected.

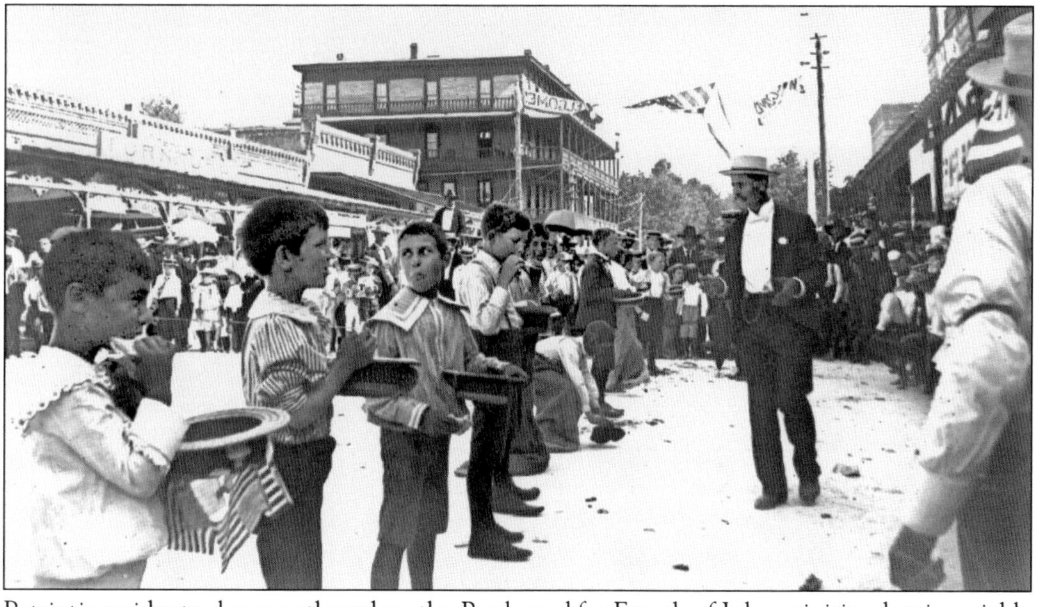

Patriotic residents always gathered on the Boulevard for Fourth of July activities that invariably included a parade, music, and some type of contest. Children are intent on beating each other in an eating contest judged by a DeLand mayor in this early recreational street scene. From the grimaces on the boys' faces, they did not seem to relish the taste of the game. Wonder where the girls were for this sport? Maybe they made the food?

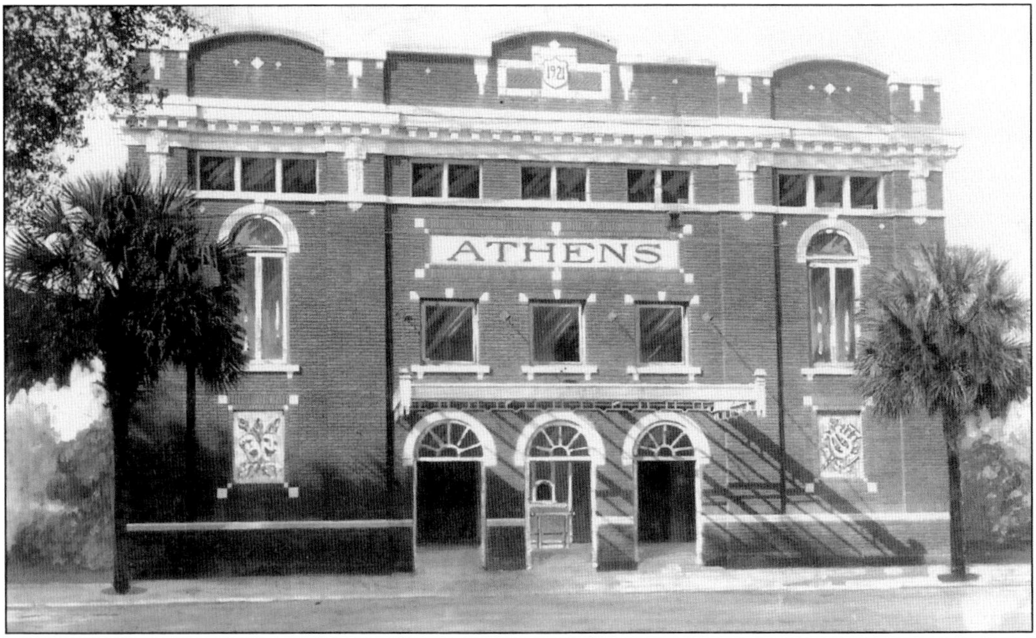

By 1921 the quality of motion pictures had improved to the point that investors saw the advantage of building deluxe theaters to accommodate both a stage for live shows and a screen for moving pictures. Hence, not one but two such theaters were built in 1921 in DeLand; the Athens (above) and the Old Dreka Theatre (below). The Dreka no longer exists but thankfully the Athens does. At present it is in its final stages of restoration thanks to the MainStreet DeLand Association. Soon it will once again be a dynamic visual and performing arts venue.

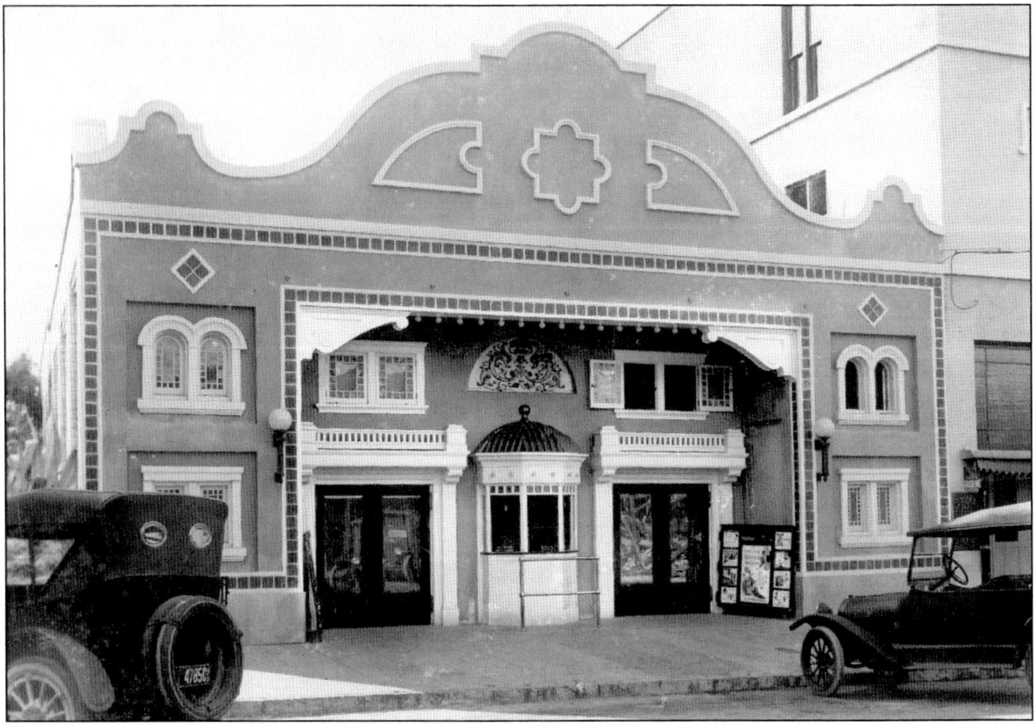

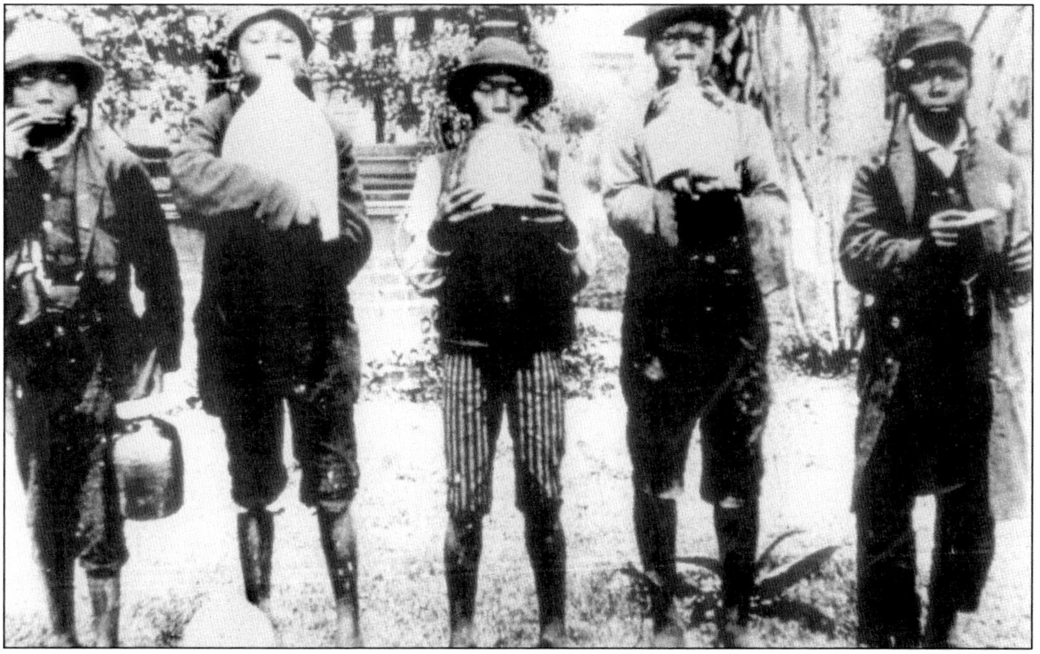

Playing for tourist coins, these barefooted boys positioned themselves ideally in front of the Putnam Hotel to entertain its visitors. They blew enthusiastically on jugs and harmonicas in the hopes that their music would bring a harmonious jingle to their pockets.

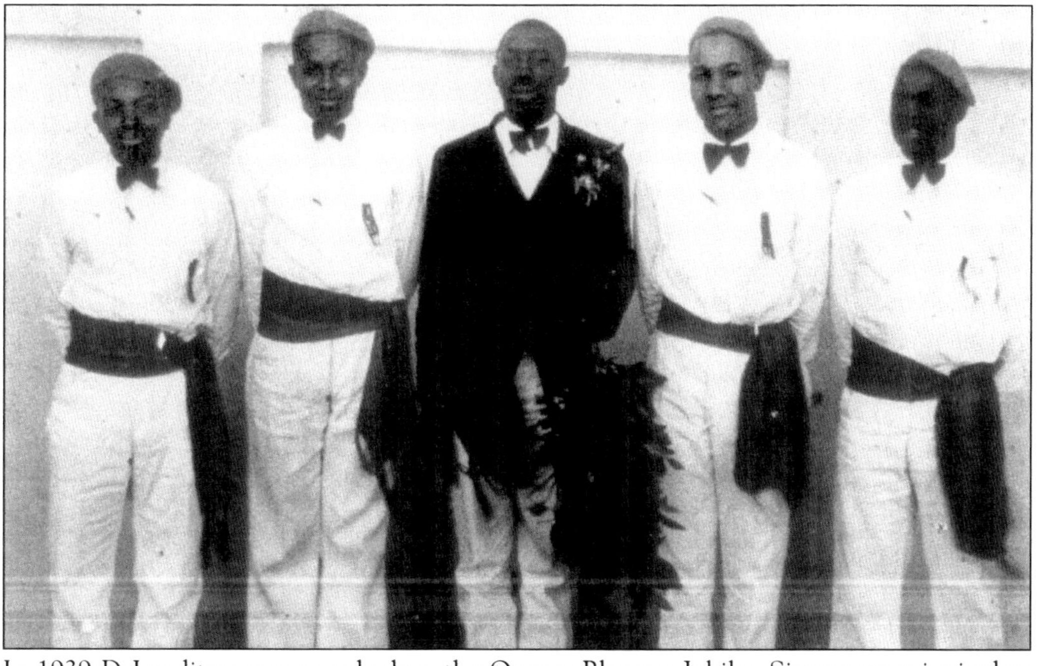

In 1939 DeLandites were proud when the Orange Blossom Jubilee Singers were invited to perform at the New York World's Fair Florida exhibit. They took an orange bough from a local citrus grove to bring them good luck. From left to right are Bradley Calhoun, first tenor; James Andrews, second tenor; Frank Griffen, manager; Robert Jackson, baritone; and Fred Durant, bass.

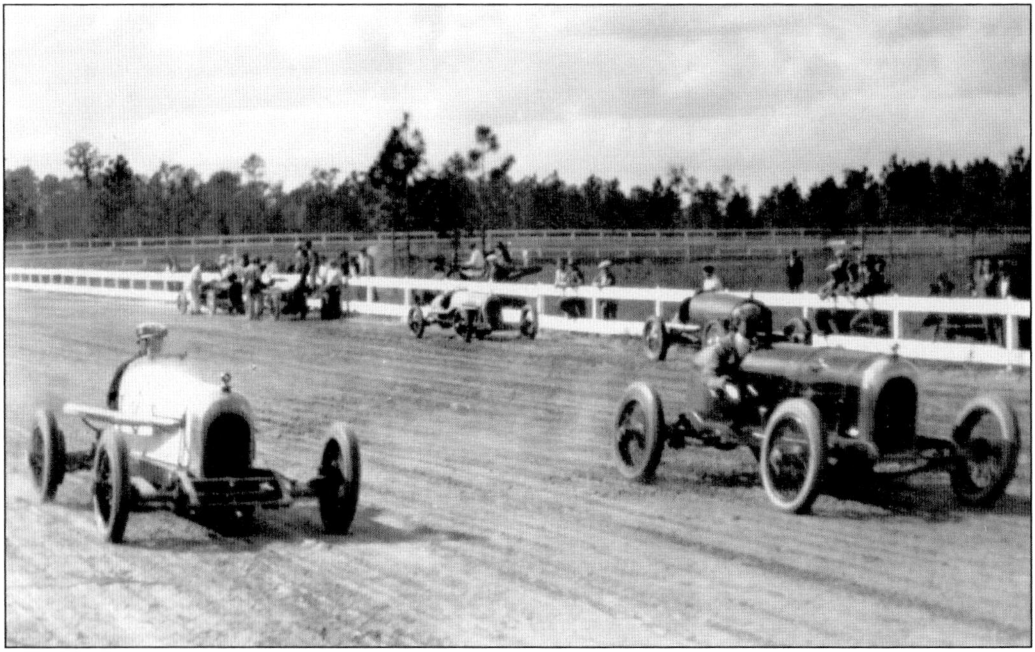

Influenced by their neighbors to the east in Daytona Beach, auto races became a common event in DeLand. The site for such events was at the Fairground's Race Track west of town and adjacent to the train station. A day at the races in the 1930s brought a crowd of gamblers, screamers, and lots of fun and thrills.

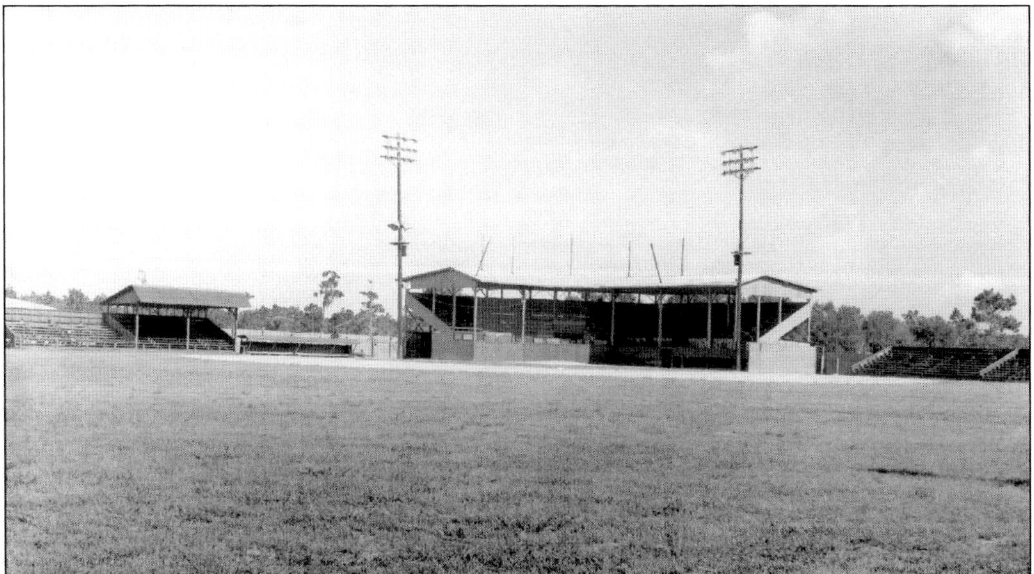

The Conrad Family donated land for the development of the baseball stadium that bears its name, Conrad Park. This picture shows the ball park shortly after its completion in 1932. The grandstand originally backed up against Alabama Avenue; however, after its $5 million reconstruction in the late 1990s the beautiful red brick façade was fittingly placed along DeLand's main thoroughfare, Woodland Boulevard. Conrad Park is home to the Stetson University Baseball Team—the Hatters.

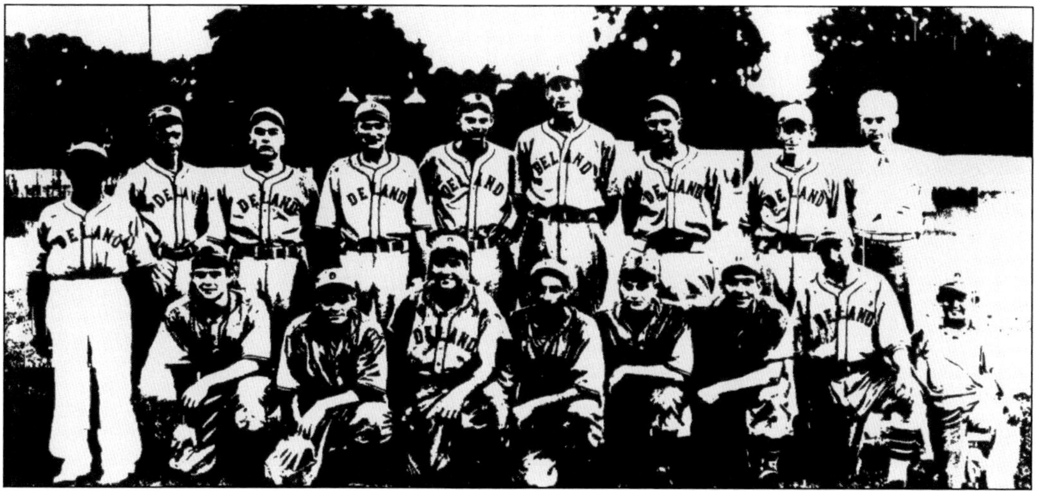

Proving that boys will be boys, the 1937 DeLand Reds Baseball Team posed smugly, eagerly waiting to hear their favorite phrase, "Play Ball!" Men's semi-pro leagues were extremely popular in the South until the 1950s. By the looks on these players' faces, who says one cannot be a kid again? Players truly played for "the love of the game." They worked all day so their families could have a place to rest their heads and food to eat, but the beauty and imaginative quality of baseball allowed them at least nine innings of play. The names of those above are lost to time but many of those below are remembered. In the front row from left to right are unidentified, Billy Sams, Bill Leitz, Jim Robertson, Stanley Culp, and Pepper Martin. In the back row, from left to right, are unidentified, Jake Owens, Winfield Mosely, "Uncle" Bill Page (Father of DeLand baseball), "Lefty" Witt Guys, John "Nut" Shirley, and Gene Fisher.

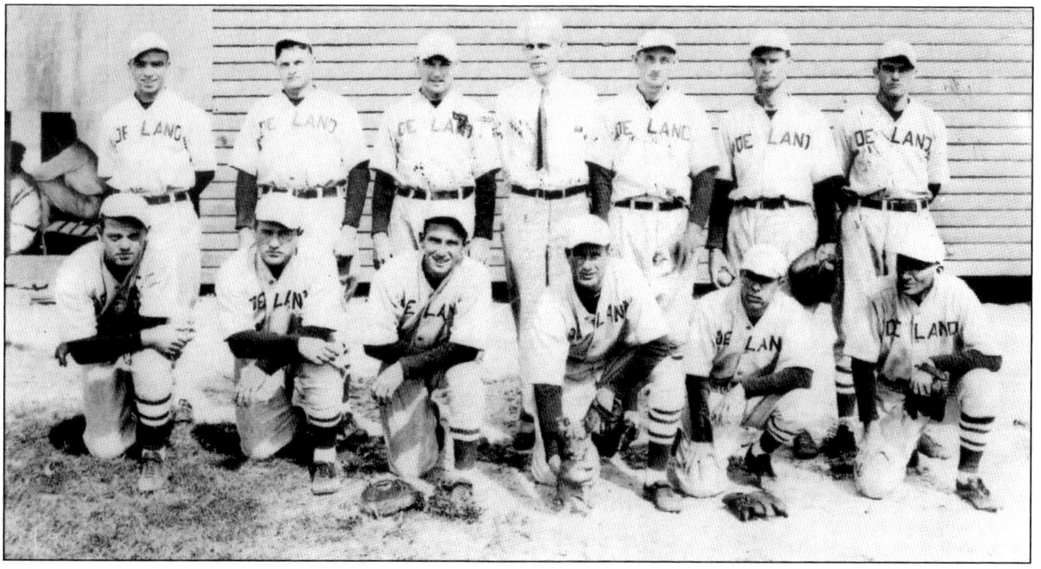

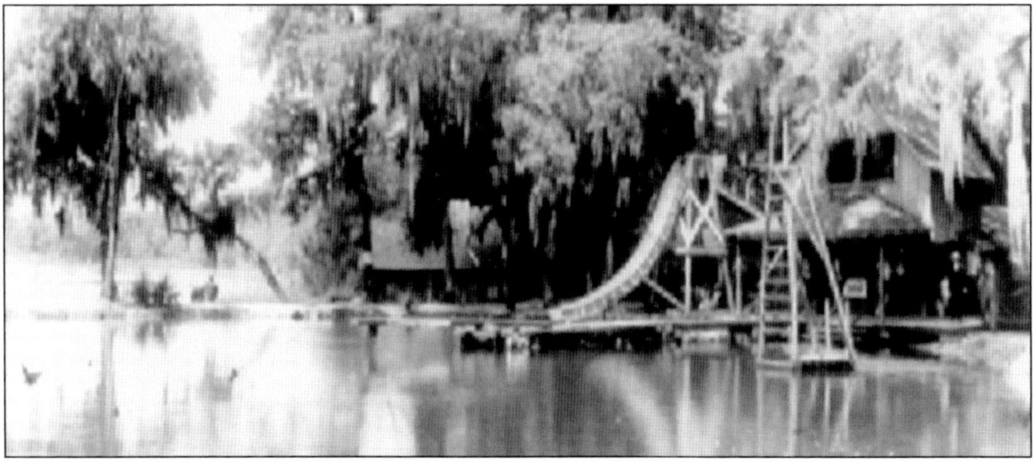

From the 1880s on DeLand offered a wide variety of playful civilities. There were all the games that men and women and children liked to do. People had a variety of transportation to enjoy, plush hotels to stay in, clubs to fraternize, and family outings to attend. And just outside the city limits to the north, south, east, and west one could also find the beautiful tranquility of water—crystal-clear bubbling springs or fresh spring-fed lakes. By 1905 DeLeon Springs, four miles north of town, offered a bathhouse and snack shop. No wonder this part of Florida was so popular.

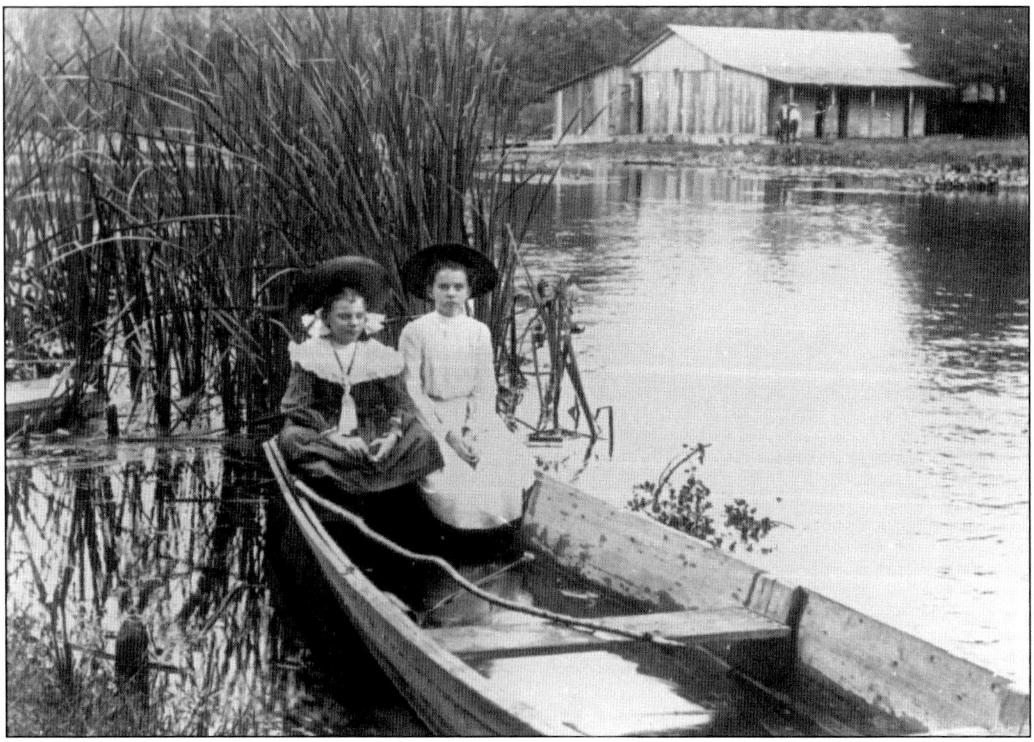

The year 1910 found prim little girls pretending to take a boat ride on the DeLeon Springs Run. Many before and many after have spent lazy days among the towering cypress and the crystal-clear waters of this hidden retreat, frolicking in the constantly refreshing 72-degree water that bubbles up from a pure Florida aquifer.

DeLeon Springs had a 45-foot diving tower that hovered above the watery boil. Many a person braved the high altitude and chilly waters to give his or her friends a thrill. Nestled amongst graying Spanish moss and majestic live oaks, the spring was a favorite gathering place for residents and their guests. The people in this 1930 crowd probably held their breath as the brave men got set to dive and only exhaled when the divers surfaced safe and sound.

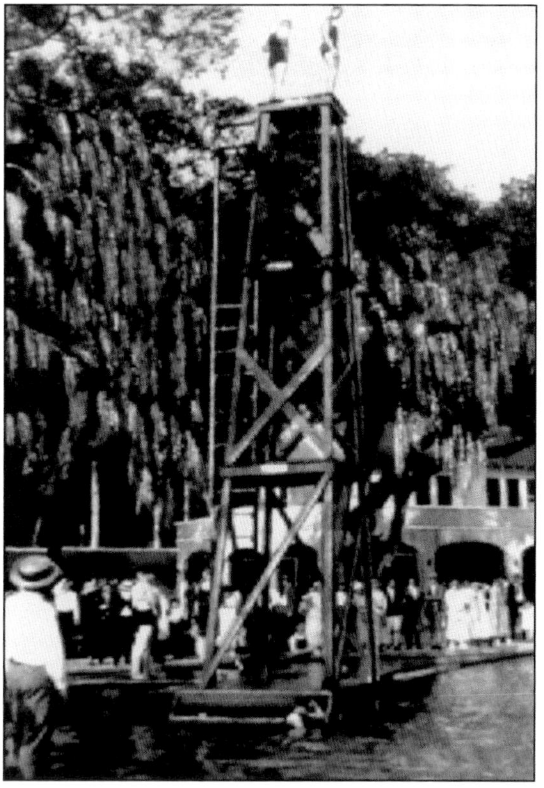

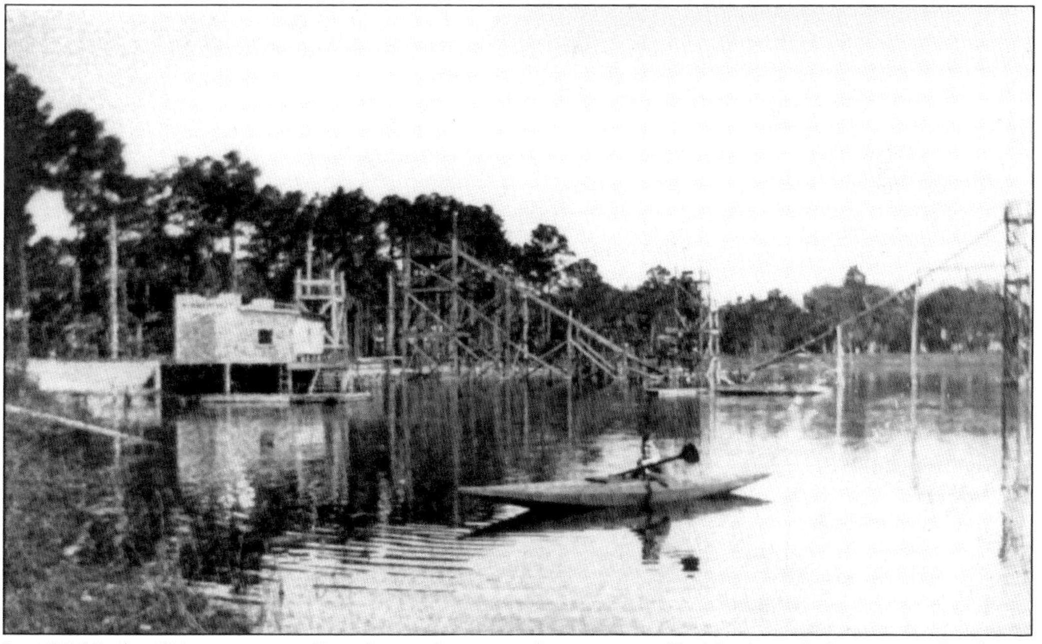

In 1935 Lake Winnemissett Beach, to the east of town, installed high, exhilarating rides down slippery slides to the blue water below. The beach was a popular destination for tourists and locals alike as weekends found the spot full of sun worshippers and bathers looking to cool down and have a little fun doing it.

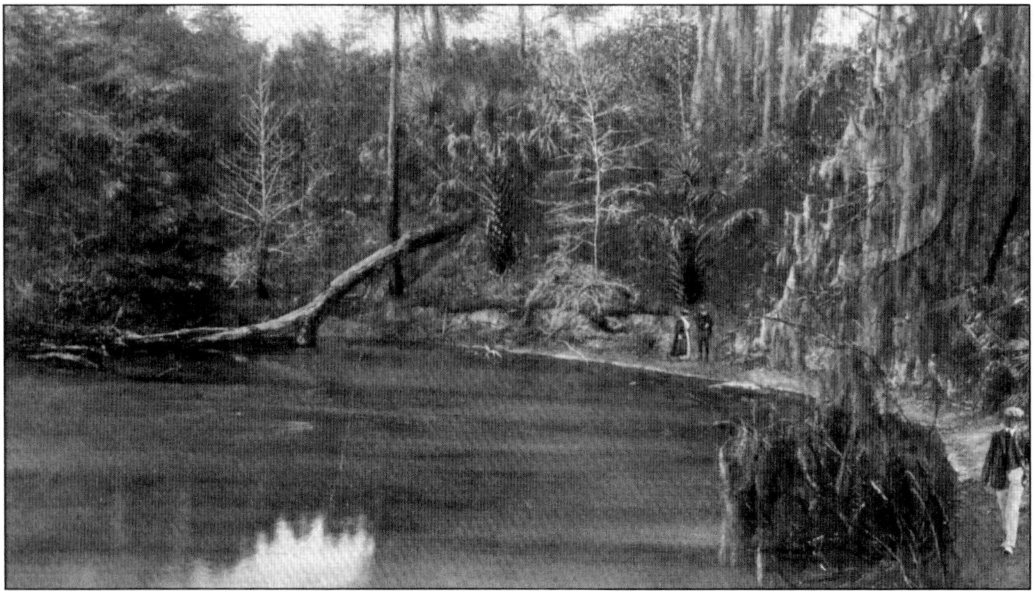

South of DeLand is the "diaphanous cerulean fountain" that William Bartram described in his *Travels*, published in 1791. Luring tourists from afar, local residents, all sorts of species of birds, and of course the manatee, Blue Spring has played a part in eco-tourism for decades, as evidenced by this 1905 photograph.

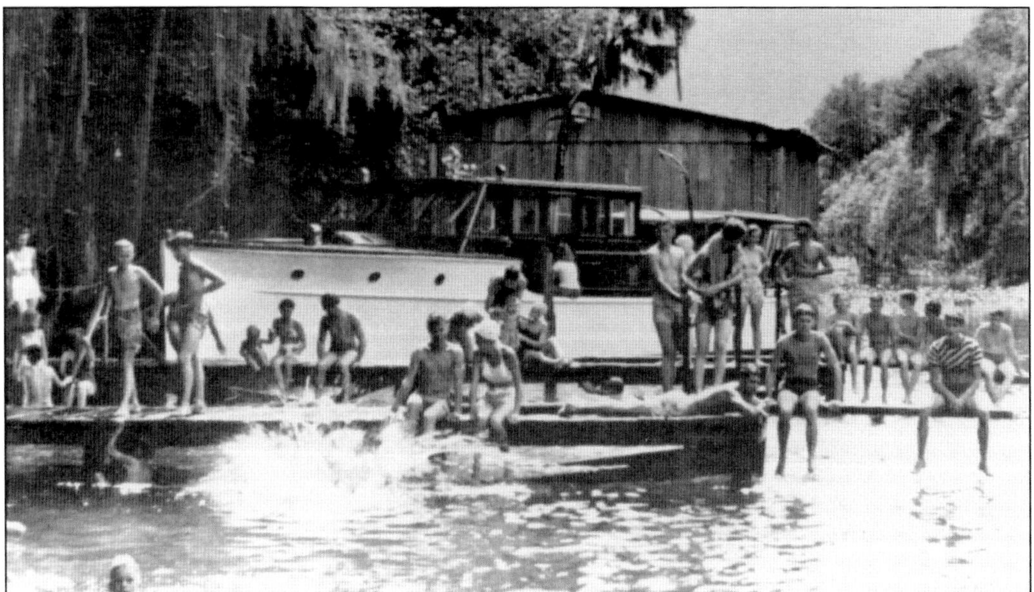

With Spanish moss dangling near the water's edge and the prospect of catching a glimpse of a manatee, (Spanish for "sea cow," the name given them by explorers), these 1945 swimmers surely take pleasure in their day at Blue Spring. Manatees frequent the spring during the winter months and are friendly, trusting creatures. Since their numbers have dwindled, the federal government has taken steps to protect the species from extinction. Blue Spring today remains one of the most popular watering holes frequented by people waiting to catch a glimpse of the spring's most unique winter residents.

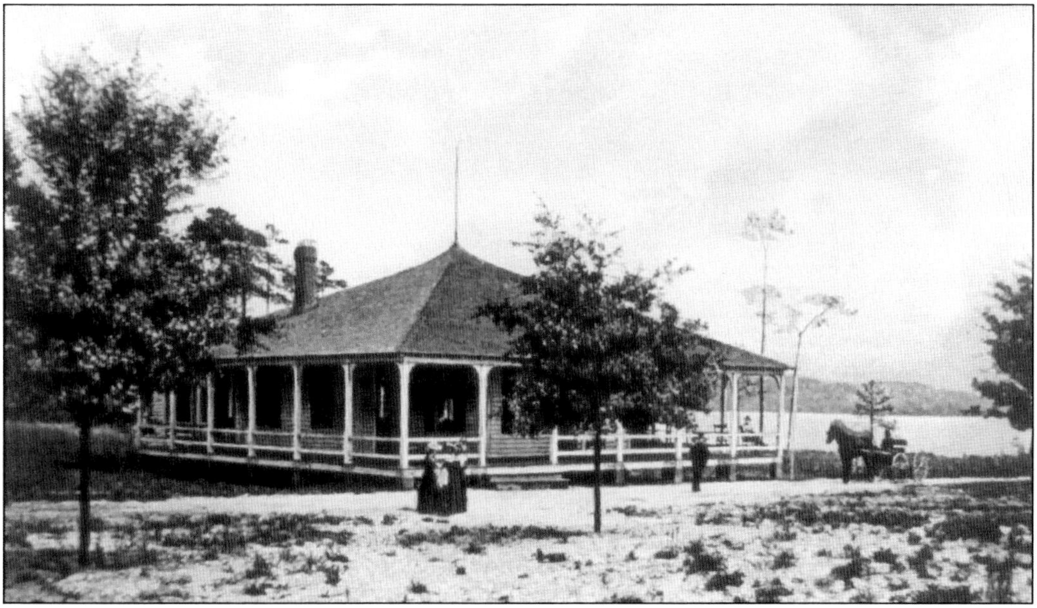

The DeLand Aquatic Club was founded in 1901, with its clubhouse built at Blue Lake on approximately 1,000 acres of land bought by the boating enthusiasts. Located east on Minnesota Avenue, the club was extolled as "a place for the sightseer or picnic party to rest . . . to lie in the cool hammocks and see the rippling blue water."

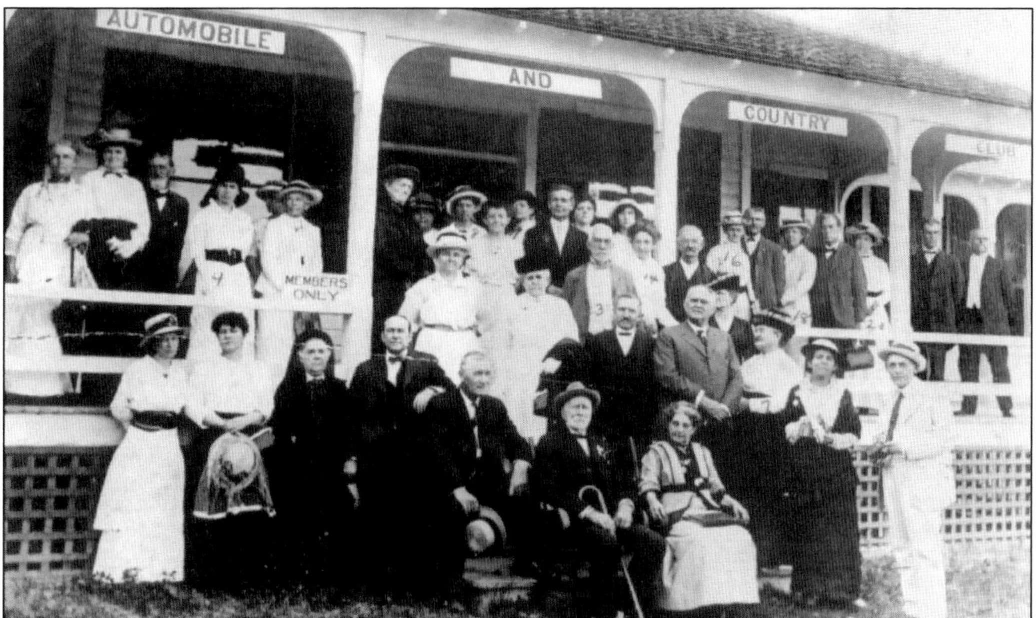

The Aquatic Club was also a popular spot for the Old Settler's Society to hold its annual meetings. In 1912 the Society posed on the front veranda of the clubhouse.

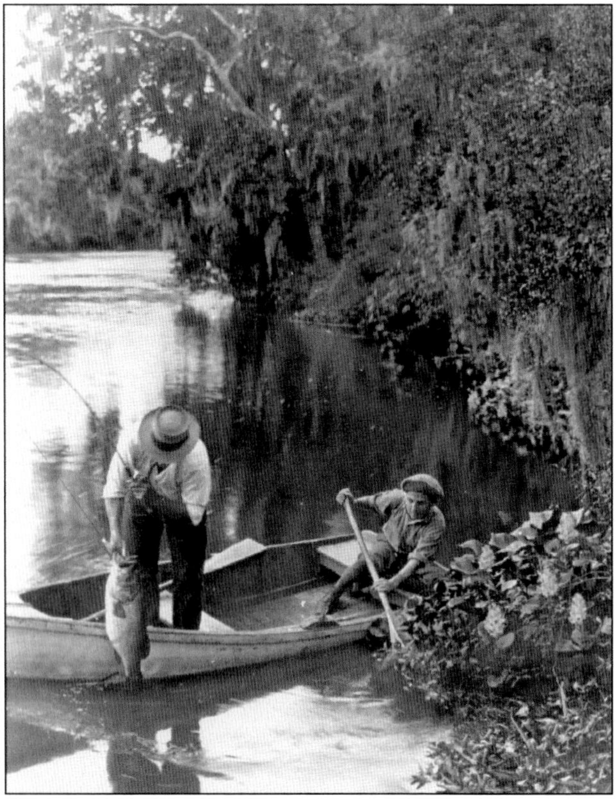

Two locals hauled in a big one in 1925. Fishing has always been a passionate diversion for DeLandites. At one time the town even advertised itself as the bass capital of the world. It is rare now to catch such a hefty wide-mouth bass. Over-fishing, loss of habitat, and pollution have caused this delicious sport to be reduced to lower and lower numbers.

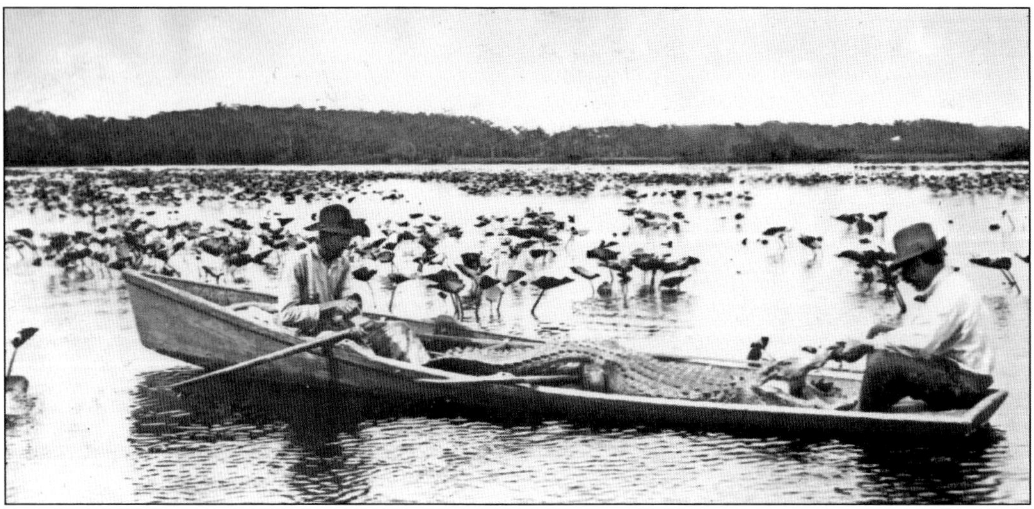

Boating, swimming, and fishing were not the only water sports—alligator hunting was immensely popular whether it was for the gator's hide used for a variety of products or the meat of the tail for its delicious flavor. In 1916 locals captured on film the proof of their 11-foot catch in Lake Woodruff. Now a federally designated national wildlife refuge, Lake Woodruff, like all of the breathtaking natural areas surrounding DeLand, adds a rich dimension to recreational activities. Lake Woodruff is protected in perpetuity, and as for the gator, he too is federally protected. But locals and visitors can continue to play along his waterways and in his ponds—if they dare.

Four

AT WORK

In the fall of 1852 Tobias Blackwelder moved his family from South Carolina to Volusia County in a wagon pulled by oxen. After settling on Lake Winona, the family cleared land and planted corn, cotton, and sugar cane. They also raised hogs. After several years of living in a small log cabin and farming his land, Blackwelder hauled his cotton by wagon to Ocala to trade it for lumber so he could provide his family with a two-story home on Lake Winona. Tobias Blackwelder understood that through hard work he could build a bright future for his family; a life where his children would have more than he, and a house his family would be proud to call home.

America was founded on the ideal of an individual's pursuit of freedom and ultimately happiness. Through the years this ideal has been achieved by those who have obtained a job, worked hard, created a family, bought a home, and built for the future. A community is a macrocosm of this ideal as citizens must work diligently to assure an even better community for their children.

DeLand's story, from its beginning as a woodsy village deep within the swampy terrain of Central Florida, is no different. The first time Henry A. DeLand visited Persimmon Hollow he had a vision of what the community could become—a prosperous town built from industrious work. He recognized the uniqueness of the area and the promise it held as a place where people would want to live.

The prospect of great wealth was evident to Mr. DeLand in the endless acres of citrus groves thriving in the area. Hailing from the industrialized North, Mr. DeLand had firsthand knowledge of what was needed to develop a modern city. One of his first actions toward that goal was to donate to the community a 60-foot wide strip of land for a thoroughfare beginning at present-day New York Avenue and extending a mile north. Land was cleared and oaks, magnolias, and orange trees were planted on both sides of the street and down the median. Hence, when Woodland Boulevard was created, DeLand's commercial district came into being.

From the beginning DeLand residents have made the downtown area surrounding the intersection of New York and the Boulevard the center of their working world. While a sense of community in America has been fragmented and in some cases completely erased by urban sprawl, DeLand residents are steadfast in the belief that their quaint downtown is and must remain the heart and soul of their city. Striving to keep DeLand's commercial district prosperous were and still are local business owners and their faithful customers, laboring together to safeguard DeLand's uniqueness.

Residents of DeLand have proven, since the town's inception, that a strong work ethic reaps dividends, that commerce and beauty can co-exist, even enhance each other, that incorporating older buildings with modern occupations can bring comfort during a hard day's work, and that preserving an historic downtown commercial district simply expressed—just works.

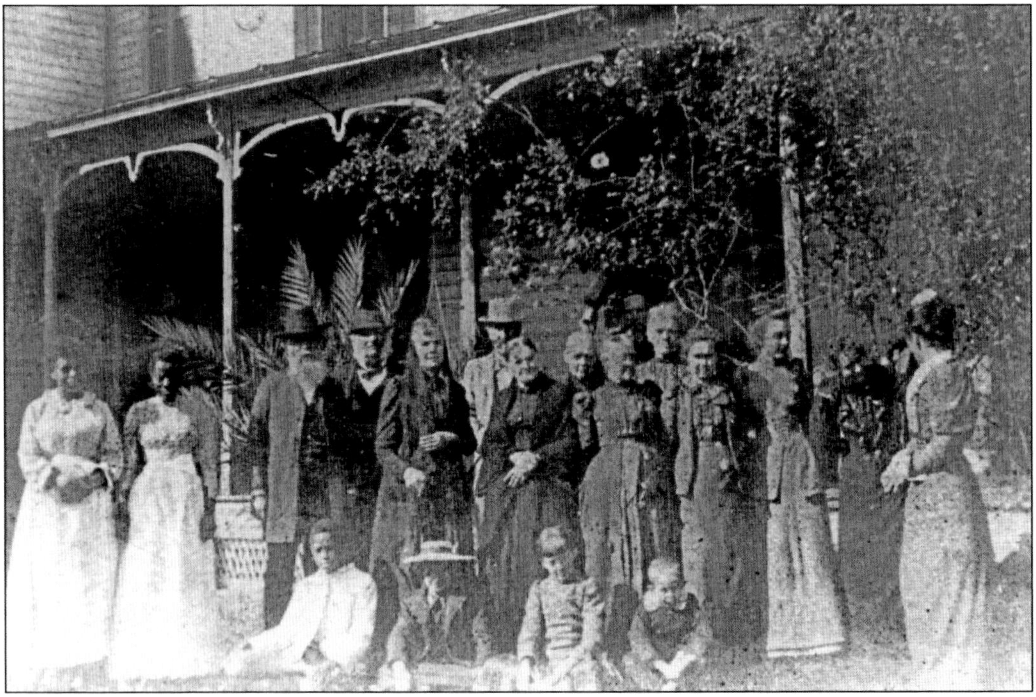

"Orange Fever" brought many to the small community of Persimmon Hollow. O.P. Terry, Henry A. DeLand's brother-in-law, was the first to catch the "disease." He bought land in the Hollow and eventually convinced DeLand to come and see what he had purchased. DeLand soon caught a case of "orange fever" along with the vision to create a thriving educational and industrial community nestled among acres and acres of orange groves. Mr. DeLand is pictured third from left and his daughter, Helen, third from right, as they stand with visitors from the North.

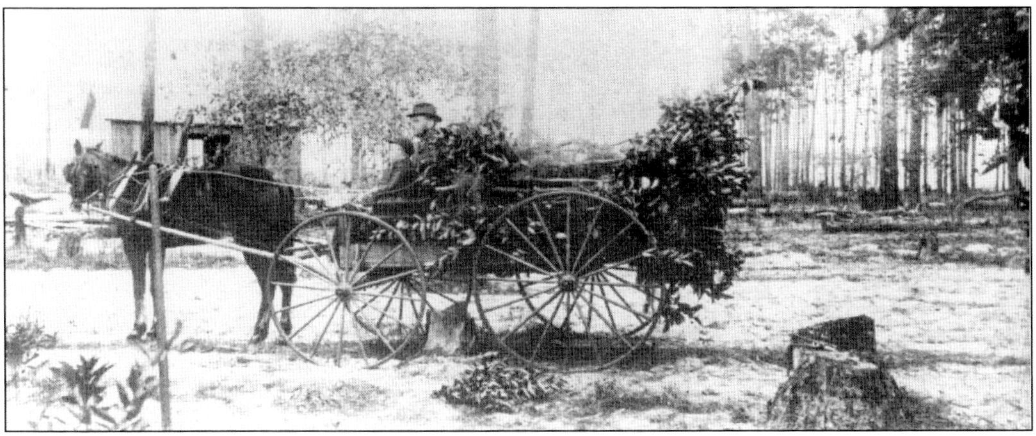

Orange trees were brought from other citrus-producing communities, transported to DeLand by wagon and mule, and planted on land that had once been a pine forest. Mr. DeLand felt so strongly about the potential in citrus production that he promised anyone who did not have a productive citrus growing season could sell their land back to him. Two freezes, one in December 1894 and dubbed the "Big Freeze," then another in 1895, almost led Mr. DeLand to bankruptcy. As a man of his word, Mr. DeLand bought back the land from pioneers who lost their citrus crops and chose to return north rather than stay and replant.

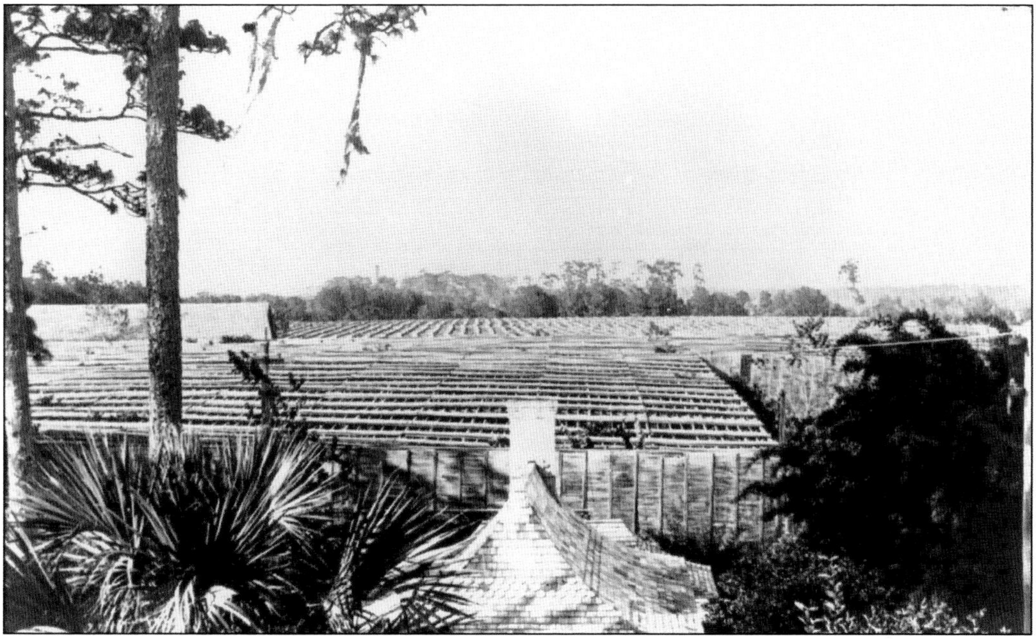

After the first "Big Freeze" most growers sought new methods for protecting their groves from replanting on high ground for water run-off or planting near water or under canopy trees to minimize frost damage. But it was the innovativeness of John B. Stetson that intrigued his competitors. He was the first to build wooden structures over his groves to mitigate extreme temperatures. Inside his enclosed 1898 grove Mr. Stetson installed rails for push carts to haul fertilizer in and cut fruit out. He and other citrus growers tried numerous ways to ensure that the economic nightmares of 1894 and 1895 would not reoccur.

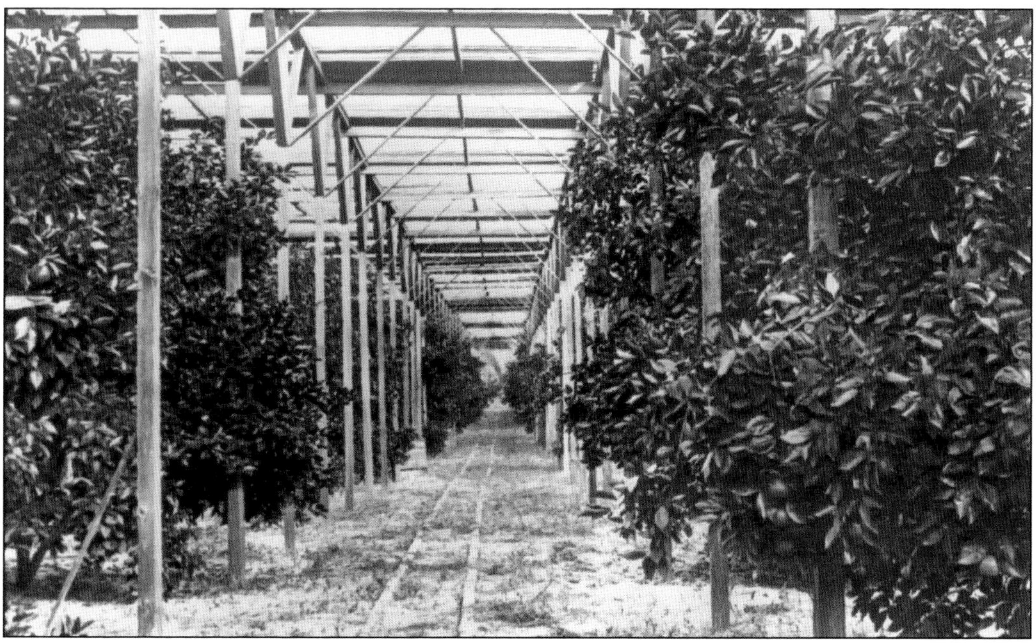

Wooden slats were cut at the sawmill and hauled to the groves by mule, man, and cart, then assembled over Mr. Stetson's delicious crop of "golden apples."

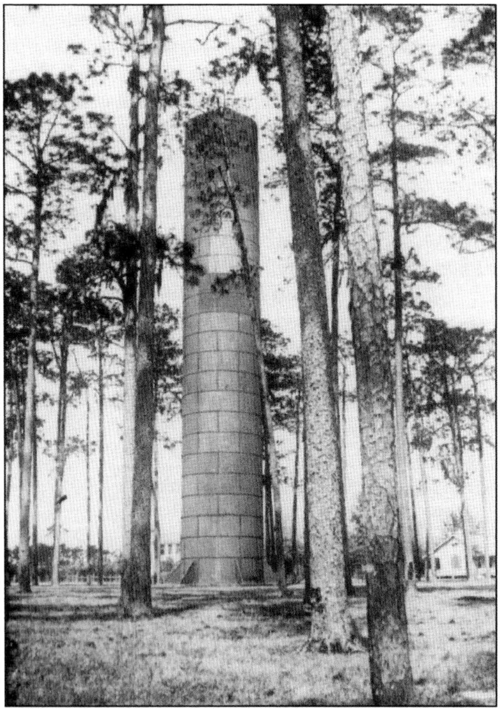

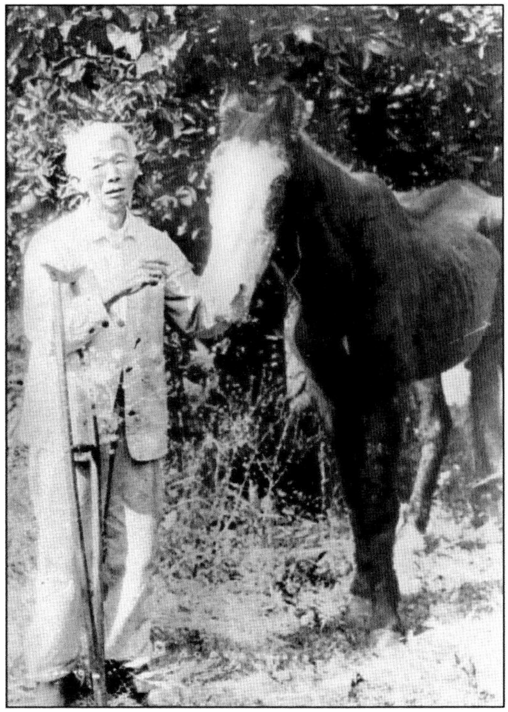

(left) John B. Stetson used this massive tank to capture rainwater for irrigating his orange groves. Some suggest that was the only known water tank of its kind in the United States. *(right)* In 1886 Lue Gim Gong, 26, arrived in DeLand to work in William Dumville's groves. When the 1894 freeze hit, Dumville returned north and Gong was fortunate to be given his property.

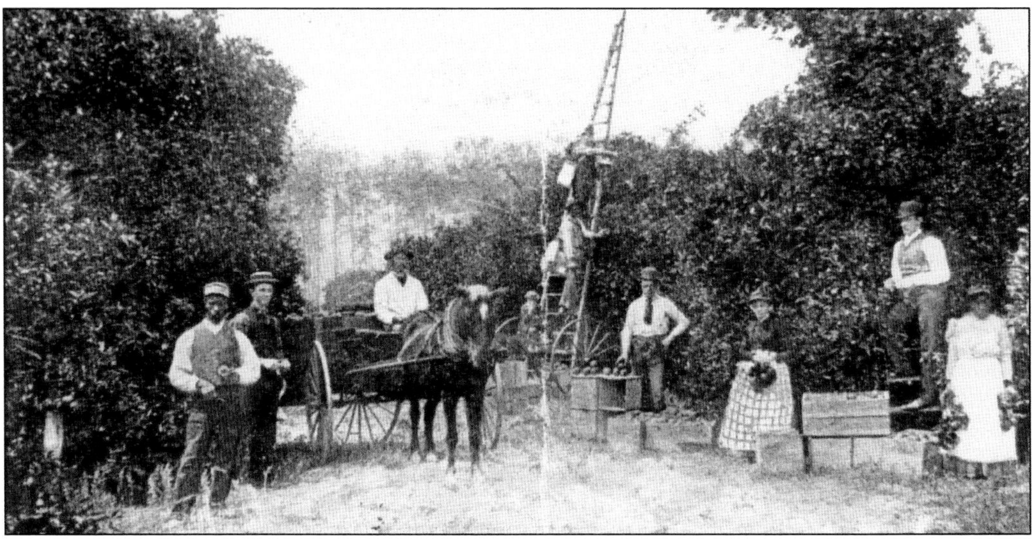

Lue Gim Gong's crew cultivated and harvested the citrus groves that had been ruined during earlier freezes. Due to his perseverance and ultimate success, in 1911 Gong was awarded a Silver Wilder Medal from the United States Department of Agriculture for cross-pollinating a "Hart's Late" with a "Mediterranean Sweet." The new orange, named the "Lue Gim Gong," ripened in early fall and was more resistant to cold weather.

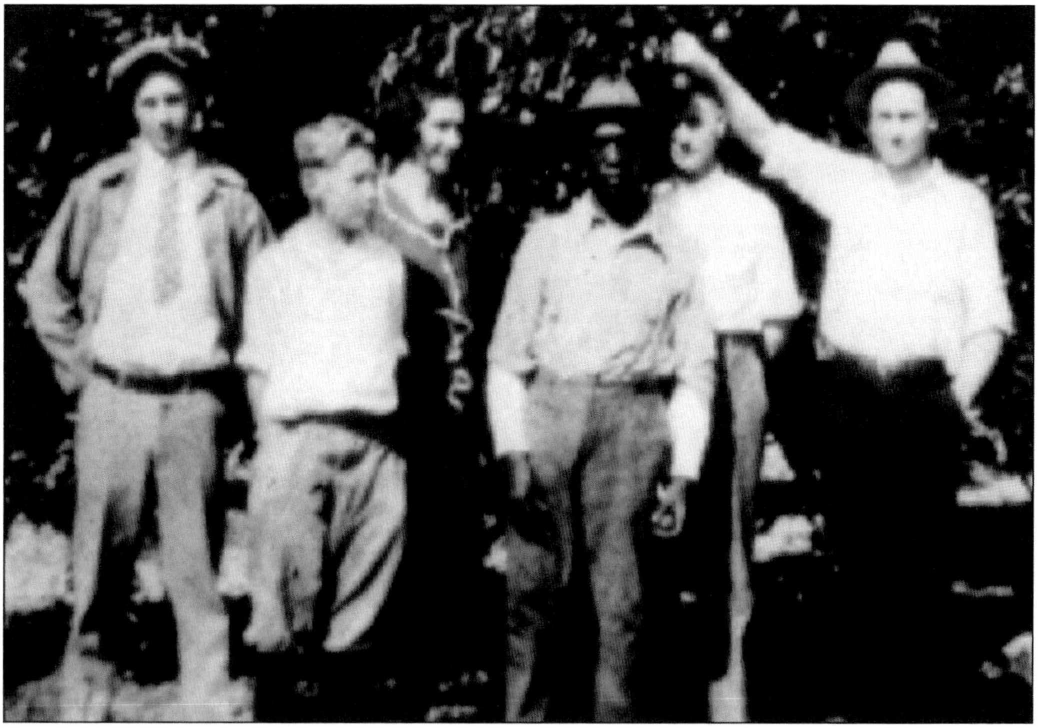

James W. Wright, an African-American entrepreneur, came to DeLand in 1890 at the age of 15 with $1.50 in his pocket and a determination to succeed. He worked five years saving every dime he could. After the big freezes of 1894 and 1895, he bought five acres of ruined citrus crop land. He worked many nights by lantern tending the groves and budding his trees. Eventually Wright accumulated 320 acres, planting them in citrus and vegetables. Wright stands in the center of his friends and young helpers amid his productive groves.

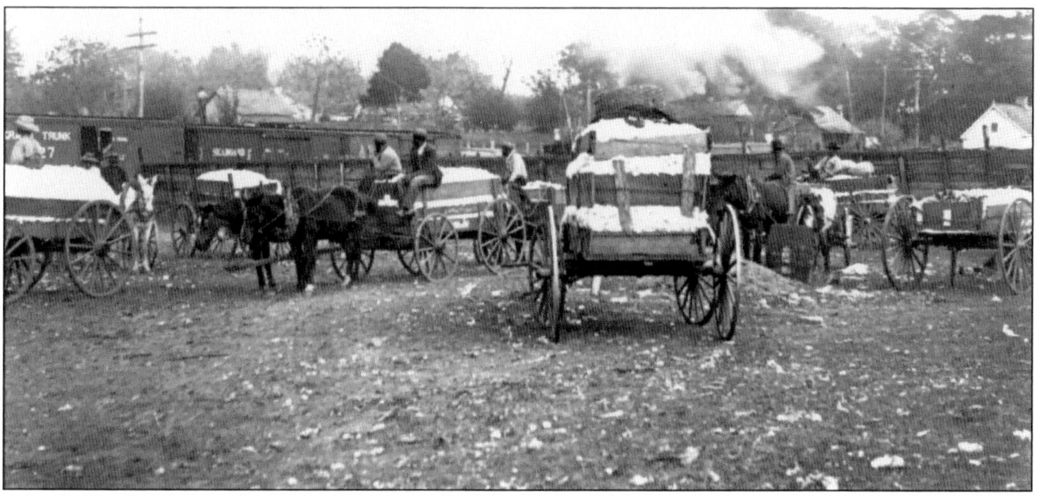

Citrus was not the only crop that gave work to the community. Popular in Georgia and South Carolina, Floridians decided to try their hand at raising Sea Island or Long Staple cotton. At John B. Stetson's railroad siding, wagons came in heavy and left empty and ready for another load. This variety of cotton was grown extensively in West Volusia although the ginning process was completed in Leesburg, an hour's distance from DeLand.

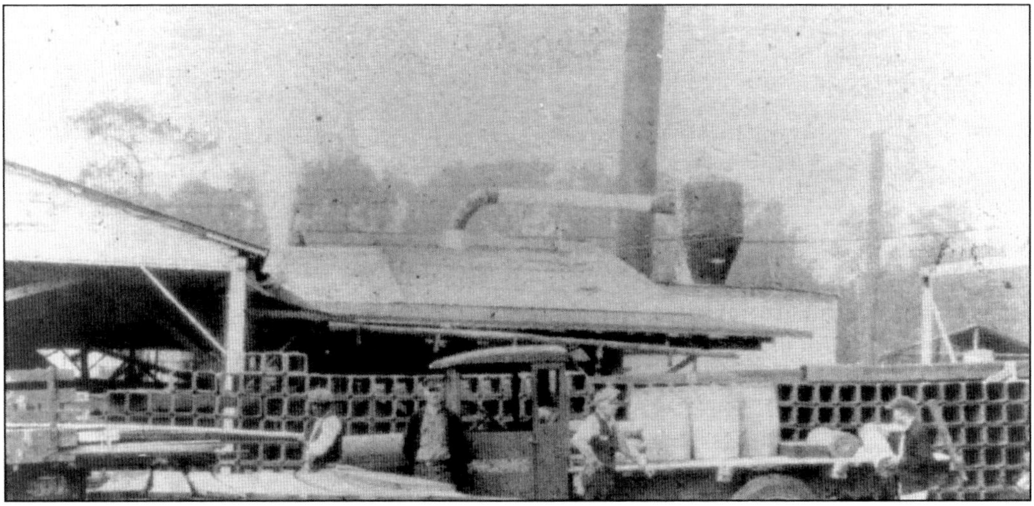

Timber was a natural product in the area so DeLandites took advantage of Mother Nature's bounty. The McCormick Lumber Company, organized in 1909, was located in the 300 block of North Delaware. Sawmills scattered about the county gave employment to many. Ever-present were the distinctive scent of cut wood and the sound of timber meeting steel. The shrill steam whistle blew four times a day to announce the beginning and ending of the work day, to let laborers take a break, and to stop for a bite to eat.

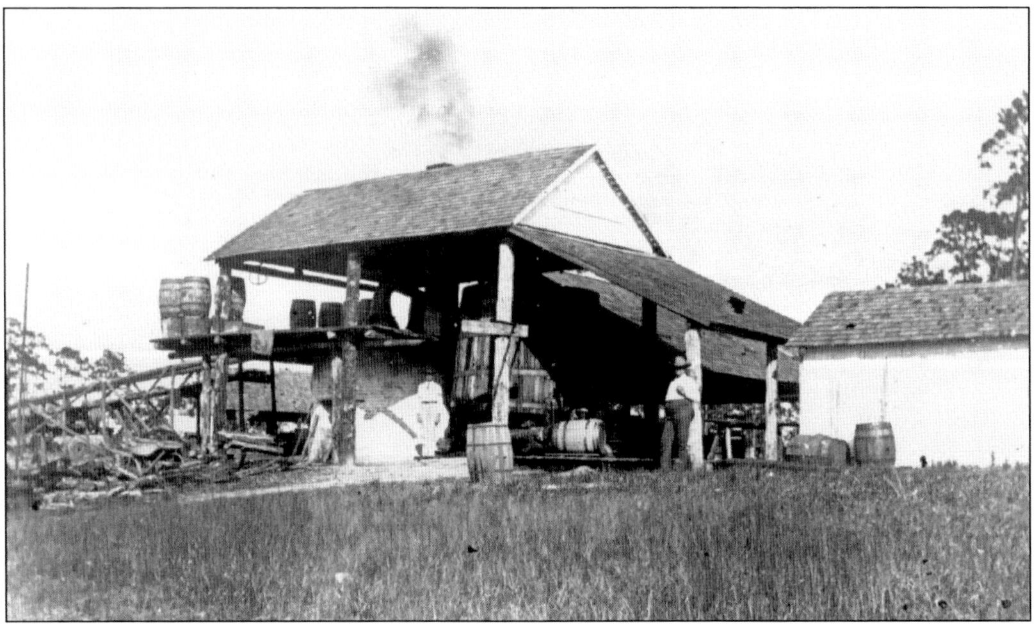

A natural by-product of pine is resin and from resin comes turpentine. Since the DeLand area had an abundance of Long-leaf yellow and slash pine, a thriving business grew among the pines. Turpentine was used as a thinner in paints and varnishes, for medicinal purposes, and in the manufacture of celluloid and eventually plastics. Between 1890 and 1935 numerous turpentine stills operated in the area. One owned by Mr. Paxton was located on the old Daytona Road. These stills usually consisted of shabby framed buildings abandoned once the forest had been decimated. There was little thought in those early days to conserve natural resources. Workers seemed to think that trees were there for the taking and need not be replenished for future use.

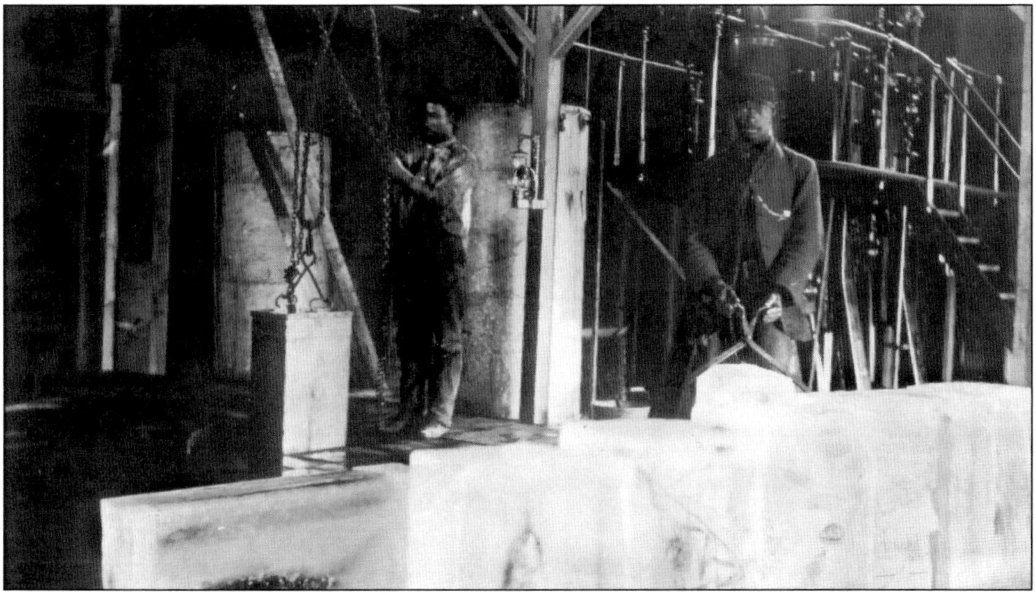

Henry M. Flagler, railroad magnate and co-owner of Standard Oil, brought ice to Florida when he developed the east coast as a winter retreat for the wealthy. But it was John B. Stetson who brought this coveted luxury to DeLand when he opened his ice plant in 1886. So important was this event that blocks of ice encased a newspaper, oranges, roses, and even a bass. An 1888 souvenir pamphlet issued by the *Florida Agriculturist* described the ice factory as "furnishing DeLand and other towns...with the purest of ice...delivered at our doors every morning in any quantity, and at a low price."

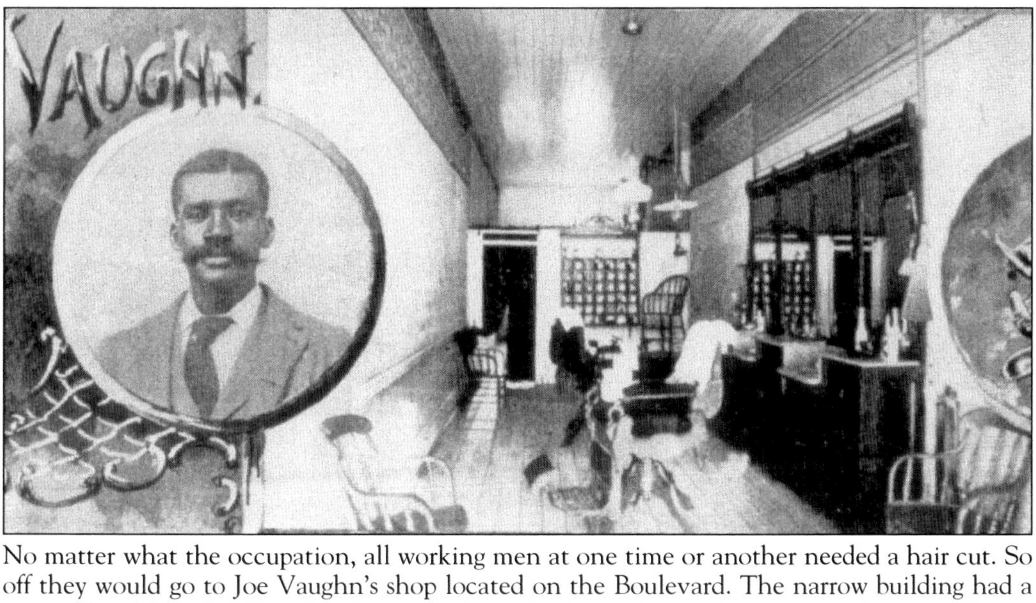

No matter what the occupation, all working men at one time or another needed a hair cut. So off they would go to Joe Vaughn's shop located on the Boulevard. The narrow building had a stained bead-board ceiling that hovered above the brass chairs where men gathered to discuss the latest happenings. While they chatted Vaughn trimmed their hair and shaped their elaborate mustaches. Imagine the scent of cut hair mixed with aftershave that greeted a customer entering the shop. And imagine the creak of the wood floor as a client walked to an empty chair to spend two bits for a shoe shine while waiting for a trim.

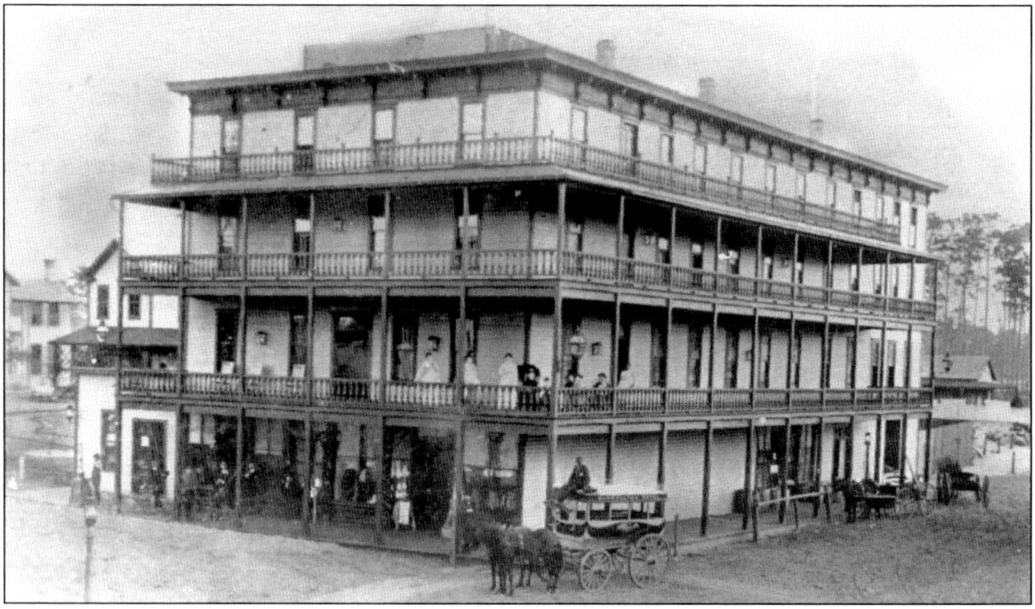

As DeLand grew and men and women no longer crafted most of what they needed, commercial shops sprang up. Located on the southeast corner of New York and the Boulevard, the 1885 Dreka & Co. Department Store used the ground floor while the Carrolton Hotel used the remaining floors. V.M. Fountain greeted guests arriving at the hotel, then returned to his job as the department store manager. Described prior to the 20th century as the department store with the most floor space in South Florida, the building was moved south on the Boulevard so Dreka could construct a new building on the site. The new Dreka Building, the first reinforced concrete structure in the county, was completed in 1909 for $50,000 and was the largest example of Mission-style architecture in the city. The 1930s photo below shows Dreka's prior to its purchase by J.C. Penney. Renamed the Whitehair Building and still extant, it is presently occupied by SouthTrust Bank and the Main Street Grill.

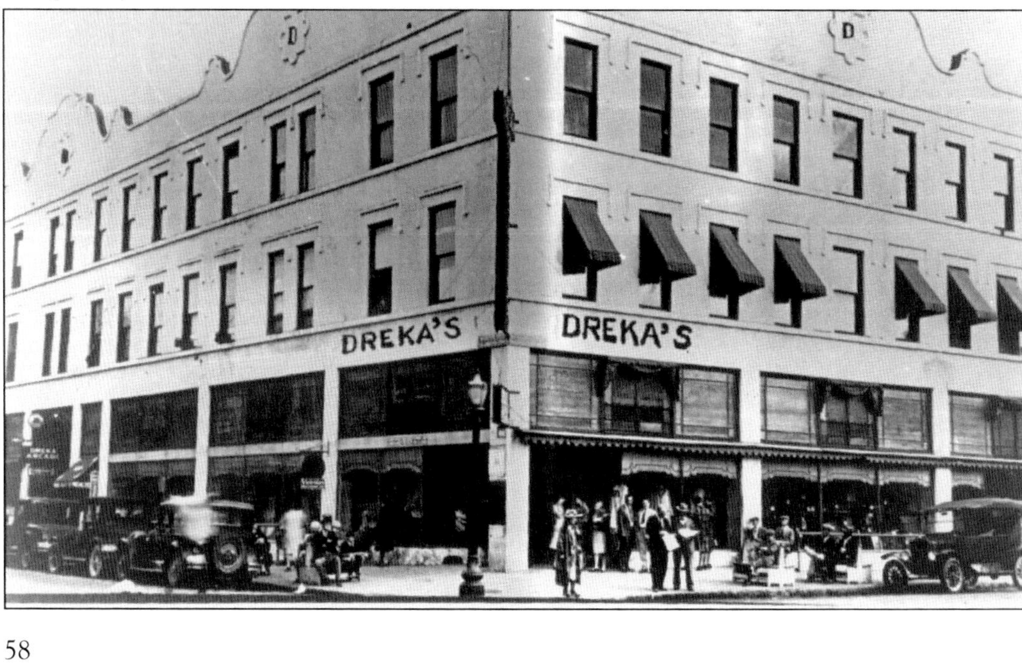

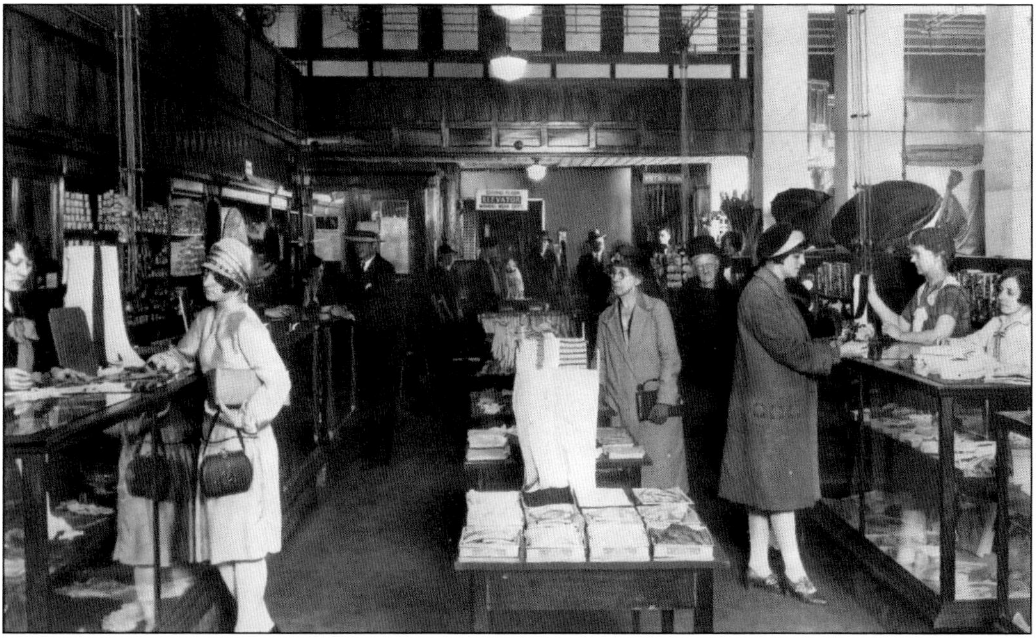

The interior of Dreka's Department Store was decorated with unique Mission-style double-armed ceiling sconces hanging from a 20-foot ceiling. When this image was captured on film, it was evidently a busy day of shopping and browsing. Glass counters accentuated sparkling jewelry offered for sale as young ladies dreamed of looking glamorous. The store's slogan was "[E]verything to eat, wear and use."

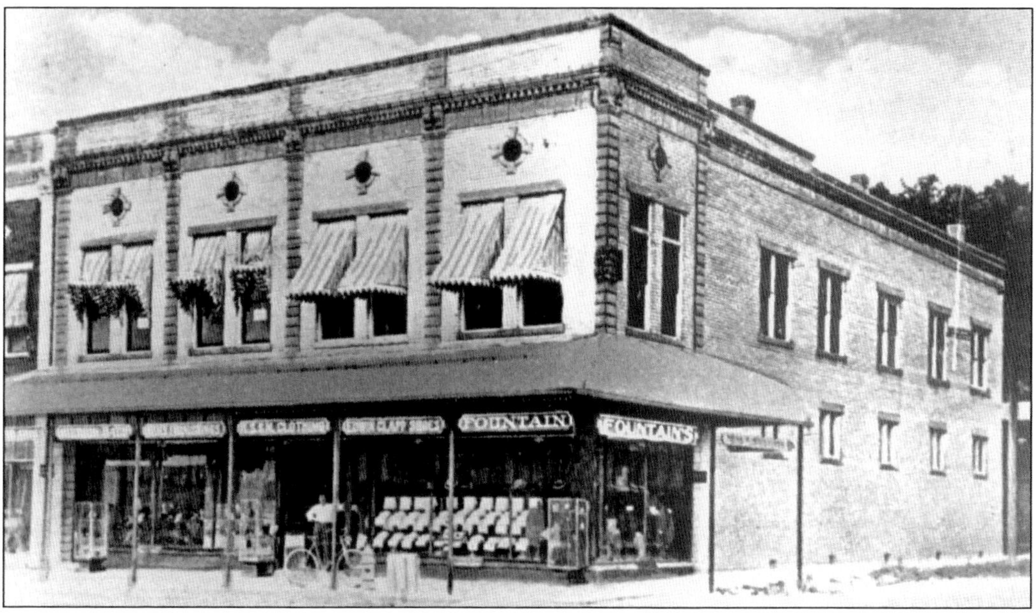

Mr. Fountain, who originally worked at Dreka's, decided to open his own clothing store. Built in 1908 for $10,000, Fountain's Men's Store was located at the northeast corner of Indiana and the Boulevard. Fountain advertised "everything for men, including trunks, slacks and satchels." The elaborate displays in the front windows showcased the latest in men's fashions. At present, the building houses the Stetson Florist Shop.

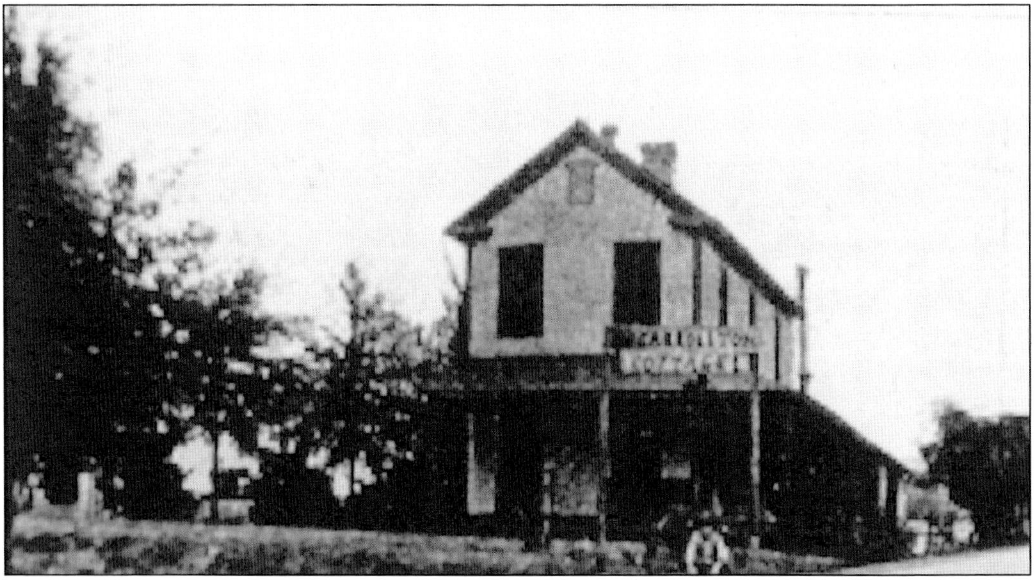

Prior to the turn of the 20th century, the Jordan-Felt General Store moved from Beresford to DeLand. Located in the 100 block of East New York, it was a community center for old timers to gather in winter around the cast iron pot belly stove and swap stories while their women purchased goods for the house. This example of Florida Vernacular sported a wrap-around porch where work-weary locals took a summer break to enjoy the comings and goings of others while being cooled by a late afternoon breeze.

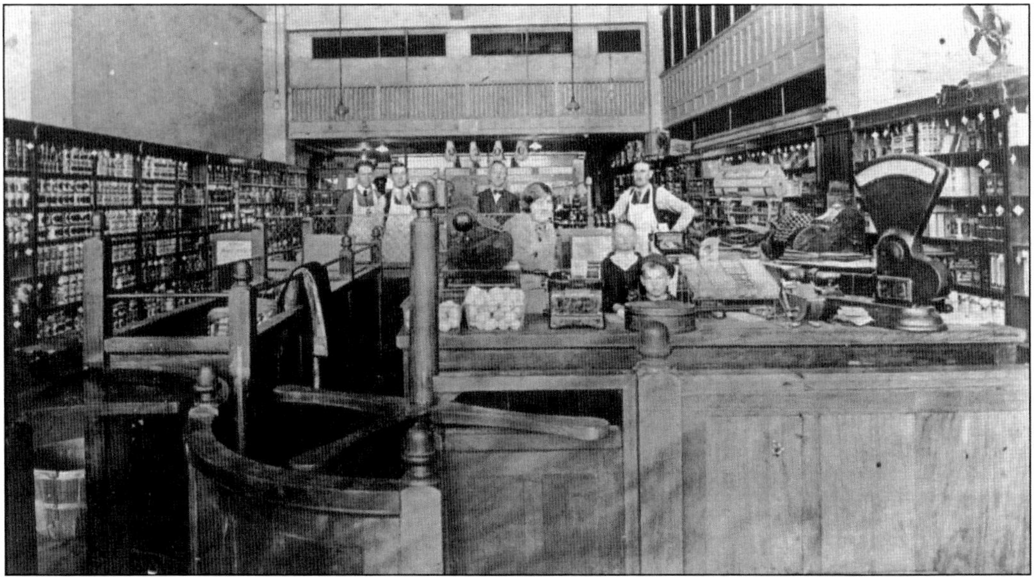

The general store eventually gave way to the grocery store. Wyatt and Emma Lou Stoudenmire moved to DeLand in 1926 to manage the Piggly Wiggly Grocery Store on East New York. They were so good at their job that they opened their own store at 142 North Woodland Boulevard. Eventually Wyatt turned the store over to his son, Truett (pictured above in open shirt) to carry on the tradition. Truett did so until his retirement in 1983. The key to the Stoudenmire's success was their customer service skills. Patrons could order groceries over the telephone, have them delivered to their door, and pay by credit. What convenience!

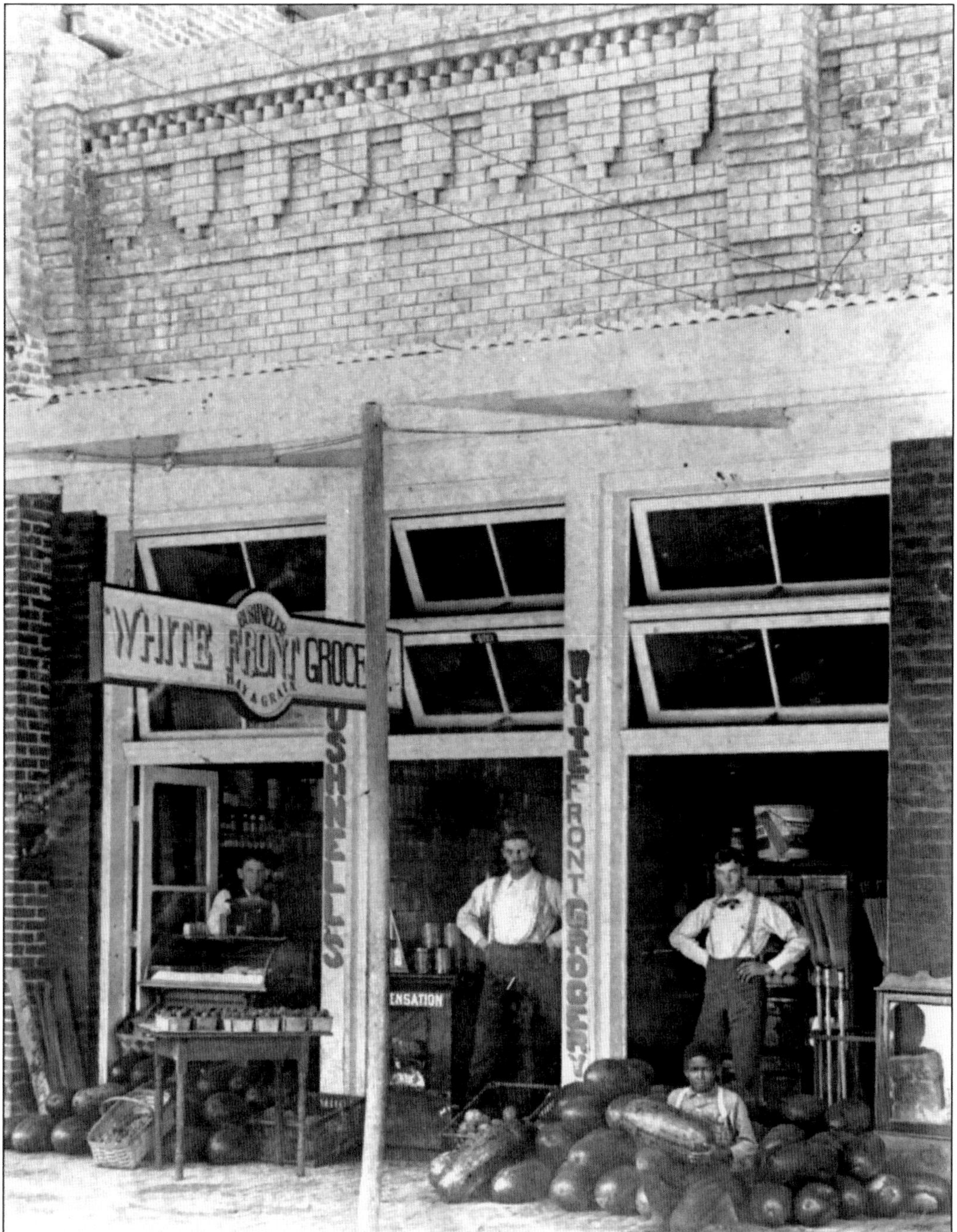

With a strong afternoon breeze weaving through the open doors and windows of Roswell Bushnell's White Front Grocery, customers shopped for weekly rations, which just might have included a watermelon during the dog days of summer. They were probably greeted by Mr. Bushnell (standing to the left). Whether it was fresh produce, brooms, or a variety of candy, almost anything could be purchased at a reasonable price down on "Bushnell's Block" once located in the 200 block of North Boulevard.

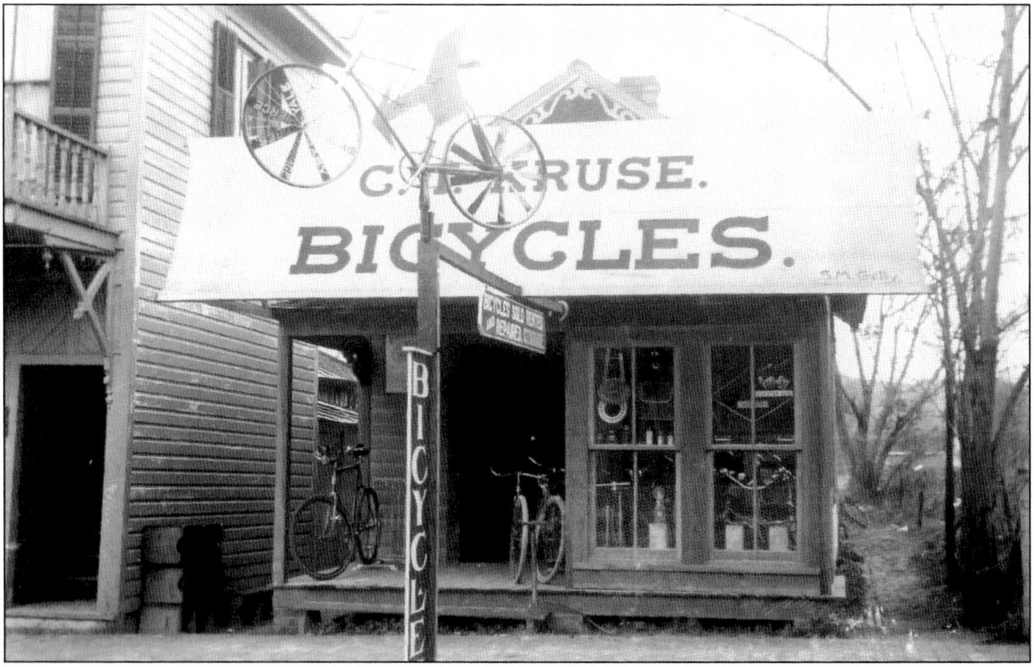

In 1913 Carl Kruse probably made a pretty decent living selling and repairing bicycles on the west side in the 300 block of North Boulevard. Bicycling was a popular form of transportation for kids as well as for adults living in DeLand so business was always busy. Kruse later moved his shop to his home on the corner of West University and Clara.

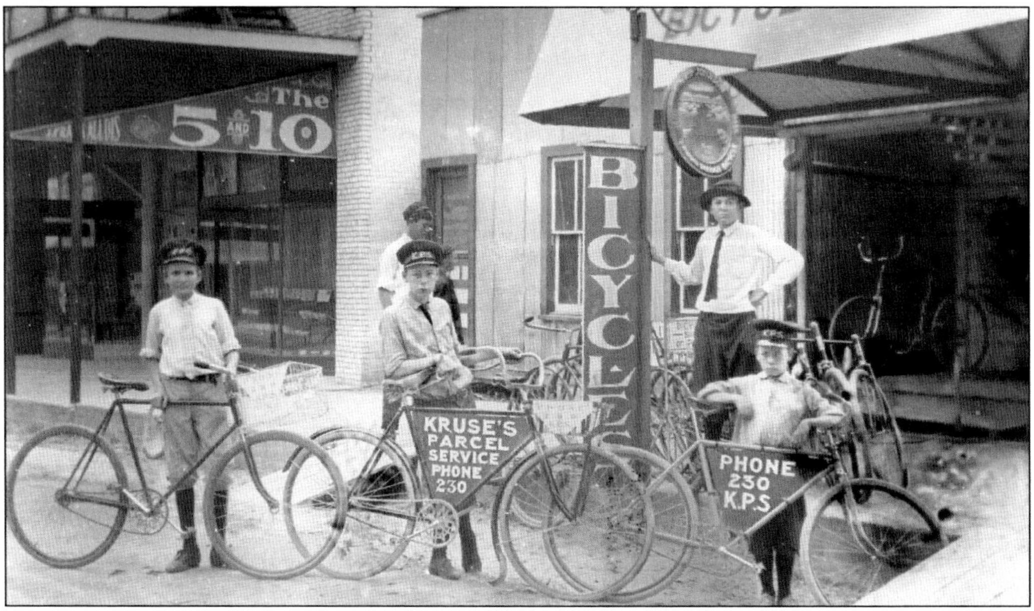

Waiting for their next assignment, these delivery boys patiently paused for a photo advertising their occupation. Kruse's Parcel Service employed five to ten young men to deliver packages of all kinds to DeLand residents. After starting off on a delivery, speeding across town down dusty streets in order to make good time, the delivery boys often arrived filthy and sweating but with the hope of a generous tip for their hustle.

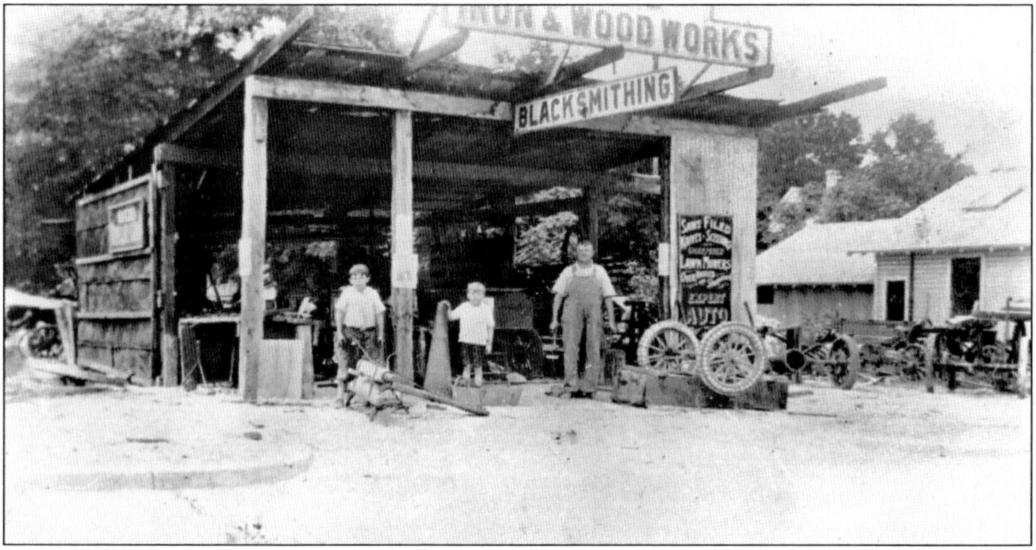

This 1922 photograph of the Dixie Iron & Wood Works and Blacksmith, located on Georgia Avenue, shows Albert G. Gunther with his sons. The blacksmith shop was a sweat intensified job but Gunther's business was productive and popular. Whether he was shodding a horse, fixing someone's broken axle on their automobile, or filing saw blades from the lumberyard, Mr. Gunther could always be found under the open shed manipulating steel and iron with skill.

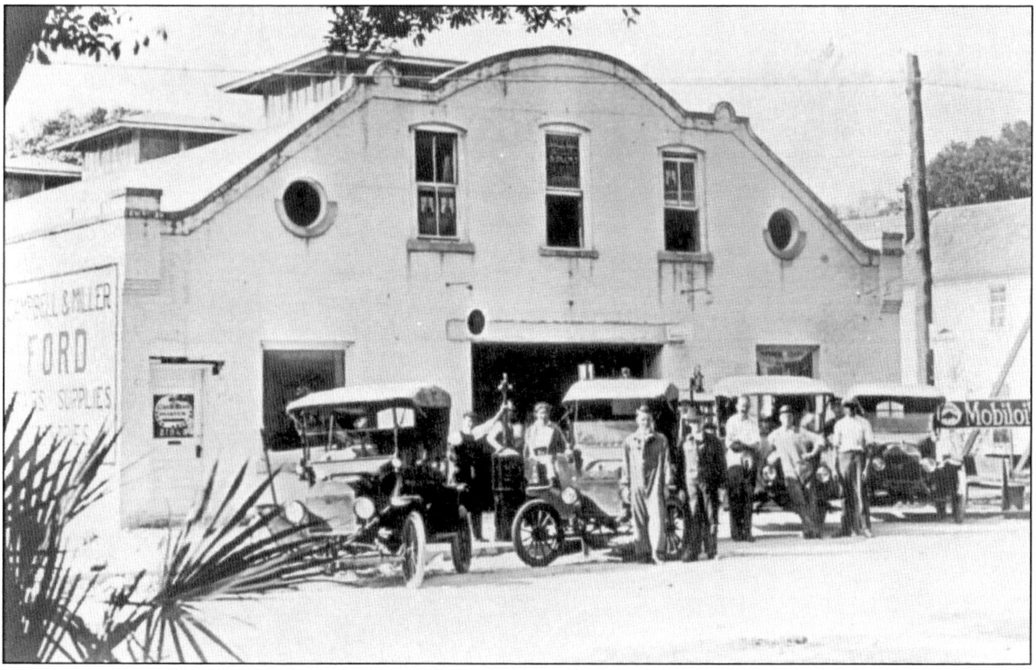

Located on West New York, the original Campbell & Miller Ford Garage did great business during the Roaring Twenties and the Florida "Boom Days" as DeLandites bought automobiles at a frenetic pace. The most popular car was the Model T Ford. The local garage shipped cars up the St. Johns River on large barges that often held up to 20 vehicles. The cars were driven off the barge and into town where they were washed clean after their long trip, then parked in front of the garage to be seen, test-driven, and hopefully sold.

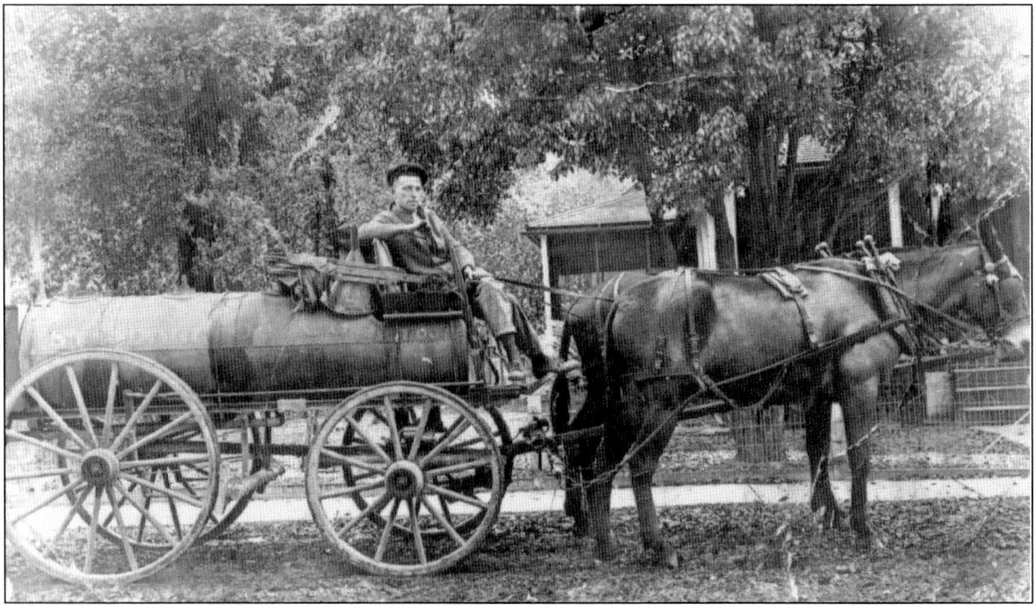

In 1919 Guy Glasgow posed high upon his horse-drawn wagon used to transport kerosene and motor oil to his customers. Covering as far north as DeLeon Springs, Barberville, Volusia, and Pierson, Glasgow made a decent living providing petroleum products. Whether he was selling heating oil for someone's home or fuel for the new-fangled horseless carriage, Glasgow played an important role in the economy of the community.

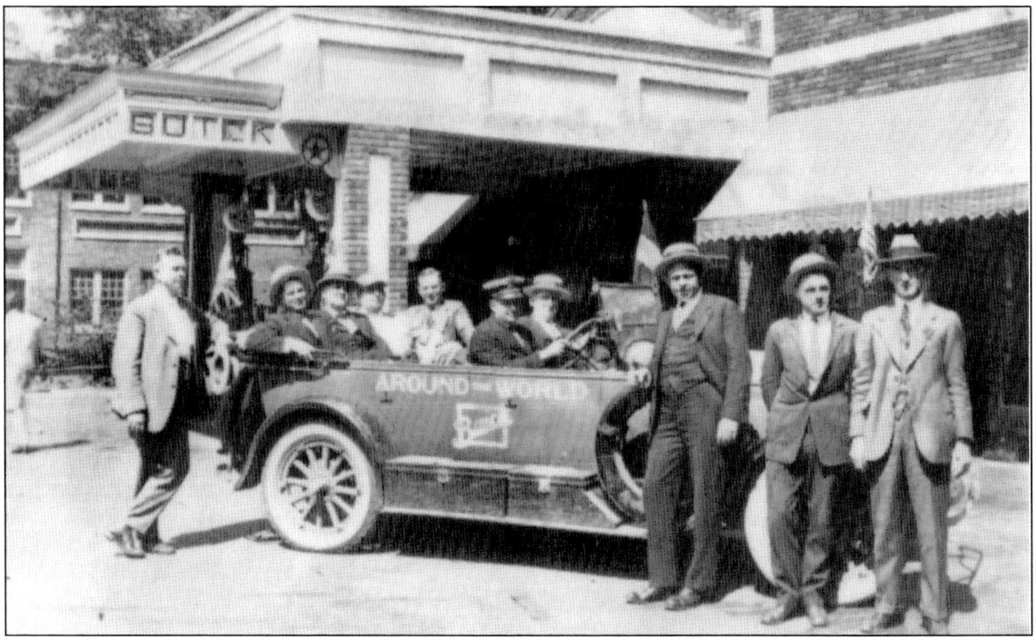

During the 1920s the car industry launched cross-country car tours to promote its product and to sell as many cars as possible during this "Boom" time. In this 1925 photograph, a group of DeLand businessmen and politicians took time to pose in front of a swank Buick convertible. Although there was still plenty of work to do for the day, these men knew when to let up a little and smile for the camera.

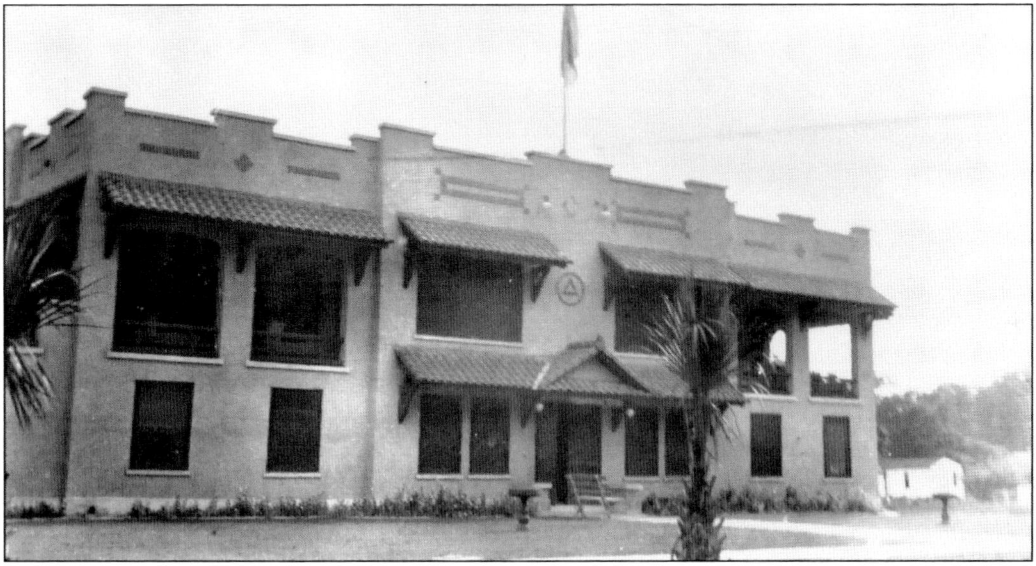

In the early 1920s DeLand's mayor Earl Brown had the Commercial Club built on the southwest corner of Florida and West New York. Also occupying the building was the DeLand Chamber of Commerce. The club was used for annual meetings of the Old Settler's Society, for business meetings for local organizations, for parties, and for other events that were just an excuse to visit with one's neighbor. Eventually this Mission-style handsome brick structure gave way to the bulldozer and the need for a parking lot.

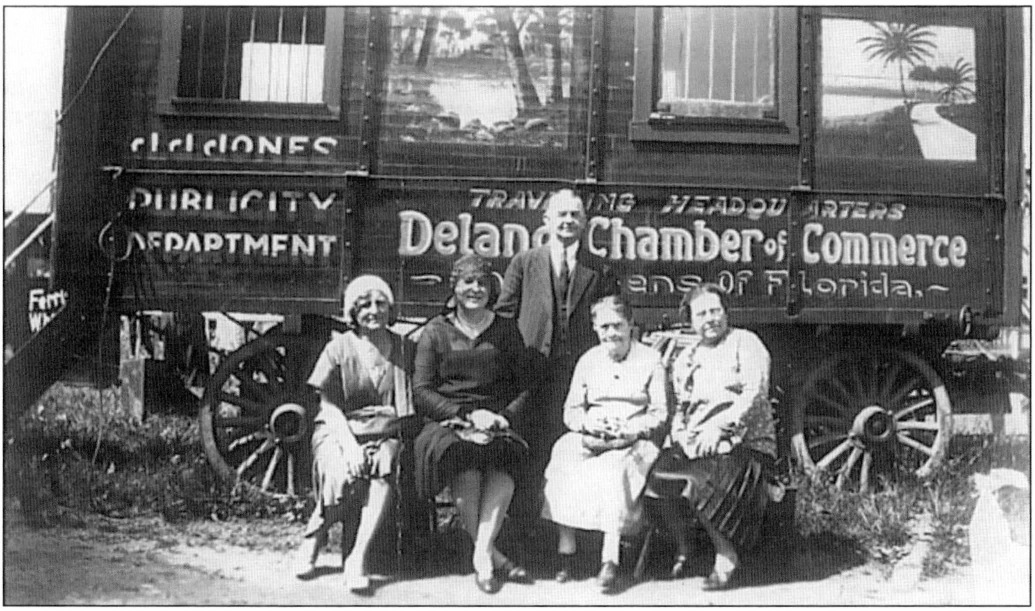

The Jones Circus advertised DeLand all over the United States with a sign painted on its traveling headquarters declaring that DeLand was "The Athens of Florida."

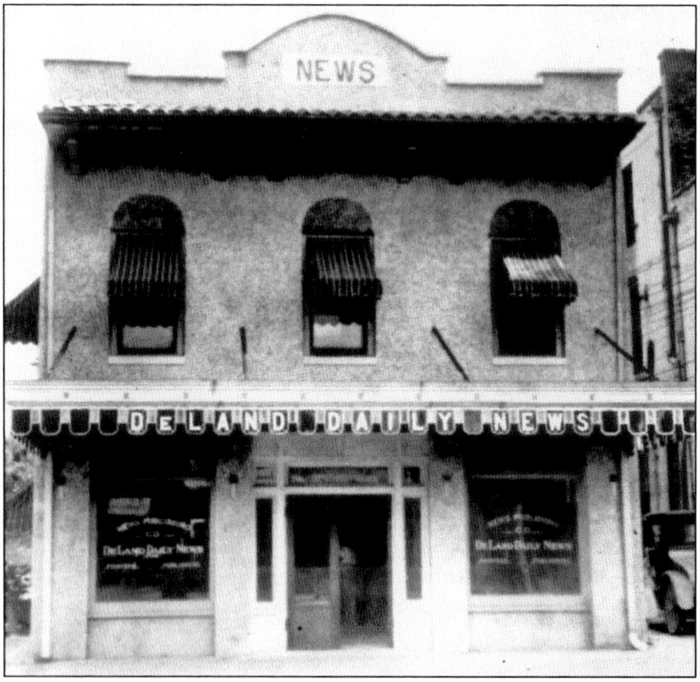

Another much-needed business was spreading the news. Constructed in 1905 on West Indiana, this building, for over 100 years, housed the *DeLand Daily News*, its predecessor the *DeLand Daily Sun*, and its successor the *DeLand Sun News*. Spanning almost the entire life of the town, the newspaper reported the activities and happenings of area residents before relocating to another site.

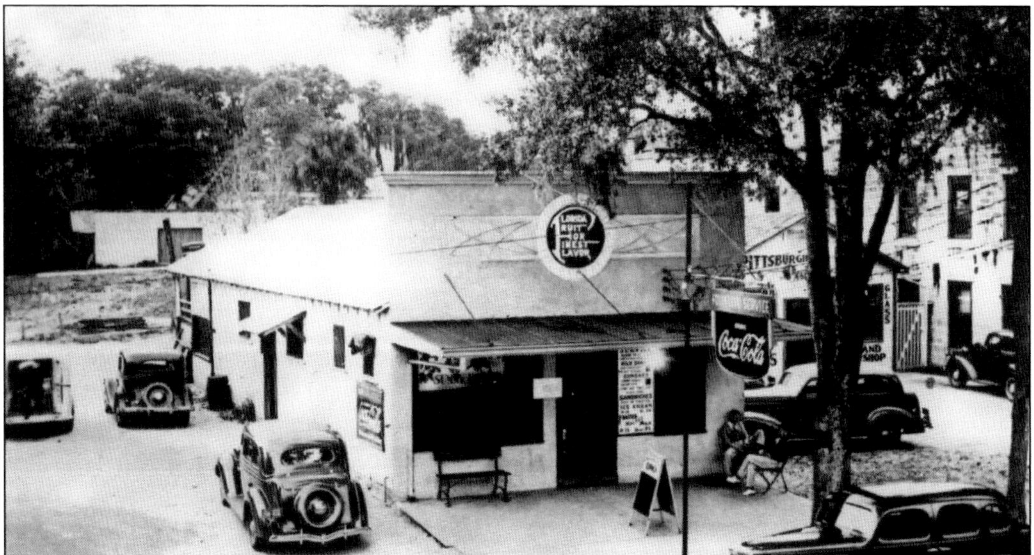

It is fitting to end the story of work in DeLand with a bit of play woven into the fiber of the town's commercial enterprises. And surely no town is complete without the culinary delights of a restaurant! Frenchy's, once located in the 100 block of West Rich, was owned by Frenchy and Mary Noriega, and offered the first malted milkshake in DeLand. Frenchy's Restaurant was a popular hangout for teenagers to socialize over burgers, fries, and the latest music on the jukebox. After school or on Friday and Saturday nights, it was not uncommon for the small restaurant to be packed with customers, most of whom were still in high school. But always during a work week, local businessmen and women could be found seated at a table taking a break from the occupations needed to maintain the life of a community.

Five

A Civil Society

Public servants are the bones of a city. The city is fleshed out by those who live there, who need city and county services, and who pay for those services. But oddly enough, those who serve the people of a community are generally underpaid, overworked, and often unappreciated.

When the settlement was a mere hollow east of the St. Johns and only a few pioneers were farming the land, civil responsibilities were pointless. But when Persimmon Hollow became DeLand and the town was eventually incorporated, the city had to meet the needs of its citizens. A city needs streets and sidewalks, fire and police service, educational and medical facilities, and private businesses to support those services. A city needs a council to guide its growth and development, to make laws, to delegate authority, and to make sure that the people who pay taxes to support their city are adequately provided with up-to-date services.

Henry DeLand, arriving in Persimmon Hollow in 1876 from the big state of New York, came with the knowledge required to give the settlers the guidance and financial support needed to turn the hollow into a thriving community. A main road was needed so Mr. DeLand donated land for the project. A wharf was needed on the St. Johns to provide docking for boats. Mr. DeLand estimated the cost at $300 and offered to make up the difference. Once the town got its new name on December 6, 1876, it needed a place to do business, so a building committee was formed. The community listed its needs and then met them quite adequately.

To communicate with the outside world, mail service was provided, brought up the St. Johns River by steamboat, and then transported to DeLand by mail carrier to the first post office located in J.B. Jordan's store.

In order to grow into what Mr. DeLand planned for his town, more people were needed so real estate specials were advertised in newspapers and magazines across the Southeast and way up in the North. Ten-acre lots with a two-room cottage, well, and 200-300 seedling orange trees could be bought for only $500. Add 10 acres to the package and a new settler got his or her Florida dream for $750. Forty acres with the same improvements only cost a grand total of $1,000. How could anyone not jump aboard the citrus wagon and move to DeLand, Florida?

The town moved forward with civil service to its residents by providing a schoolhouse in 1877, used as DeLand's community center and a house of worship until more pioneers came to expand the city. By 1880 Volusia County hired its first tax collector, J.B. Jordan, to ensure residents paid for their civil conveniences and necessities. The City of DeLand provided its residents their first sidewalks in 1880, wooden planks to keep leather shoes and bare feet dry during the rainy season.

Until a city garbage ordinance was passed in 1885, settlers dug large pits, shoved in their trash, sprinkled a bit of lime and soil over the refuse, and continued the practice until the hole was full. Then they would cover it over and move to a new spot. Needless to say that early custom has afforded both professional and amateur archaeologists with vital cultural artifacts and information so as to teach residents about their town's past.

All civil societies need electricity. DeLand got its first electrical plant in 1887. Water and sewer systems were installed in 1916 with an order from city officials to remove outhouses. Indeed, DeLand was booming.

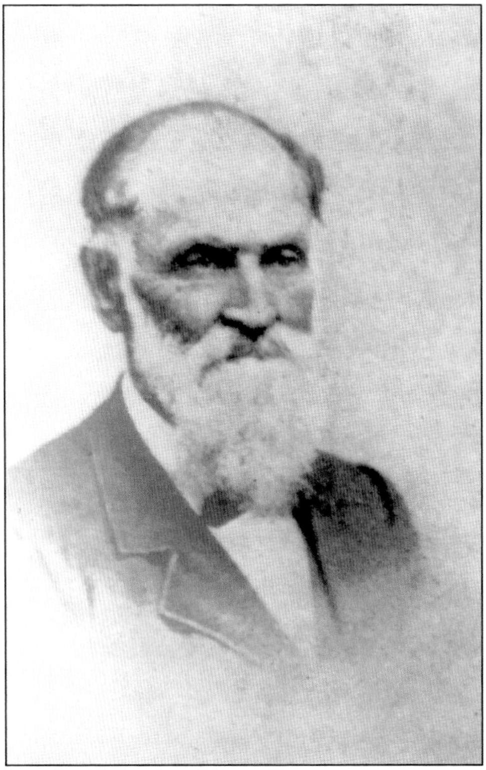

On March 11, 1882, serious business occurred at the little one-room schoolhouse on the Boulevard. Minutes from that early meeting read: "Record of registered voters who were present and voted at the first municipal election held in DeLand, Volusia County, Florida.... The canvassing of the ballots was done forthwith in the presence of the electors, by the inspectors.... ...[T]here were thirty-nine votes cast, all of which were for incorporation." C.H. Wright (at left) was elected mayor, H.C. Strack, clerk and treasurer; Aldermen were J.Y. Parce, C. Codrington, J.J. Banta, G.A. Dreka, H.C. McNeil, Vincent Kirk, George Fearn, J.D. Bohanan, J.A. Huffman, and J.W. Miller. David Cooney became the marshal and collector. Swearing-in of officials took place on the evening of March 13th, in the Rich Cabin, at the time occupied by Judge Wright.

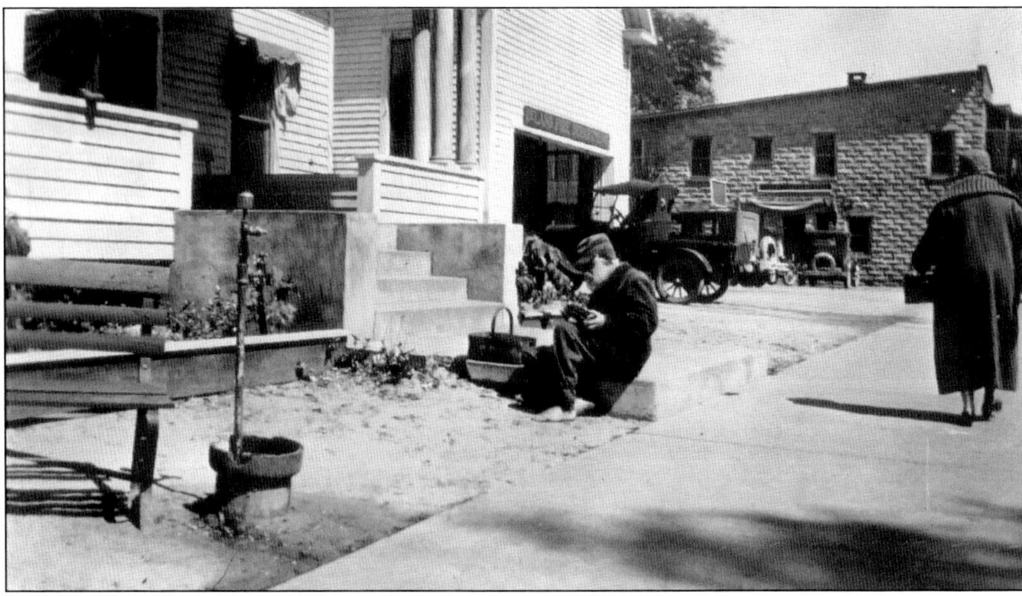

DeLand's first City Hall was constructed c. 1905 at 100 West Indiana. Soon after the complex was completed, civil servants enjoyed a lunch break out-of-doors. This innocent practice of eating on the steps of a publicly owned building was discontinued due to complaints by some rather stiff-backed individuals. Eventually the building was moved to North Amelia but in the 1980s was demolished. Had it survived man's weary wastefulness, it would have been the oldest civic building in DeLand.

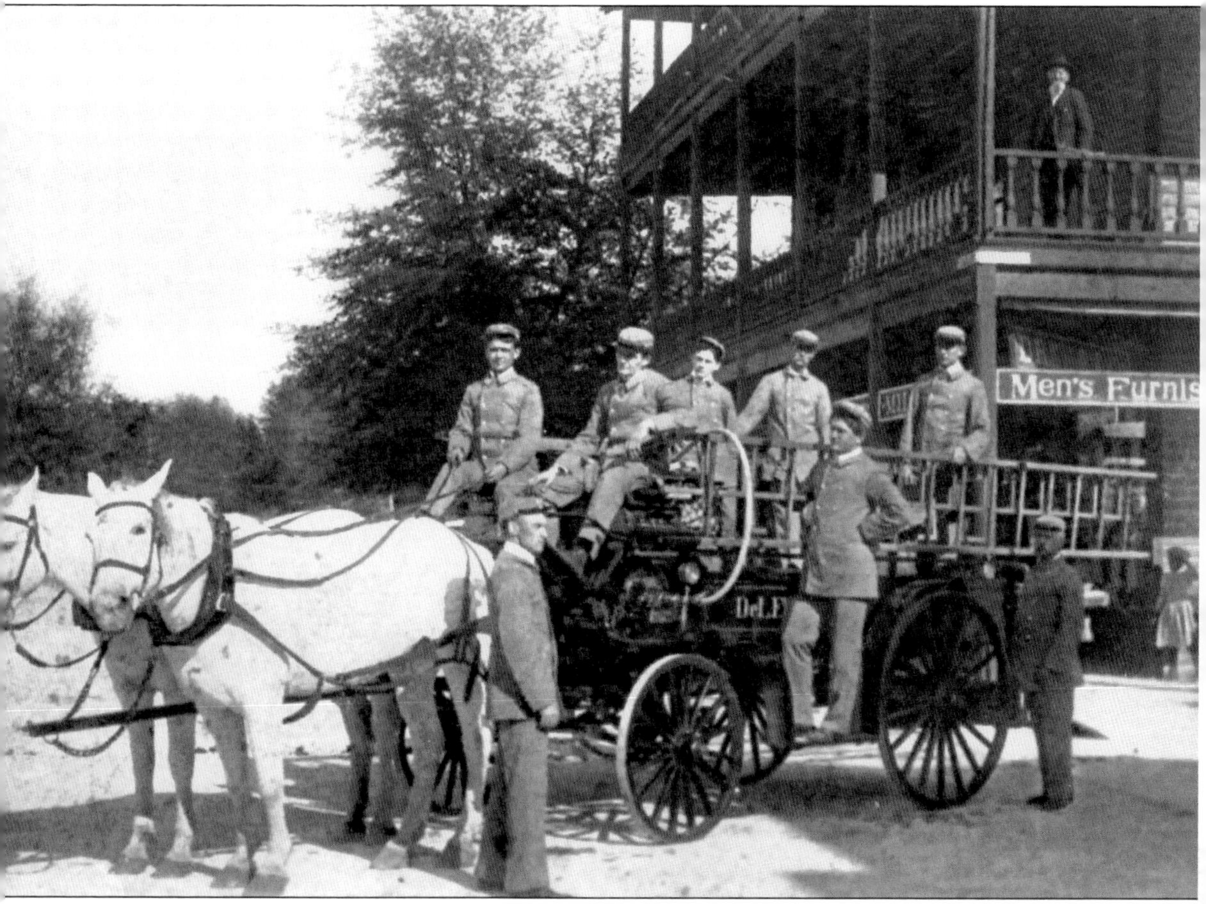

Fire is a natural disaster that brings terror to the heart. And when a town is built of wood, fire service is desperately needed. On September 27, 1883, DeLand organized its first fire brigade, appointing William B. Fudger fire chief. When a fire alarm sounded, usually the clanging of someone's bell or a holler of "fire!," volunteers ran from their respective buildings with bucket in hand to form a line from the water-tank truck to the blaze. Cisterns and water tanks supplied water to the tank wagon. When the Civil War ended in 1865 and the Confederates marched home, many of them did so in their worn gray wool uniforms. How to recycle a used Confederate uniform? Reactivate it for public service as these firemen did. Coincidentally, three years to the day that the fire brigade was formed, fire struck the frame town. Fat lighter burns well and it burns rapidly. The men did the best they could with what they had: two horse-drawn chemical wagons each holding 30 gallons, a hook and ladder truck equipped with two five-gallon portable chemical extinguishers, hand-held buckets, volunteers, water tanks, and cisterns, as well as all the carbonated water the drug store could supply! The first old schoolhouse, abandoned as a church, housed the brigade's equipment. It was not until 1913 that a fire department was created and the first motorized vehicle purchased. For years men were summoned only as needed and paid a dollar an hour for a night call.

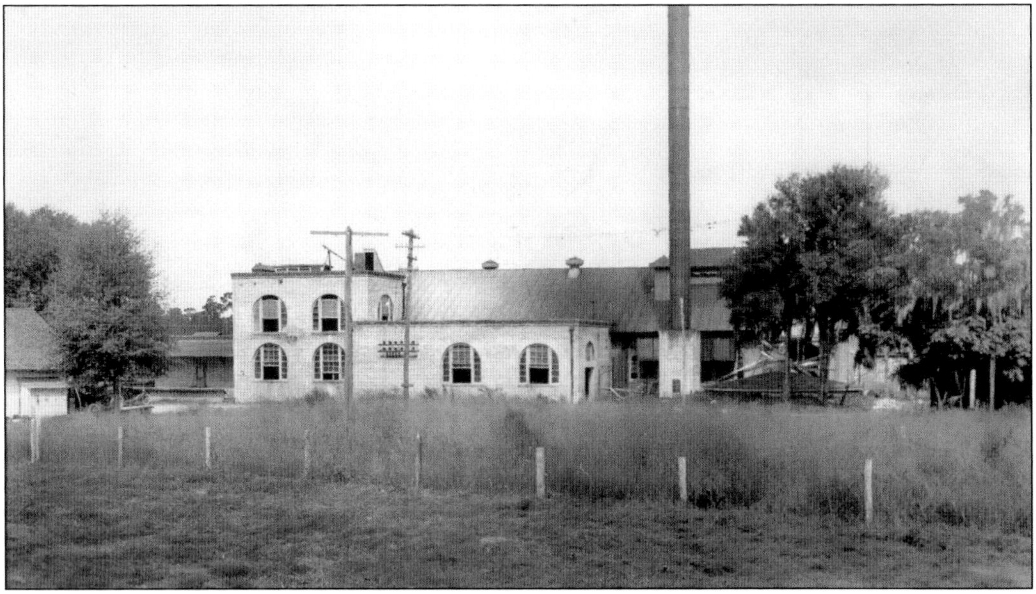

DeLand saw the light with its first electric plant in 1887. Soon after, street lights began appearing all about town. Initially there were two 25-kilowatt generators. Then c. 1900, one 50-kilowatt generator was added. These were arc lights which gave off a strange ethereal glow. Initially they were used from dusk until midnight, then later from sunset to sunrise. DELPICO, for DeLand Electric Light, Power, and Ice Company, was located on Rehbehn, west of present-day SR 15A. DELPICO sold out to the Florida Public Service Company in 1924, which sold to Florida Power (now Progress Energy) in 1944.

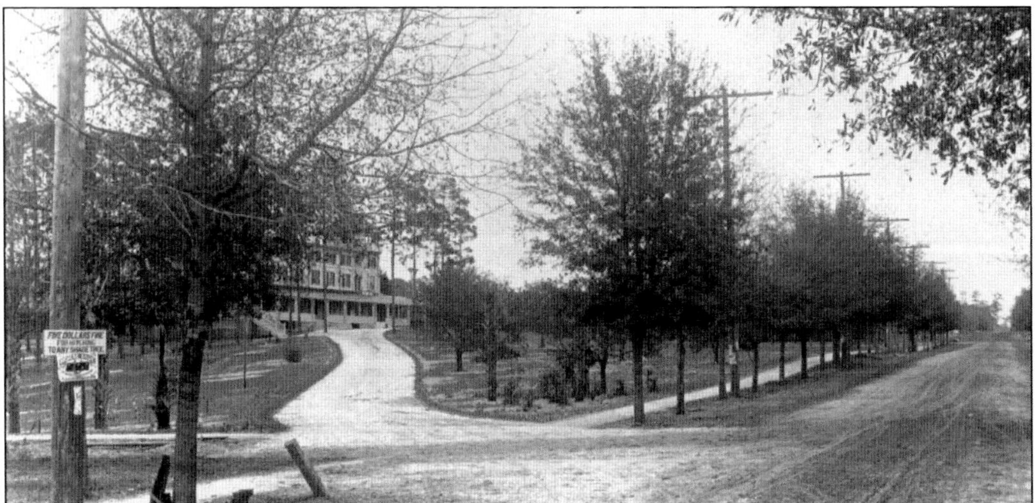

As the need arose, town council passed laws: humane treatment of all animals; dogs to be licensed and collared; vicious animals could not run loose; and birds could not be trapped or killed. City officials also declared that bars could open at sunrise but must close by 11 p.m. Riders were prohibited from galloping horses more than five miles an hour downtown. Riders were also warned they were to stop hitching their transportation to public trees since the practice was killing the trees. As the c. 1908 sign posted to a utility pole in front of the Hotel College Arms threatened, "Five dollars fine for hitching to any shade tree."

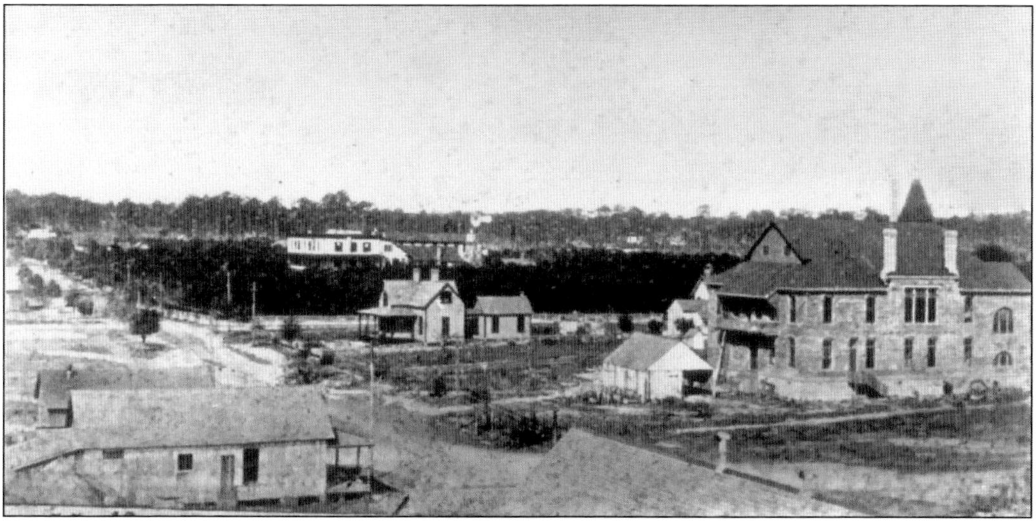

Movement was afoot in the 1880s to relocate the county seat to DeLand from Enterprise, the small community south of town and adjacent to the St. Johns River. Citizens were split on the issue. Both a verbal and voting fight ensued that eventually culminated in DeLand receiving a majority of votes on April 3, 1888. Henry DeLand donated land for the courthouse. Mr. DeLand, John B. Stetson, and Fred S. Goodrich contributed $15,000 toward construction. This view is looking west along New York toward the Putnam Hotel in the distance. In the foreground is the rising new courthouse in continual use until it was demolished in 1927.

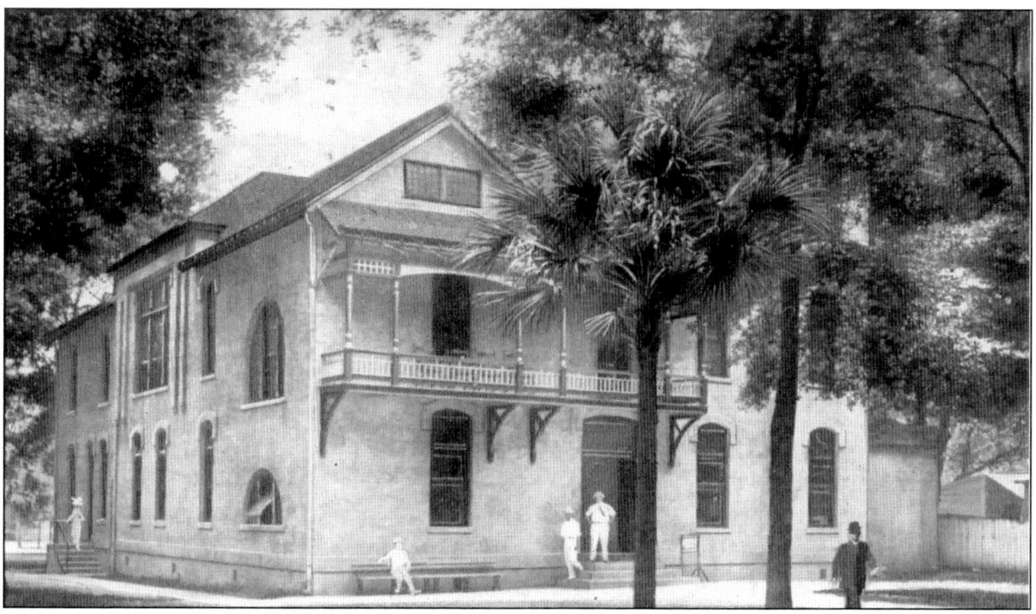

The second county courthouse, built in 1890 and demolished in 1925, sat on the site of the present historic courthouse on the corner of West New York and West Rich.

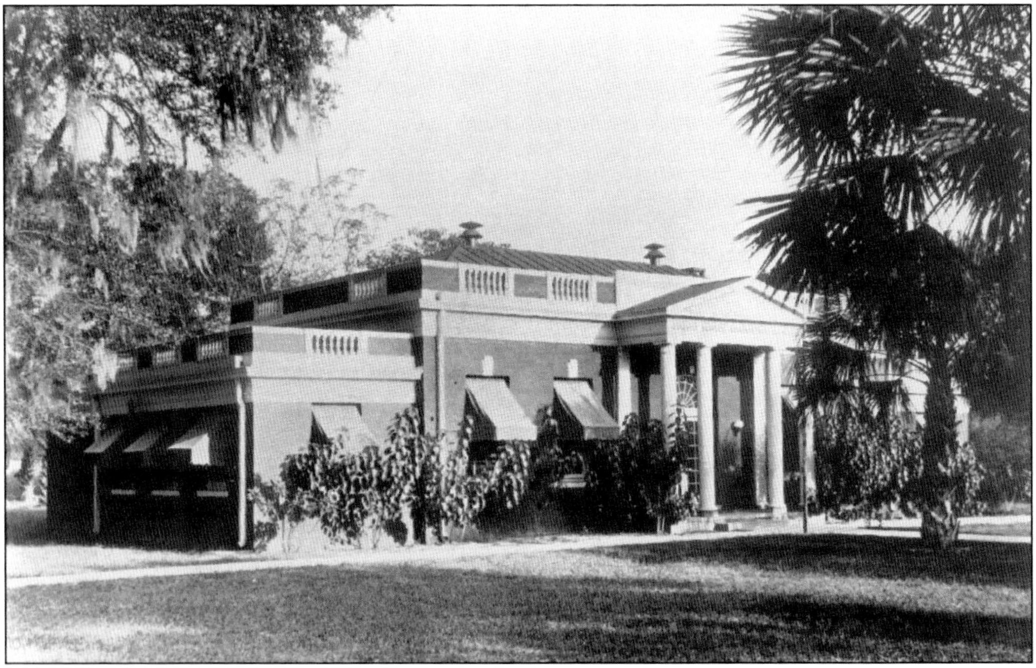

The first Volusia County Jail in DeLand was built c. 1890 and used until 1910 when a new jail was constructed in the 100 block of West New York. At that time the superintendent of public instruction moved into the building. Until its demolition in 1987, this beautiful Greek Revival structure was the oldest governmental building still in use in the city.

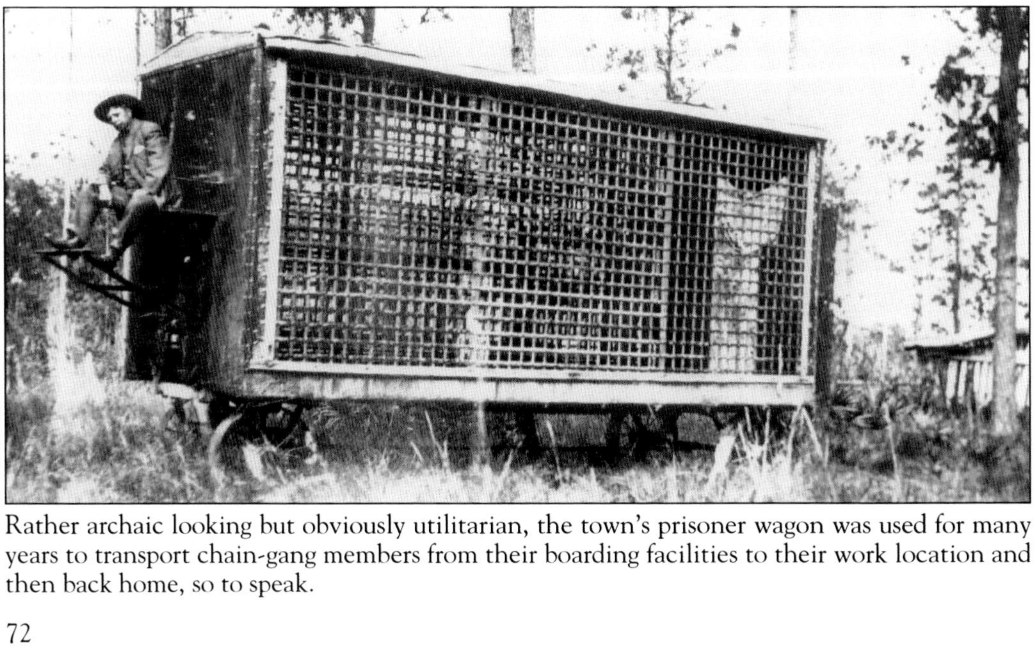

Rather archaic looking but obviously utilitarian, the town's prisoner wagon was used for many years to transport chain-gang members from their boarding facilities to their work location and then back home, so to speak.

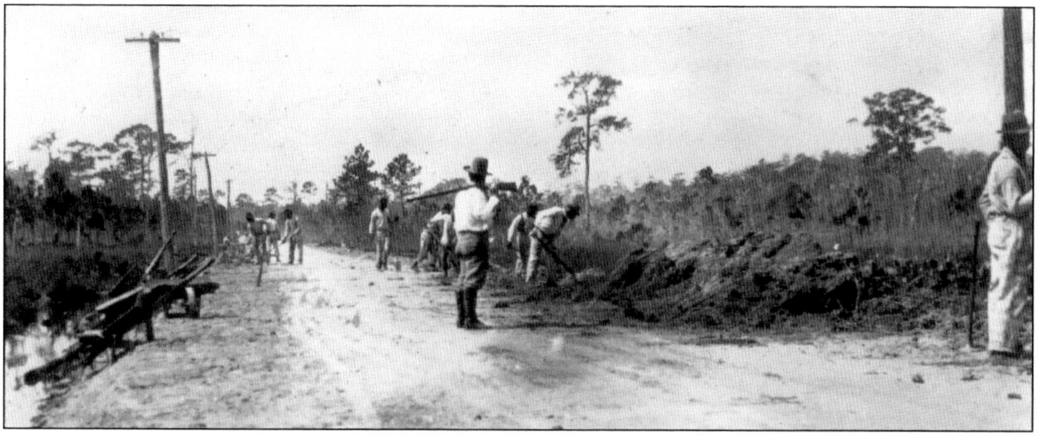

Around the turn of the 20th century, Florida adopted the philosophy that prisoners should earn their keep—thus the state initiated the "chain gang." Chain-gang members cleaned roadways and assisted in numerous other public projects while wearing a long chain about their ankle to which a large steel ball was attached. When they walked, they had to carry the ball or drag it behind them. Occasionally shackles were removed from trusted prisoners to allow them more freedom of movement. By mid-century the cruel use of chains was abandoned, but prisoners still worked for the state. Evidently these were trusted prisoners as they worked unfettered in 1917 clearing land for the new road from DeLand to Daytona.

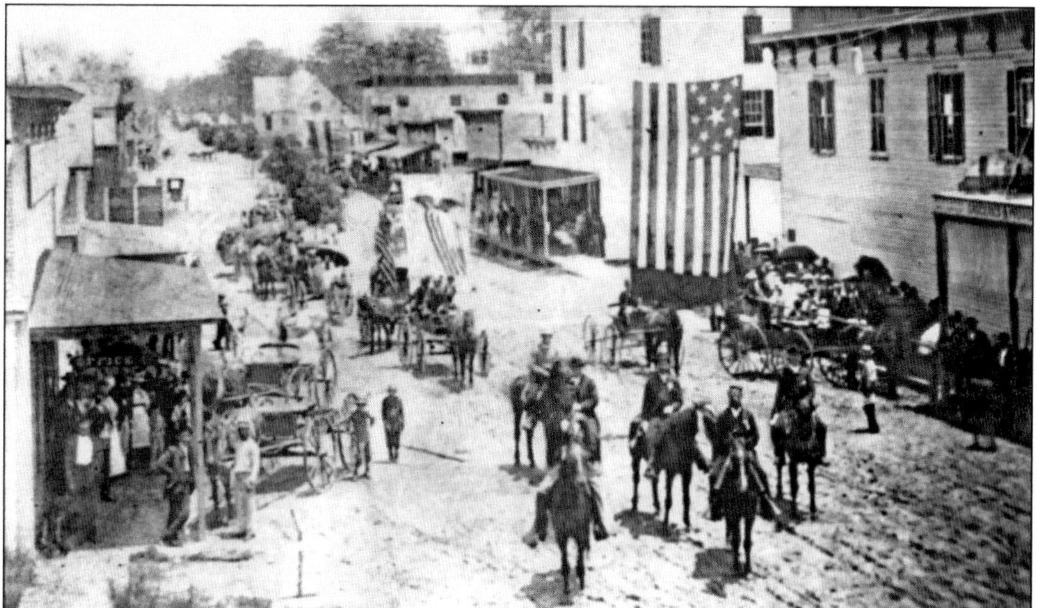

In 1887 city officials flexed their muscles with the decision to improve the town's sandy dirt streets by appropriating $200 to purchase a mule, wagon, and hire a driver to haul sawdust from the sawmill to spread on the streets. Some citizens were furious because they played horseshoes in the street and thought sawdust would ruin their game; others protested the money was being wasted. But dirt creates mud and mud creates a mess so the city fathers won. However, by the early 1890s the town council decided pine needles were the way to go and cheaper at only $50 a mile to spread. Toward the end of the 1890s, city leaders again improved the streets, this time paving them with crushed shell for a cost of $1 per yard.

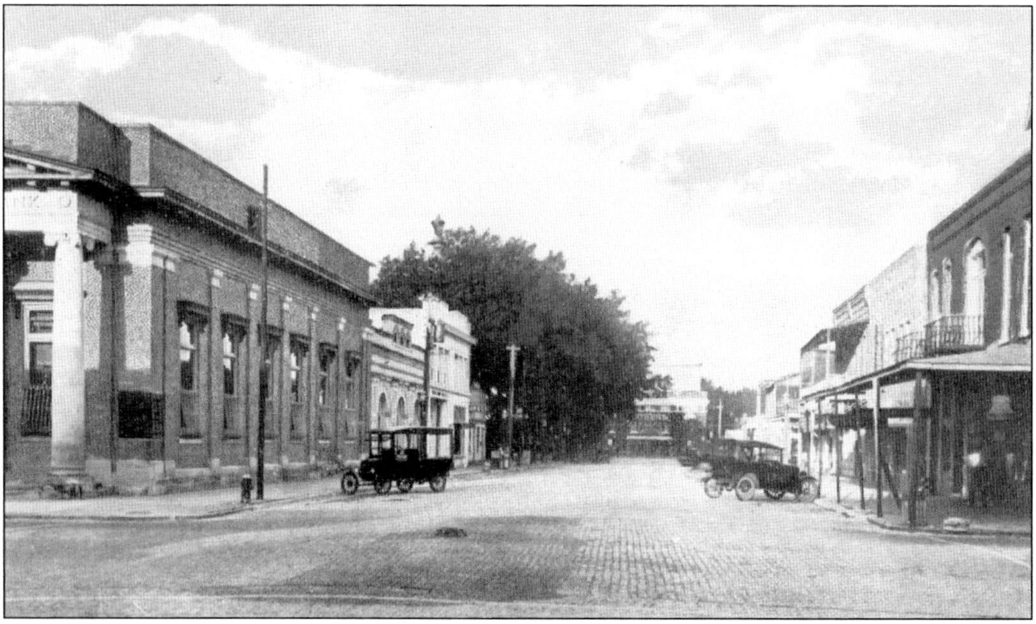

By 1925 city officials flexed their muscles again and ordered that the streets be bricked. The 1940s found them concreted; the 1960s asphalted. Now farsighted officials have chosen to enhance some of the downtown streets by re-bricking them! History often folds back onto itself after reflection and rational rethinking.

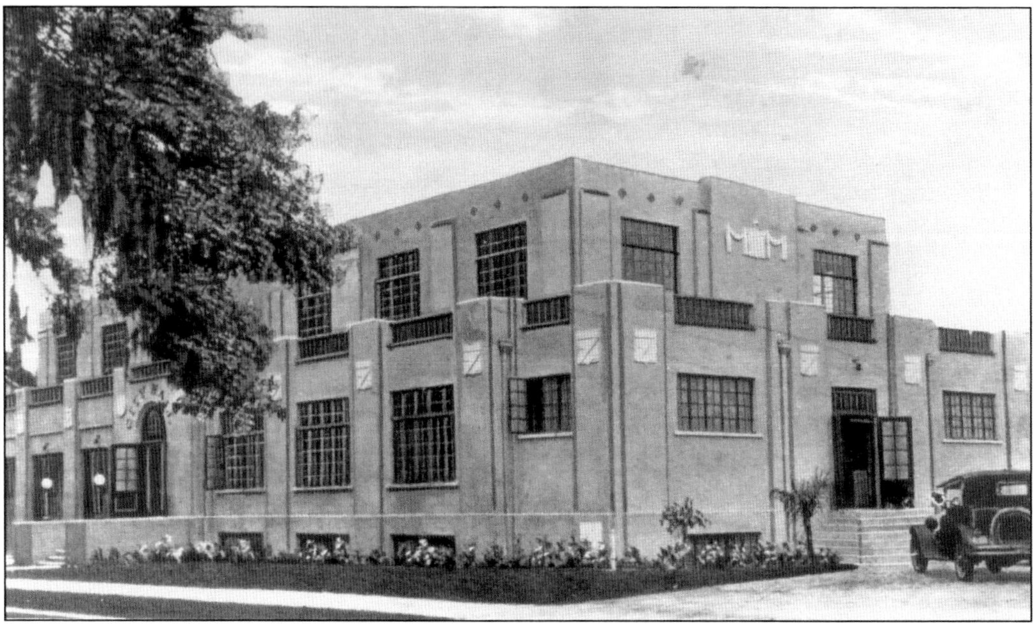

A city governmental complex was built in 1921 at 120 South Florida Avenue. Originally the north end was city hall and the fire station was at the south end. The firemen slept on the second floor during their shift. The police were housed in the basement of the complex. The building remains in use today as City Hall but with a new fire and police complex to the south.

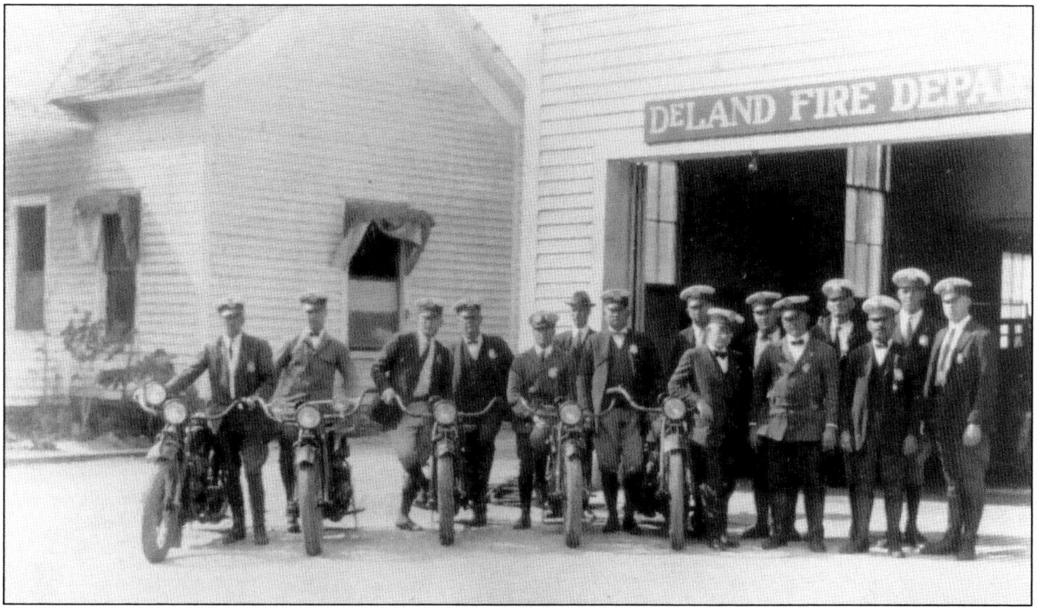

The DeLand police force posed with their speedy equipment in front of the DeLand firehouse in the 100 block of West Indiana prior to moving to their new complex. The old city hall is to the left.

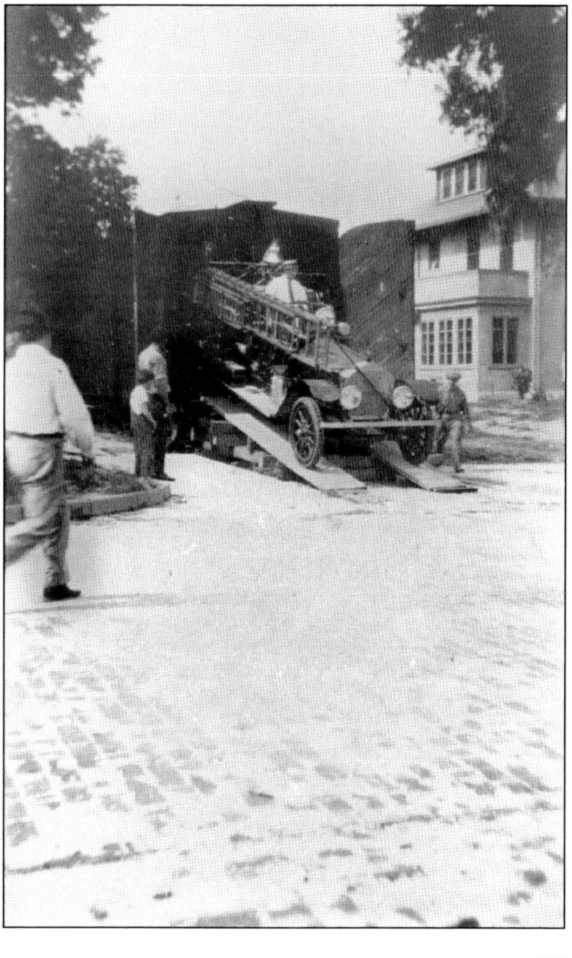

By the 1920s DeLand had acquired three fire trucks. This 1926 modern beauty was unloaded at the corner of Amelia and East New York. In 1952 the city had four trucks ages 39, 31, and 21 years, and one purchased in the late 1940s. The oldest relic was sold to Stetson University where it sat on campus for many years as yard art for a fraternity. Another was sold to the city of Lake Helen.

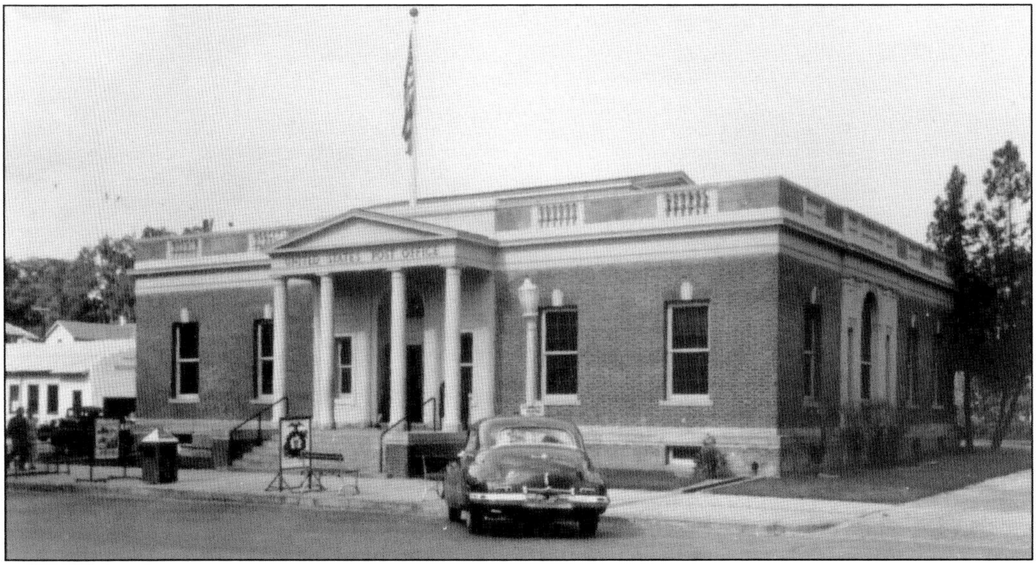

In 1916, two blocks north of where the new City Complex would one day be built, the federal government built DeLand a state-of-the-art post office on the northeast corner of Indiana and Florida. This 1940 photograph captured the time and design that went into governmental buildings during the early to mid-1900s. Buildings were practically constructed but with a classic beauty and pride in workmanship. The post office survived until 1987 when it was razed to build a modern county administrative center.

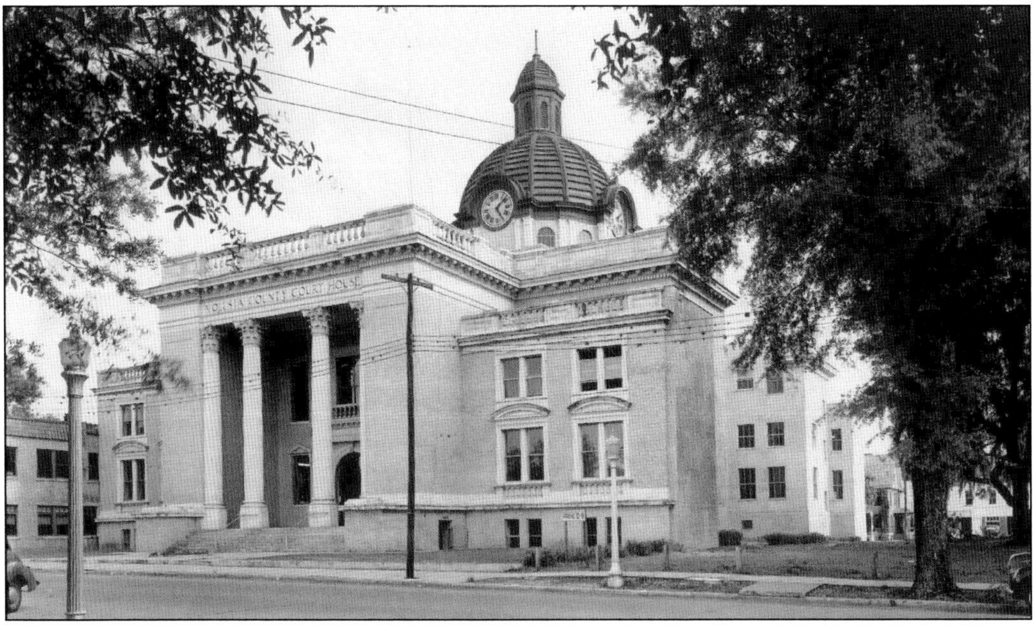

In 1929 Volusia County built a 60,000-square-foot courthouse. Constructed of Georgian pink marble with a copper-covered dome, this classic beauty with Corinthian columns was in service until 2002 when a new courthouse was built. State and local funds restored the building to its original grandeur. The county's first courthouse was located on this site at 126 North Indiana and removed to make way for this third courthouse, which was later placed on the National Register of Historic Places.

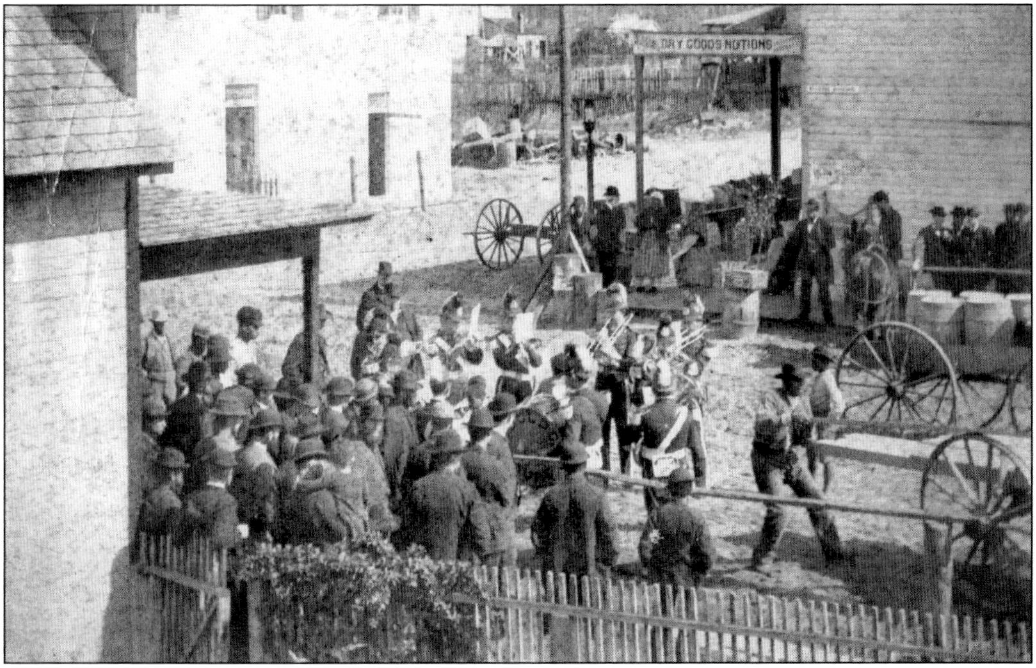

Until the community could afford a "real" hospital, the public fell victim to the typical medicine men of the times. The year 1885 found "Dr. Golden's Magic Discovery" being touted on the corner of New York and the Boulevard as *the* cure of all cures.

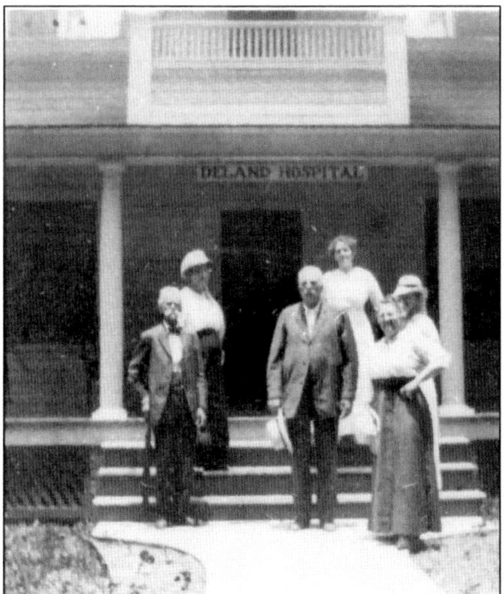

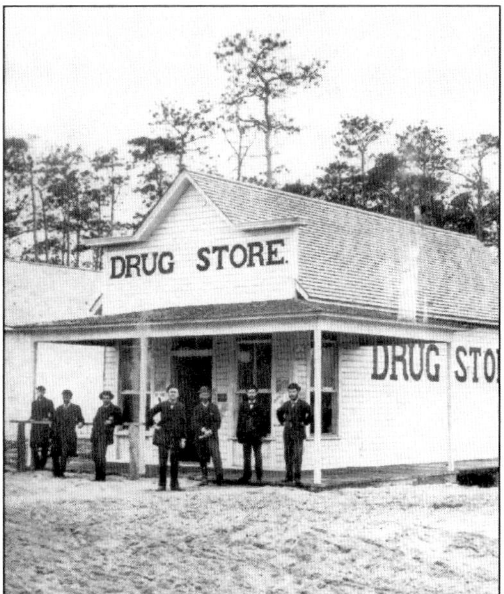

It was not until sometime around 1915 that the city provided proper medical services to its white citizens. Blacks were excluded. The first hospital (left) was located in the Willows Hotel on the north side of the 100 block of East Rich. The staff at the hospital stood on alert prepared to serve their patients' physical needs. Fisher Drug Store (right), the second in town, was located on the southwest corner of New York and the Boulevard and conveniently within walking distance of the hospital.

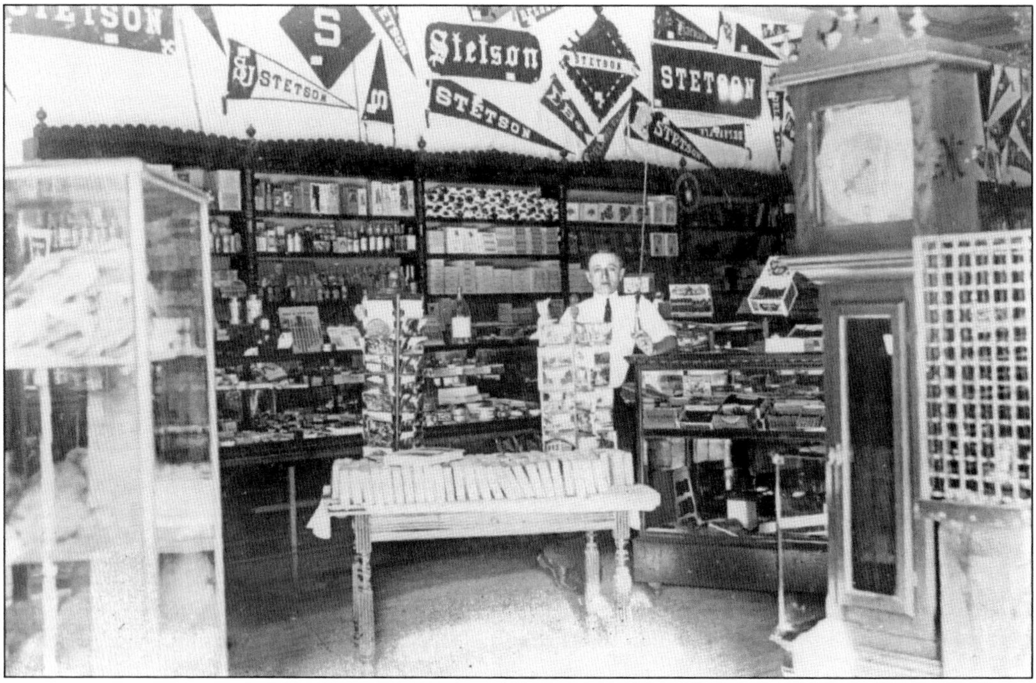

Growth brings greater needs for a community, especially in medical services and servants. Allen's Drug Store, built c. 1900, was located on the southwest corner of Indiana and the Boulevard. Its well-supplied shelves offered assorted items other than those used for medicinal purposes. Evidently the druggist was a John B. Stetson University fan as his walls were covered with college pennants. Ambulance service was also modernized and could be called when a citizen needed the services of a hospital or a mortuary.

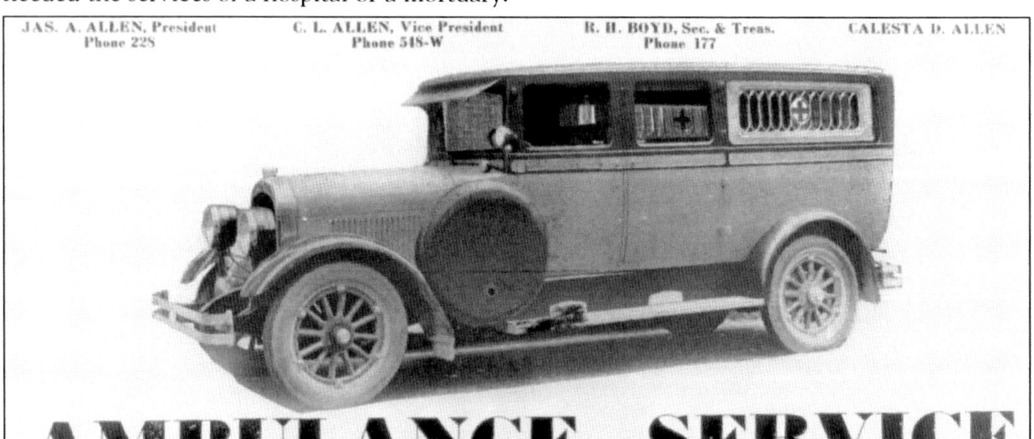

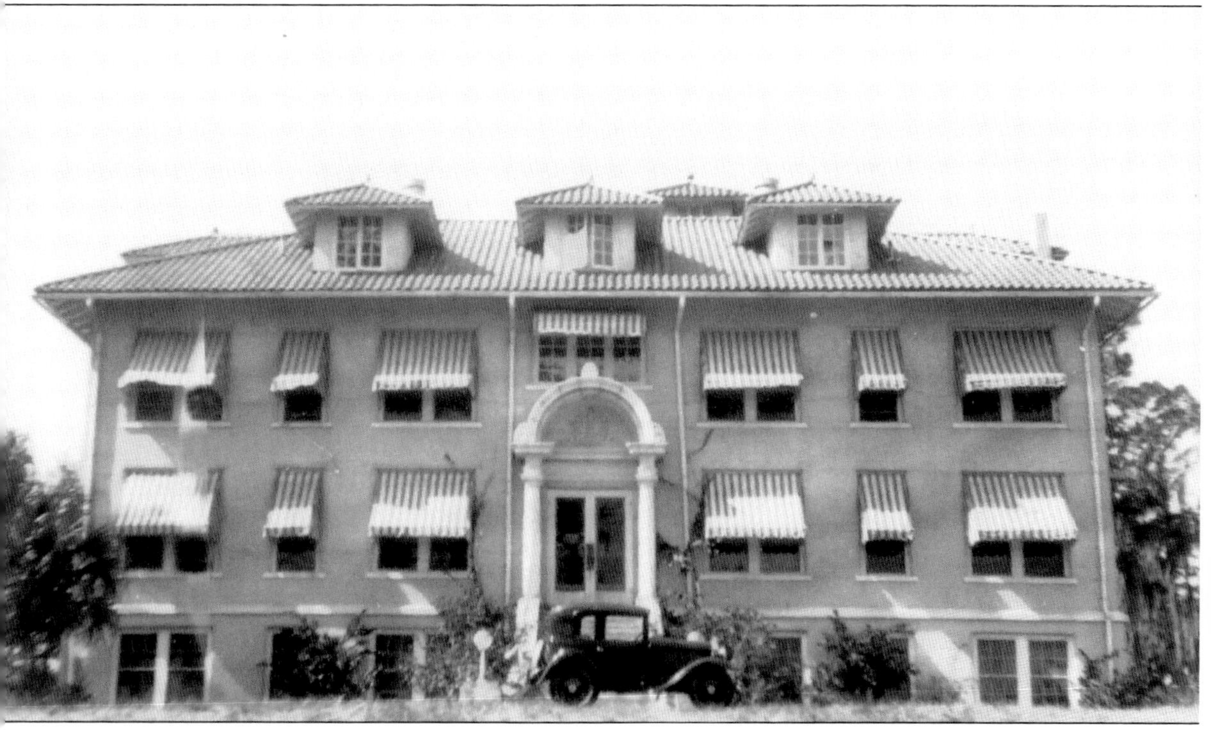

A much-needed modern hospital was constructed in 1923 with public funds. The four-story Italian Renaissance DeLand Memorial Hospital was located on North Stone Street on property donated by Mr. and Mrs. Smiley of New York, whose son, Charles, had been killed in World War I. Initially the hospital had 20 beds and four private rooms. Guests of the Hotel College Arms donated furnishings for one of the more elite private rooms, which had a price tag of $6 per day. Lesser-quality rooms cost $5 per day and ward beds were only $3—a real bargain compared to today's rates. In 1948 the hospital moved to the DeLand Naval Air Station in preparation for its new location in 1952 on the site of what was once the grand Hotel College Arms. The old hospital became a fraternity house for Stetson men, then later it was converted to offices for the county school board. Abandoned for years, the city eventually received a grant from the state to restore this architectural gem. Listed on the National Register of Historic Places, it now contains the city's recreation department and a museum.

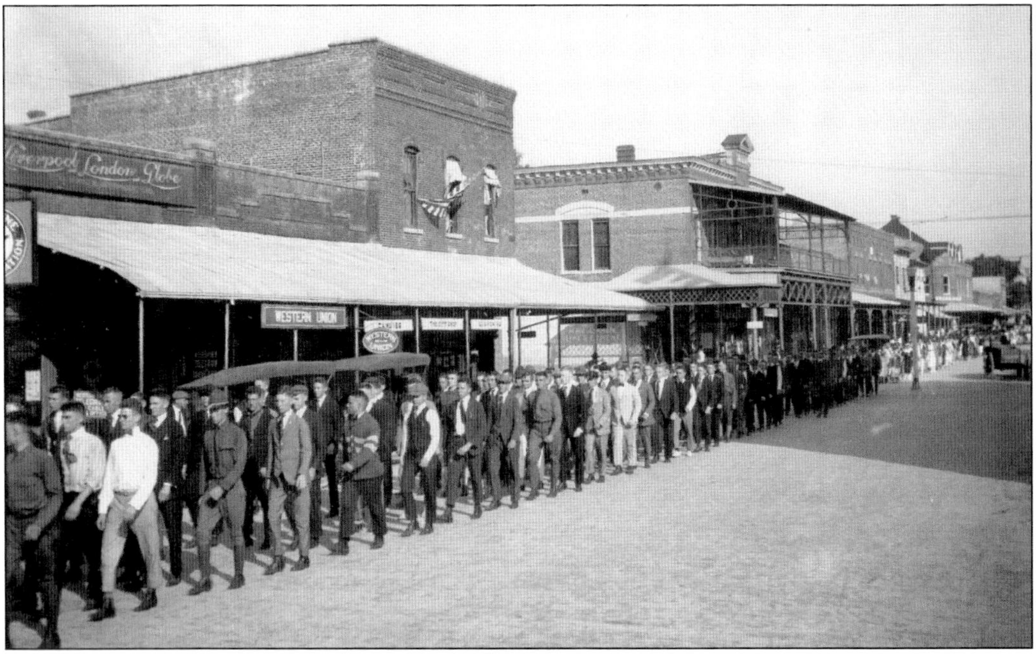

The bravest of all civil servants are those who march forth to battle. When World War I began, the draft of 1917 called up DeLand's finest. Patriotic young men summoned to duty and women who volunteered moved in unison down the Boulevard, heading toward the registration office.

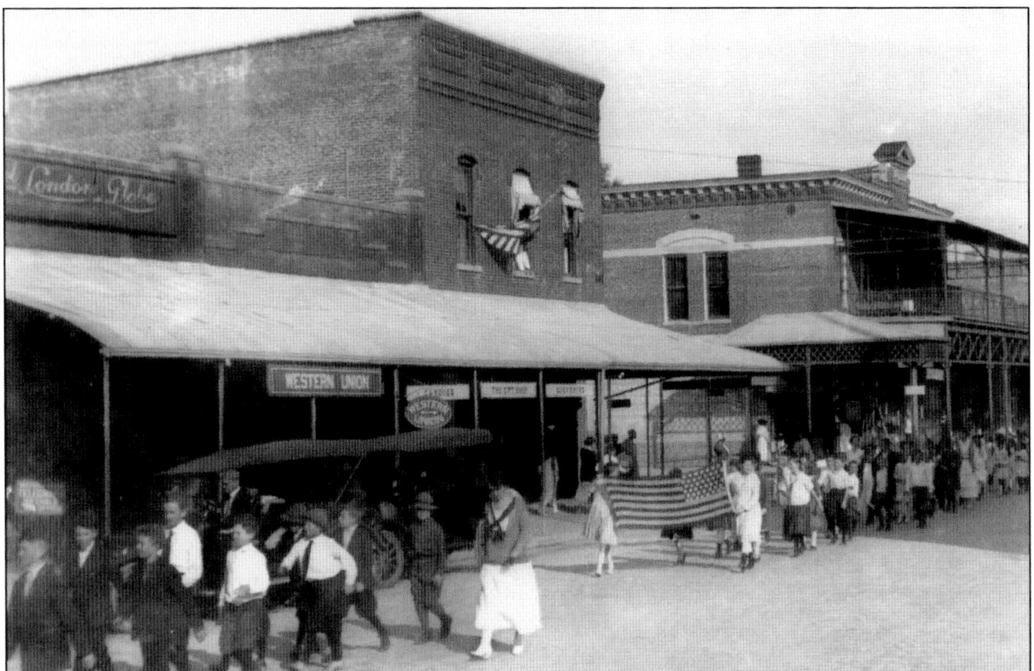

The children of those who marched to battle in 1917 took to the street to march down the Boulevard on Veteran's Day in honor of those who defended their country.

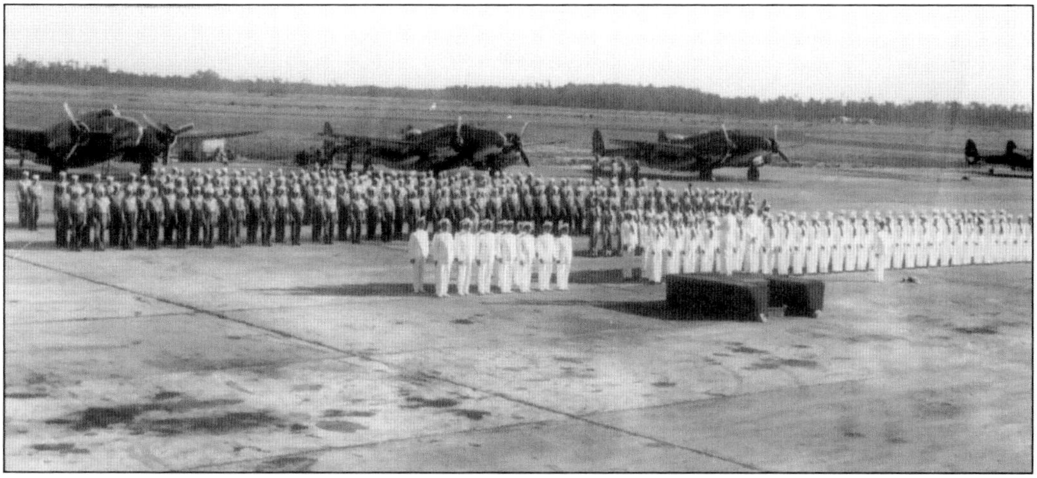

The next call to civil service came in 1941 when the United States declared war on Japan. DeLand's Naval Air Base, located north of town, was the training site for yet another generation of young people called to risk their lives to protect and preserve their democratic society.

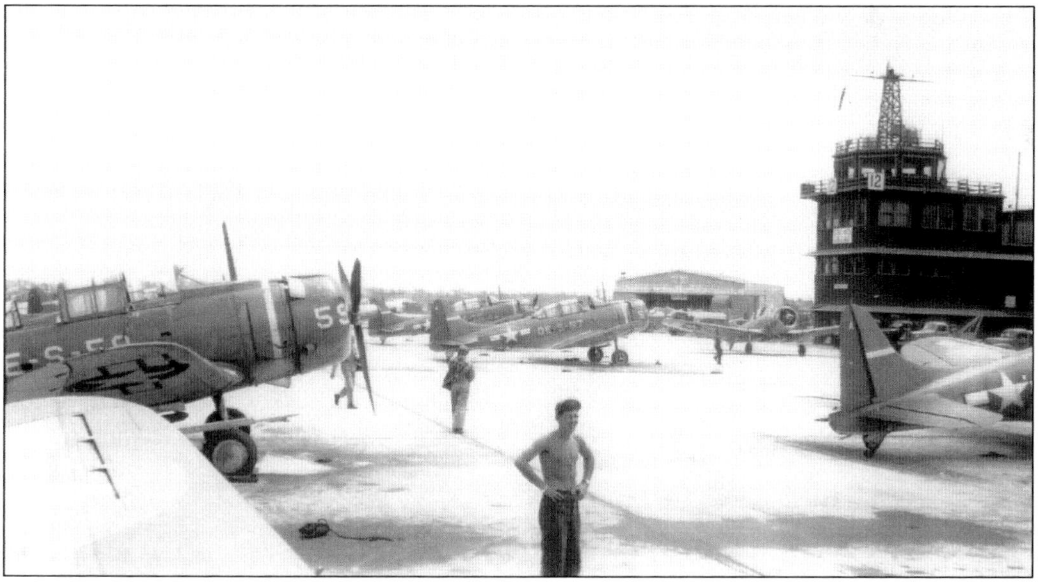

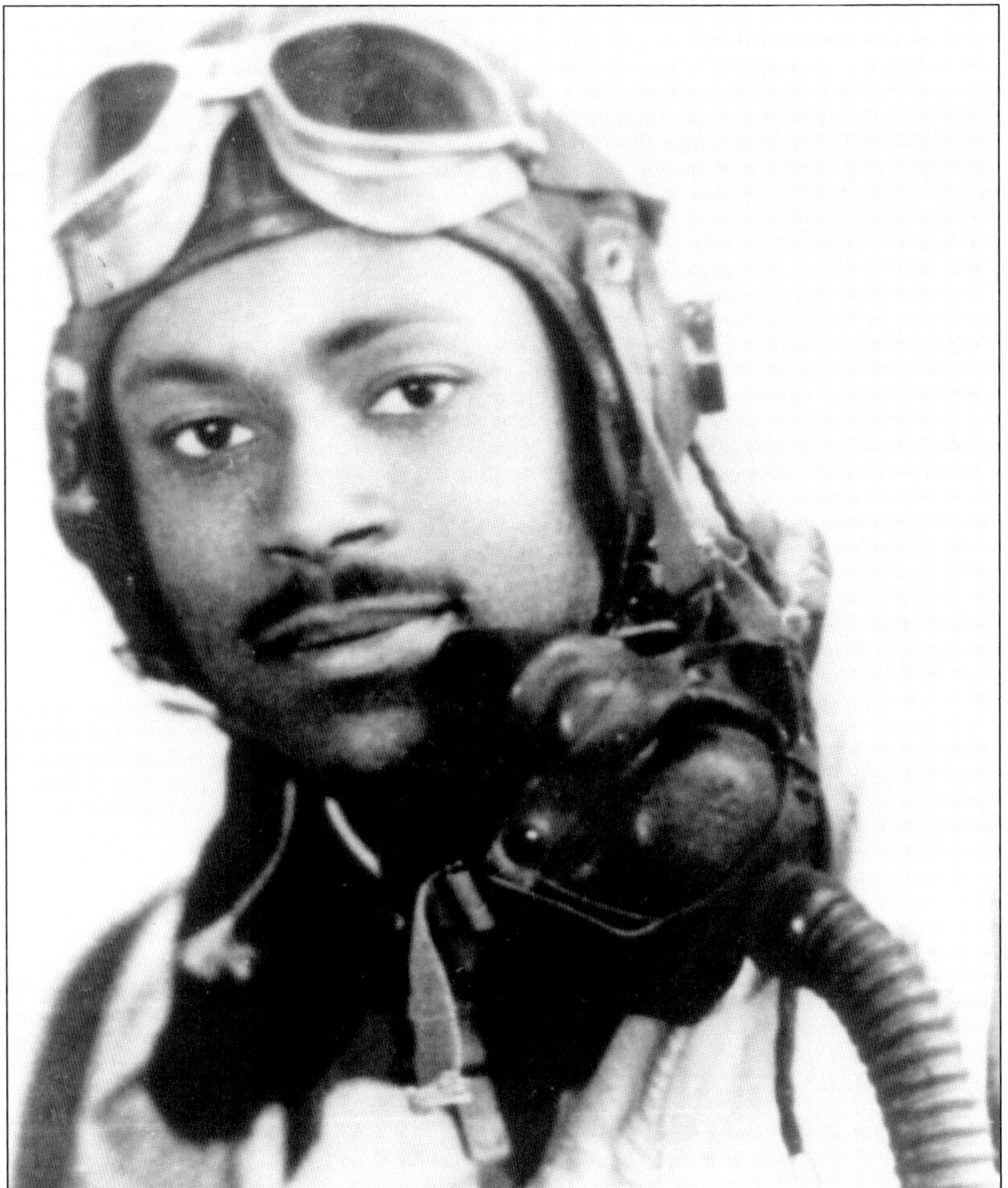

Charles T. Bailey, a native son, took to the air as one of the famed Tuskegee Airman of World War II. Fighter and bomber pilots, flight engineers, and gunners were trained in Alabama by the AAF at the Division of Aeronautics of Tuskegee Institute. By the end of the war, 992 men had graduated from pilot training at Tuskegee, 450 of whom were sent overseas for combat assignment. The Tuskegee Airmen, because they were African Americans, were not allowed to fraternize with white soldiers or use the officer's club. They were discriminated against until their brave refusal to capitulate to those unjust practices finally led to President Harry Truman's 1948 desegregation of the Armed Forces. Charles T. Bailey is a hero in his hometown of DeLand and an outstanding example of the men and women who gave and will continue to give their time and their energy and their lives in order that we remain free.

Six

MOVIN' ALONG

In April 1875 John Rich and his father-in-law, Cyrenius Wright, took the long journey from Beaufort, South Carolina down to Central Florida looking for just the right place to settle. After an extensive search, Rich decided on the little village of Persimmon Hollow. One of Rich's partners was O.P. Terry, who also purchased a large portion of land in the area. It was not long before Terry convinced his brother-in-law, Henry DeLand, to visit this serene land. They traveled by train down to Jacksonville, took a steamship up the St. John's River to Enterprise and after a night's rest at the Brock House, mounted a one-horse rig and made their way along a primitive trail to the Wisconsin Settlement (now Orange City).

Once the weary travelers reached the outskirts of the little village fittingly called Persimmon Hollow, Mr. DeLand caught wind of the waxy white blossoms dangling in every direction, a fragrance like no other. As the wooden wheels of the rig rattled to the top of rolling hills, Henry A. DeLand caught a glimpse of endless orange groves laid out before him, and he fell in love.

Travel initially played a huge part in developing the little village. It continued to do so as more and more people from the North set their sights on Florida and its winters of leisure. In 1885 travelers from the North could board one of the major steamship lines out of Jacksonville. By 1886 tourists could board the Jacksonville to Tampa Railroad all the way to Beresford near DeLand. Eventually the line was extended into DeLand. With so many people coming and going by carriages, wagons, steamships, and eventually trains, DeLand was movin' along toward the future.

In order to make traveling around town easier, city officials ordered roads paved with crushed shell. An earlier mixture of dirt and wood chips caused carriages to get stuck after a hard rain, often making travel virtually impossible. After V.W. Gould and James W. Perkins located a nearby mound of shells, the city purchased the property so it would have an infinite supply of material. The City of DeLand had its own way of movin' along its residents.

The future eventually lead to a gas-powered vehicle—the automobile. In 1907 Charlie Yeargin bought one of the first automobiles in DeLand. Driving was not very easy and not always appreciated. Many considered the new invention a noisy contraption that not only frightened horses but gave off an awful odor. Those still using horse-drawn carriages firmly believed that automobiles should be banned from roadways. Yet change was inevitable. The luxury of strolling along without the congestion of moving vehicles and traffic lights or signage or police had been a delightful moment swept aside by progress.

By the late 1920s Florida's "Boom Days" busted with the Great Depression, causing soaring travel to screech to a halt. But by the late 1930s the Depression was in the rearview mirror of time as new inventions were absorbed into the lives of citizens on the go. DeLand became a part of America's mobile society with the construction of paved roadways and the building of an airport.

No longer did visitors from afar have to endure tough terrain and slow, often undependable transportation. Now visitors could swoop down to this tropical paradise without having to experience hardships. But more importantly, locals could move along at a far quicker pace than ever before.

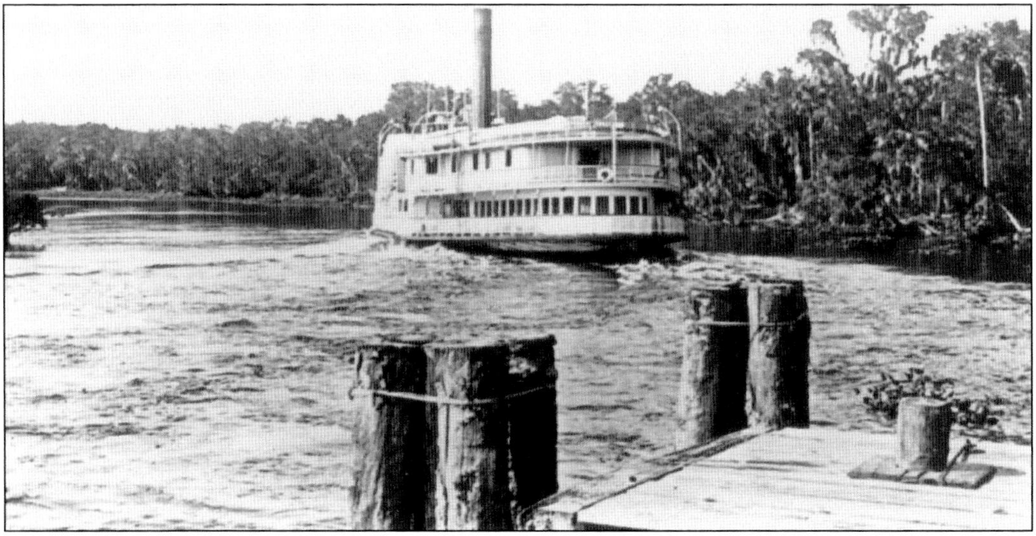

By the late 1800s Florida was growing by leaps and bounds. Winter visitors from the North traveled south floating up the St. Johns on one of many steamships which stopped at numerous small towns before reaching the end of the line at Lake Monroe and the small communities of Enterprise and DeBary, south of DeLand. The City of Jacksonville, a handsome three-storied steamer with a smoke stack that reached to the sky, plied the swift currents and sharp bends of the black water to deliver its passengers on time to DeLand's wharf.

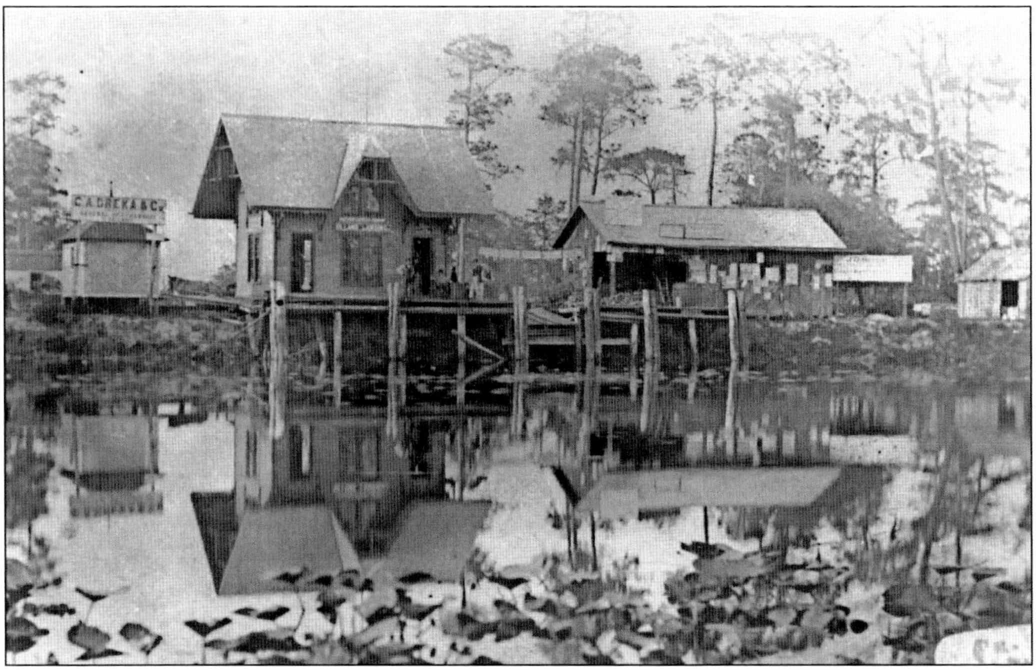

Before the turn of the 19th century a majority of the incoming traffic still took place on the water with Cabbage Bluff Landing on the St. Johns River as the docking point. An emerging form of transportation that exploded in Florida in the late 1880s was the railroad. Eventually water and rail transportation merged at the Bluff in 1884 when the first railroad was completed from the river to the community of Beresford, west of DeLand.

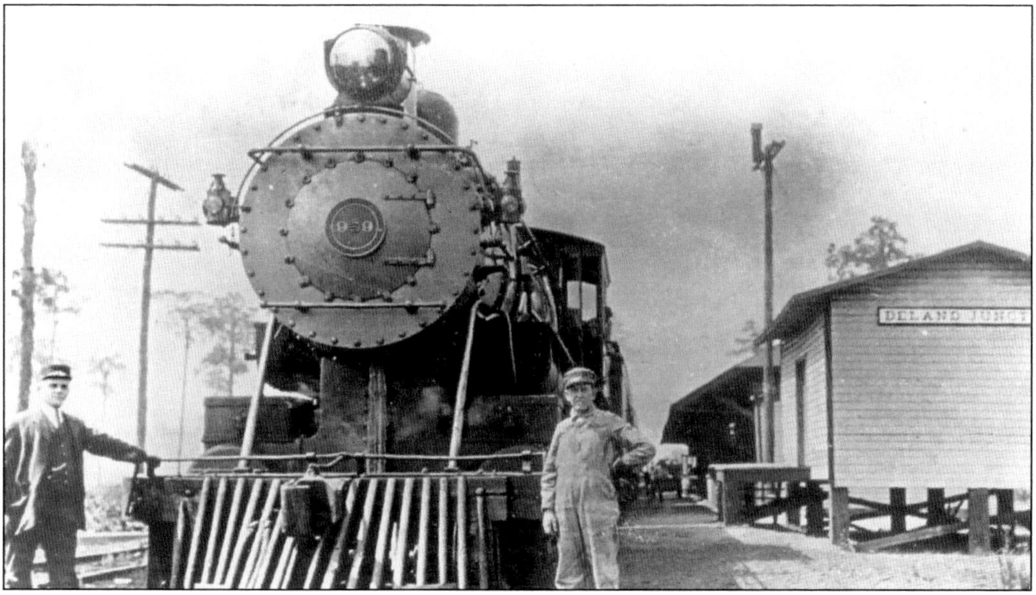

The railroad line consisted of "a narrow gauge with an engine, two flat cars, three box cars and one passenger coach." By 1910 the narrow gauge line was discontinued and the Atlantic Coast Line Depot broad gauge line was in effect, complete with a stop at DeLand Junction.

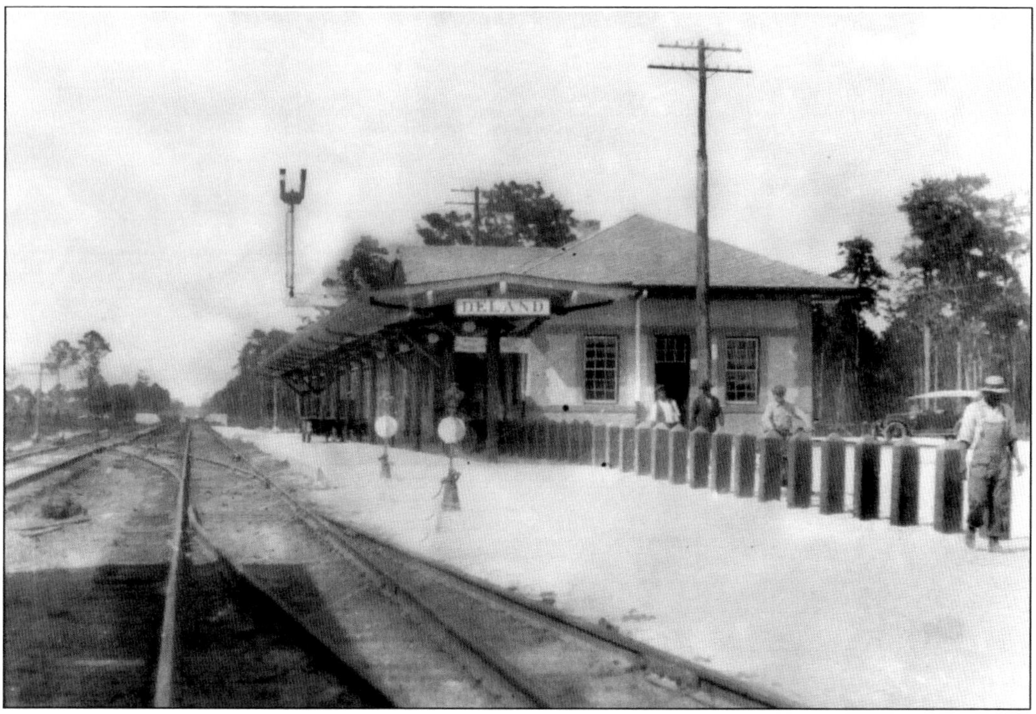

Located down old West New York toward the river, the DeLand Junction Depot of 1918 is today the Amtrak Station. Gutted by fire in 1981, it was repaired and put back into service soon after. In 1988 locals and the company restored part of the facility to its original character. It awaits further restoration efforts.

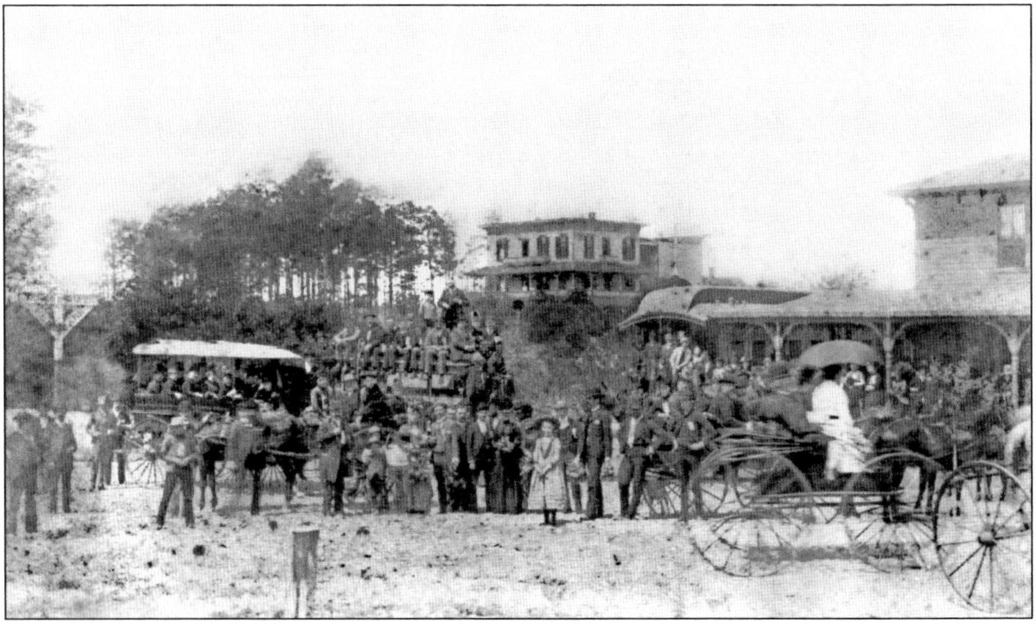

At the corner of Amelia and New York in 1890, travelers waited at the train depot to take a short ride to Cabbage Bluff for their steamship ride back north or to visit relatives and friends in the big city of Jacksonville. The Parceland Hotel is in the background. The numerous comings and goings by train caused what was once little ole' Persimmon Hollow to move progressively toward the 20th century, just like Henry A. DeLand had planned.

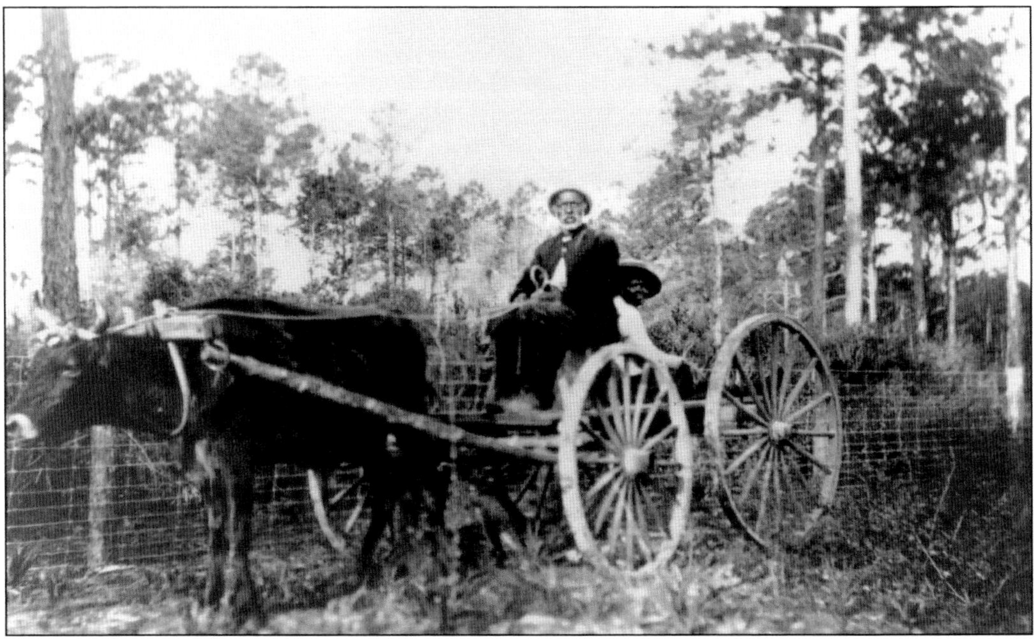

A tedious, more primitive mode of transportation during the 1800s was the faithful ox and cart. Though travel was slow, it was surely dependable and those traveling aboard had total control. All they needed to supply their lead was a little grain, a little water, and a firm giddy-yap.

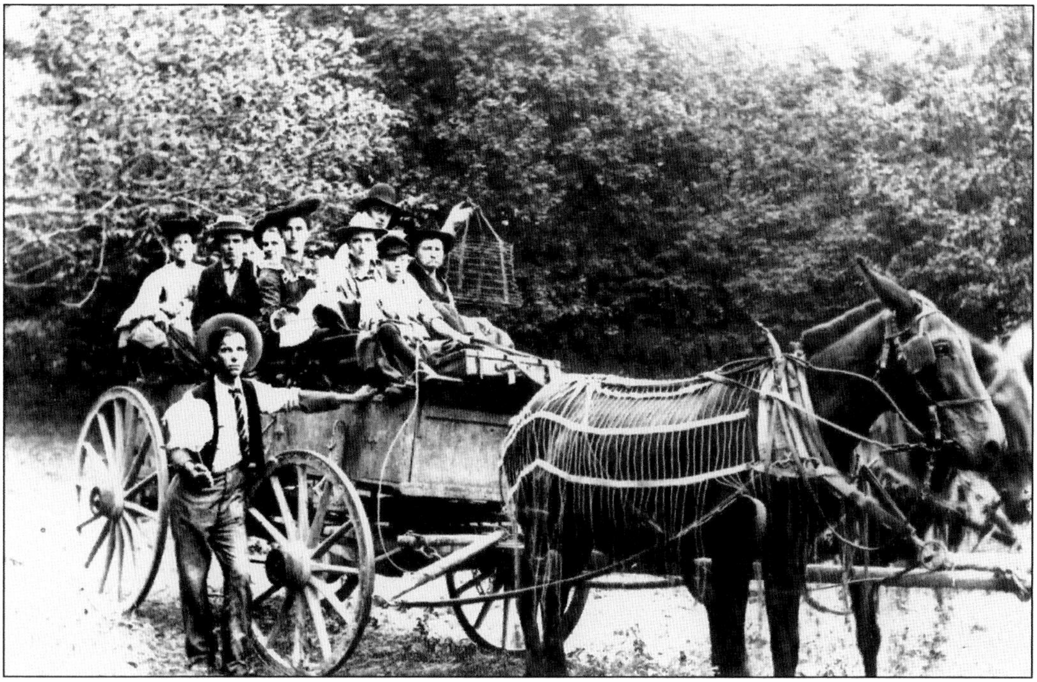

Around 1900 a fancy contraption was created to alleviate the pain that horses suffered due to the bite of a horsefly. It was called a fly-guard and though it was a funny-looking sight to see on the back of a horse, it must have done the trick. The material rolled back and forth across the horse's skin as the animal walked, keeping horseflies befuddled as to where they should try to land in order to take a bite.

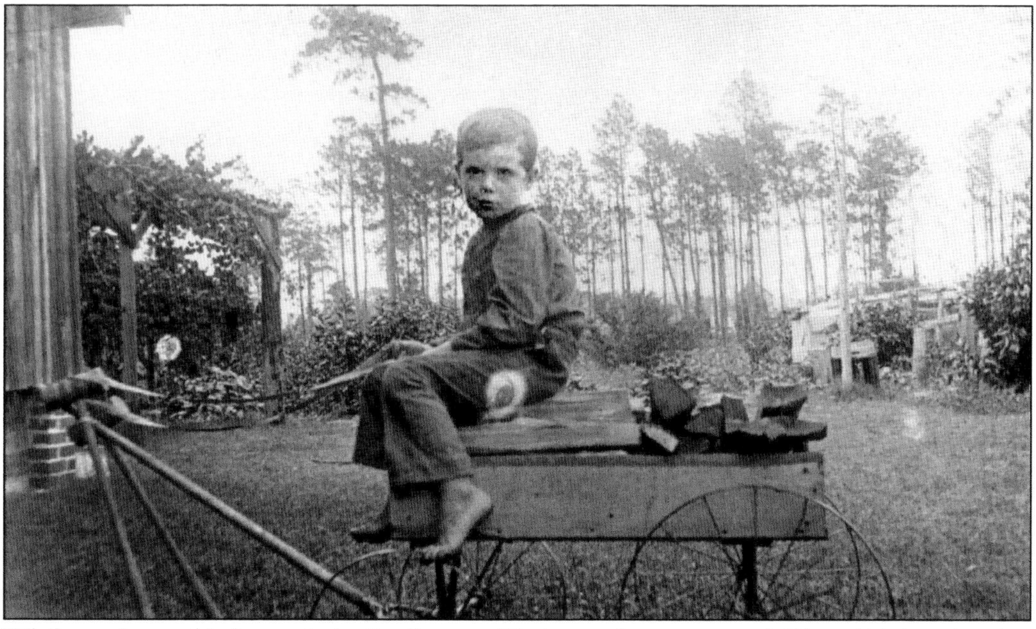

While mother and father took the family to and fro in a real wagon, one child used his imagination to imitate his elders in this 1900 photo. This youngster needed only croquet mallets and the creativity to envision himself far, far away to travel without great expense.

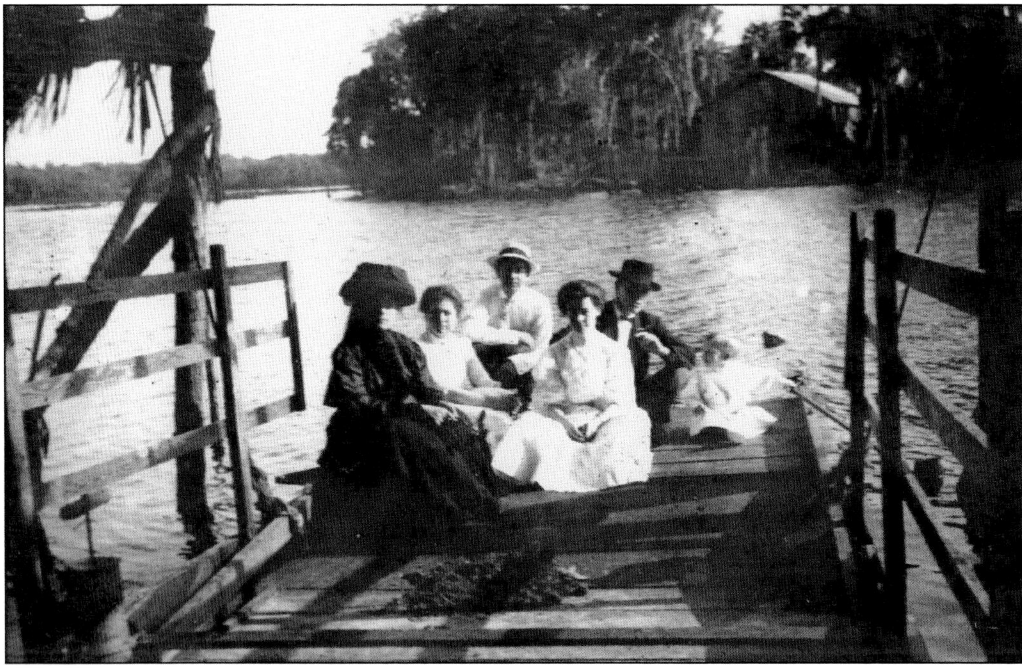

Another mode of transportation for DeLandites was the ferryboat. This floating flatboat was used extensively on the St. Johns to transport employees to their workplace, a packing house on Hontoon Island, and for visitors to see an abandoned Timucua Indian shell mound. The Timucuans, the first to inhabit Hontoon Island, ate snails as their main food source and over the years the discarded shells formed two high and sturdy mounds. This 1,650-acre island was home to Native Americans, then an orange grove and pioneer settlement, later a boat yard, and finally a commercial fishing site. In 1967 it was purchased by the state of Florida for a park. Today one must still board the ferry for a trip across the St. Johns to this majestic piece of history.

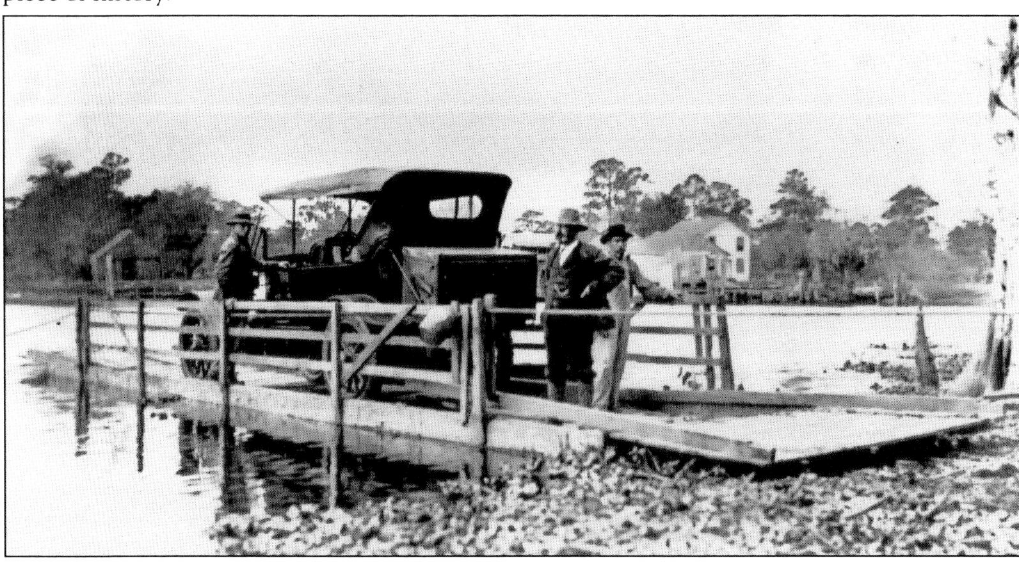

In 1913 a hand operated cable ferry at Crow's Bluff carried animals, pedestrians, and vehicles and their drivers across the St. Johns.

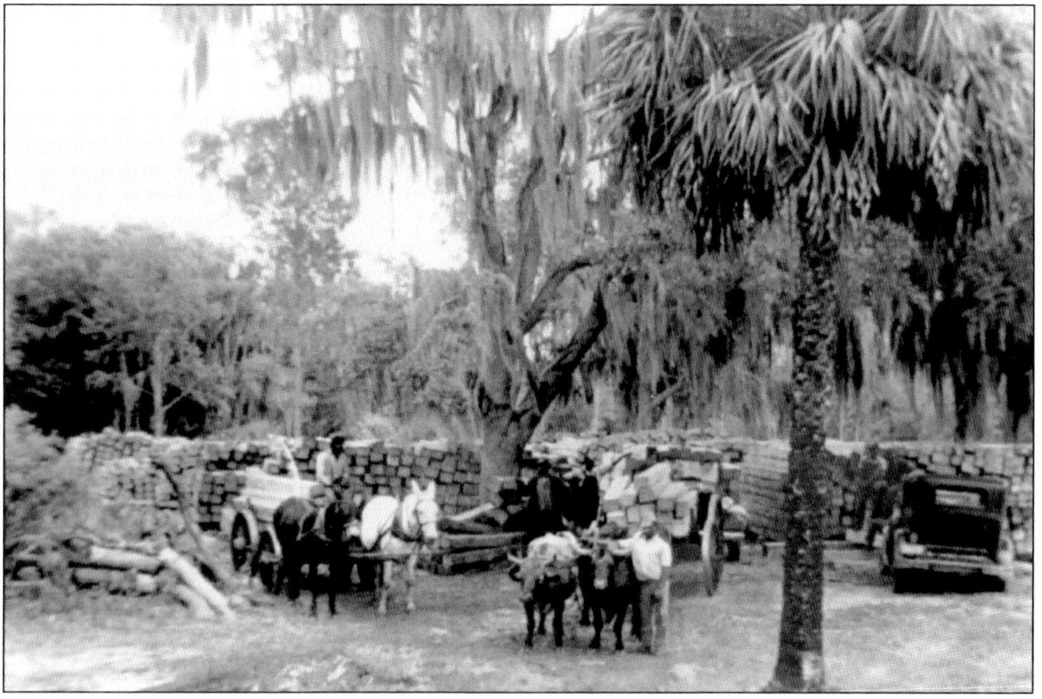

Several forms of transportation converged at Crow's Bluff. Men unloaded railroad crossties from their wagons, one pulled by oxen, the other by a team of horses. An automobile sat parked nearby, probably owned by the man in charge of the shipment of ties that would eventually be laid down to accommodate the train's rails. Times were changing toward the end of the 19th century as the evolution of how people got from one point to another was captured on film.

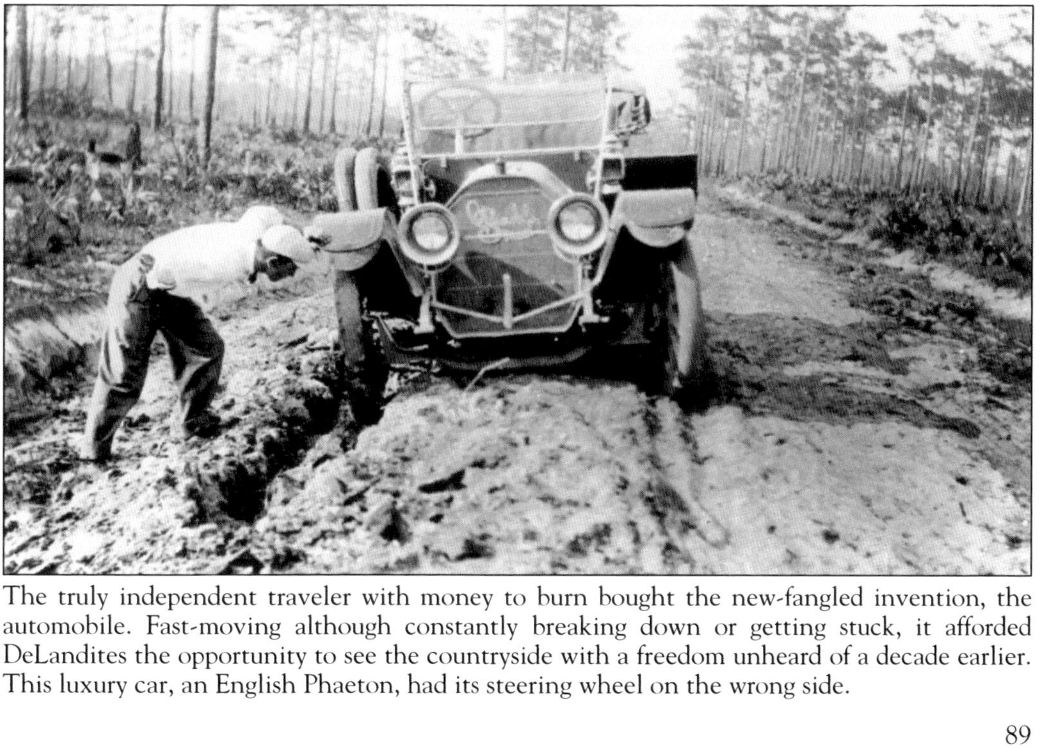

The truly independent traveler with money to burn bought the new-fangled invention, the automobile. Fast-moving although constantly breaking down or getting stuck, it afforded DeLandites the opportunity to see the countryside with a freedom unheard of a decade earlier. This luxury car, an English Phaeton, had its steering wheel on the wrong side.

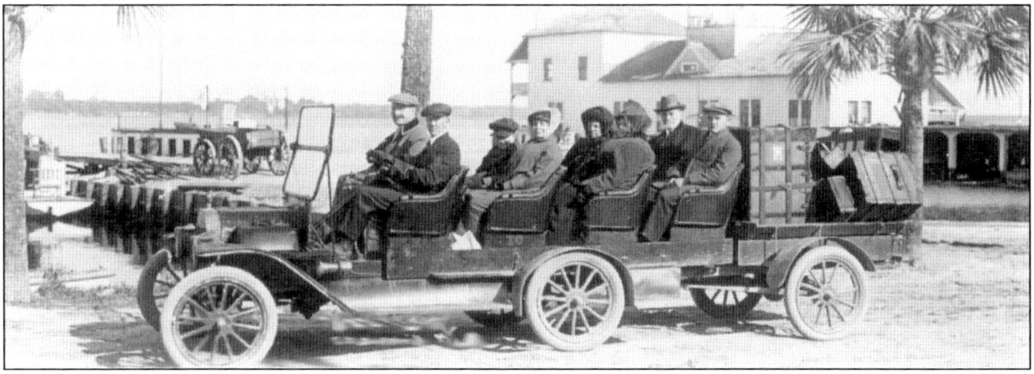

E.D. Barnhill, builder of the DeLand Hotel, also owned a transportation company known as the "Red Line" express. This 1912 postcard advertised one of his "buses" arriving at the "end of the line," the Halifax River in Daytona. The line ran between DeLand and Daytona.

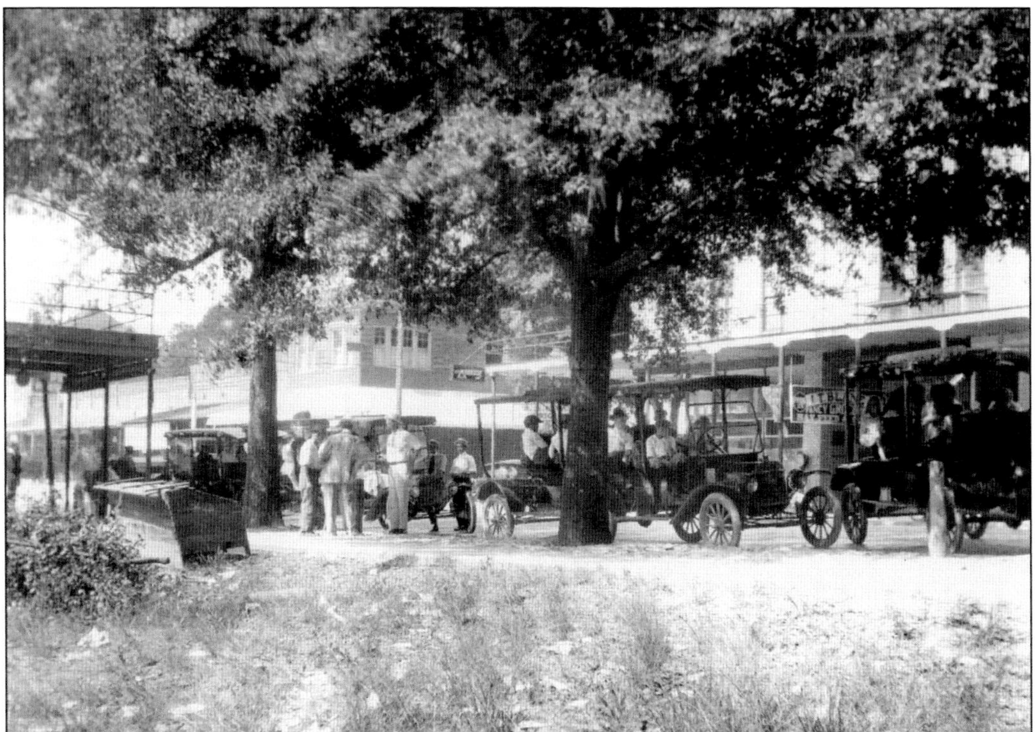

Around 1914 at the corner of Rich Avenue and the Boulevard, travelers waited to catch one of the local "air conditioned" buses that served most of the towns in West Volusia.

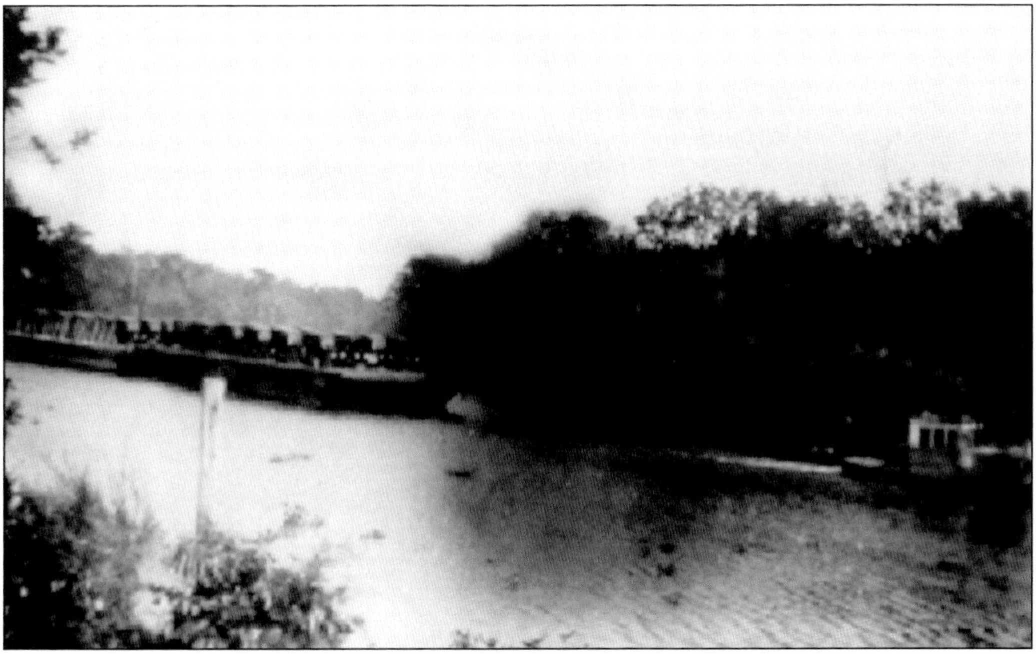

The last year the Model "T" was made was 1927. Barges carried one of the last loads to DeLand on the St. Johns River that same year. By this time the automobile was fully integrated into the daily lives of DeLand's residents. The repair shop in Nahm's Dodge Agency was filled with auto mechanics and their patients.

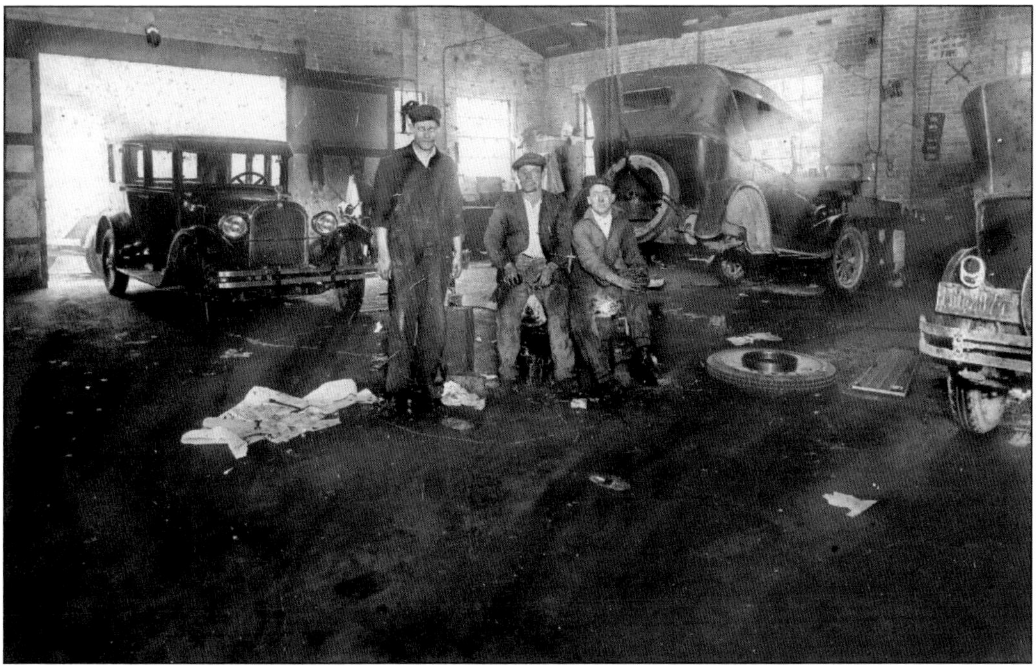

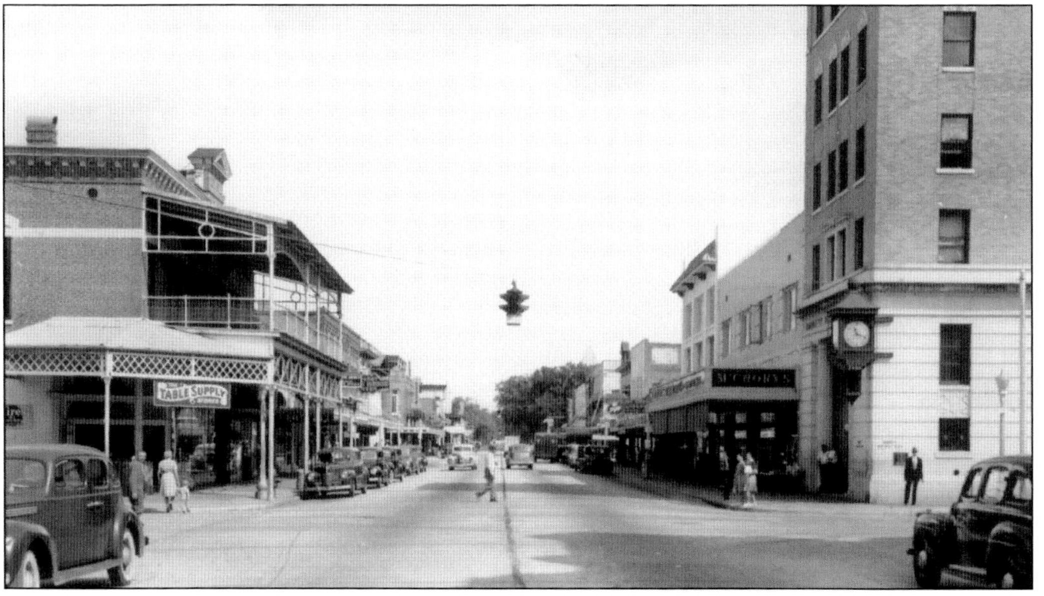

Downtown DeLand was hopping during the Roaring Twenties. By looking at this image one may experience the feel of a sense of community involvement that existed in town. More than eighty years later present-day DeLandites can take pride in the fact that this same spirit is alive and well as they stroll down the Boulevard, window shopping and people gazing.

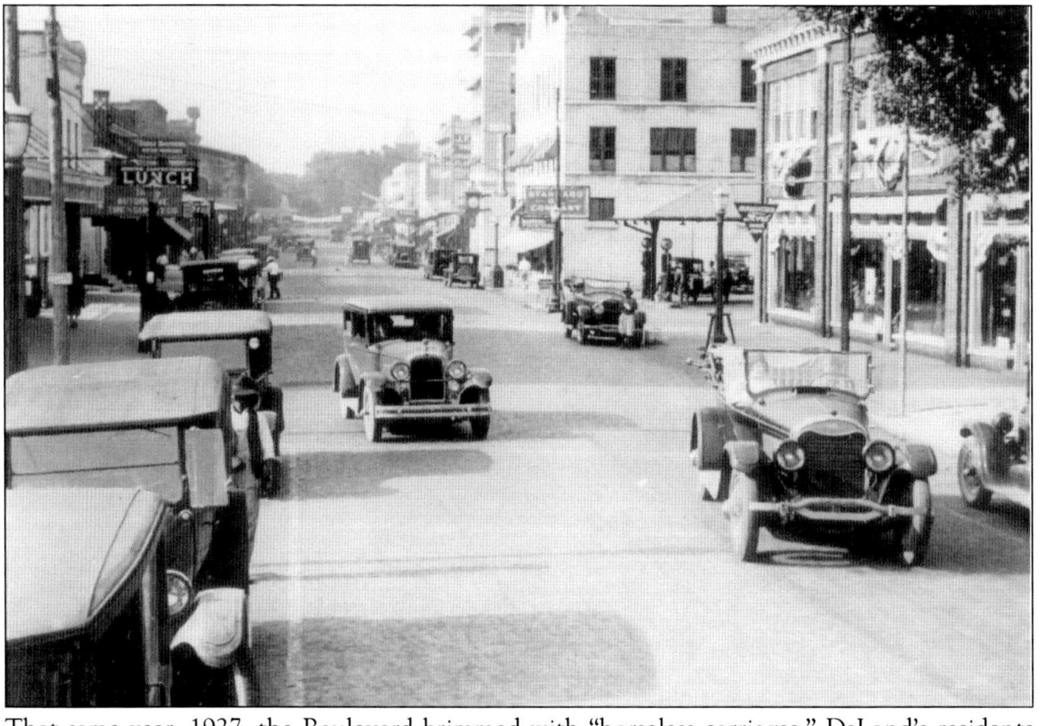

That same year, 1927, the Boulevard brimmed with "horseless carriages." DeLand's residents could travel for recreation to Daytona Beach and surrounding towns with relative ease while at the same time use the new contraption to conduct their daily business affairs. And as Henry Ford promised, one of his cars could be purchased in any color so long as it was black.

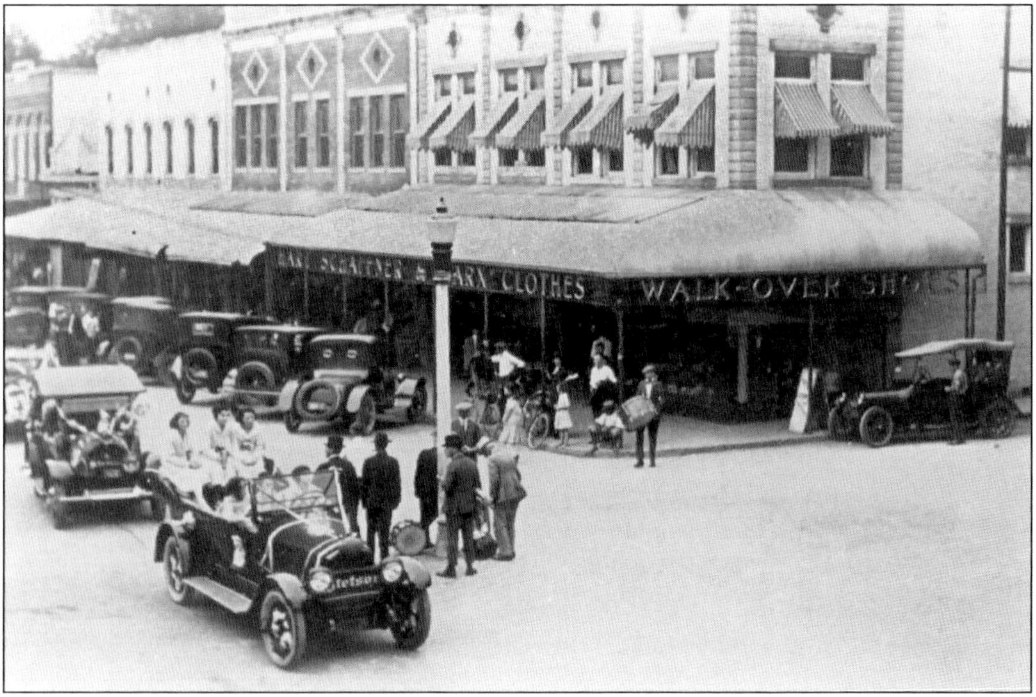

By the 1920s, as seen on the corner of Indiana and the Boulevard, life was swiftly movin' on. Gone were the horse and buggies. Gone were the mules and oxen. Gone were horseback riders. Gone were dusty streets, muddy potholes, and crushed shell roads. Gone were plank sidewalks for strolling DeLandites who enjoyed foot travel over speed. The gasoline engine had arrived, and with its advent into American society, things were never quite the same again.

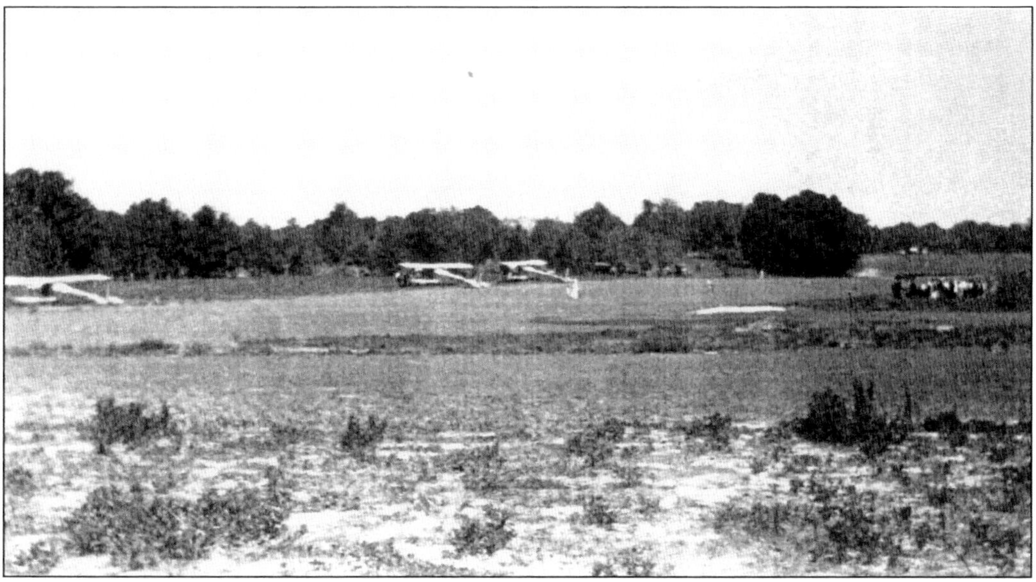

With the invention of the gasoline engine, enter the age of air travel. Before there was an airport in DeLand, World War I biplanes actually landed on the Hotel College Arms Golf Course. In 1919 planes were still very much a novelty so what a thrill it must have been for DeLandites to witness those cutting-edge machines descend on their small city.

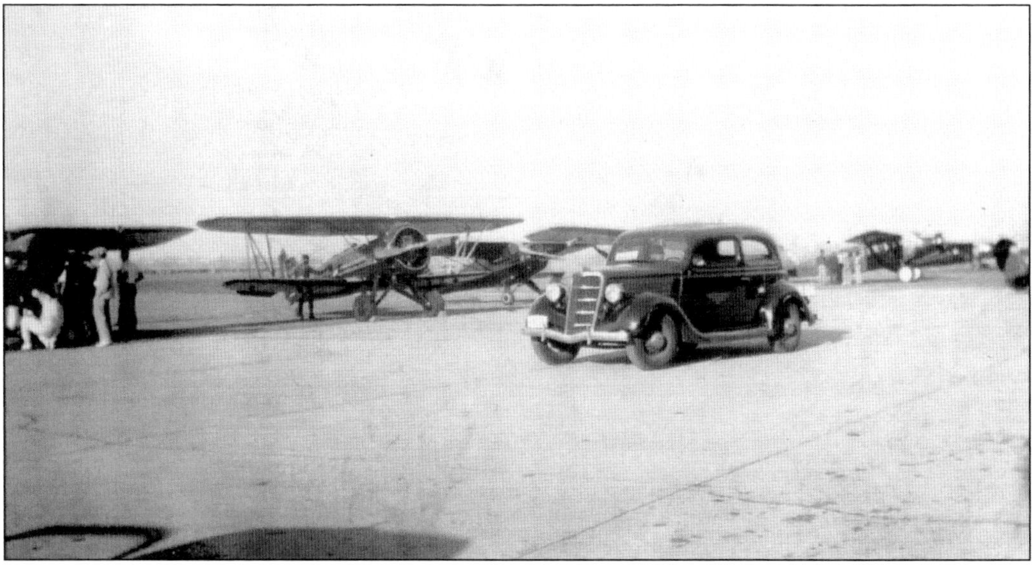

In May 1928, A.R. Brown and son, Al, opened DeLand's first air travel business, the Volusia Airways Company. By 1935 the airport was a busy intersection of traffic from private pilots to air shows to small commercial planes that brought even more people to town.

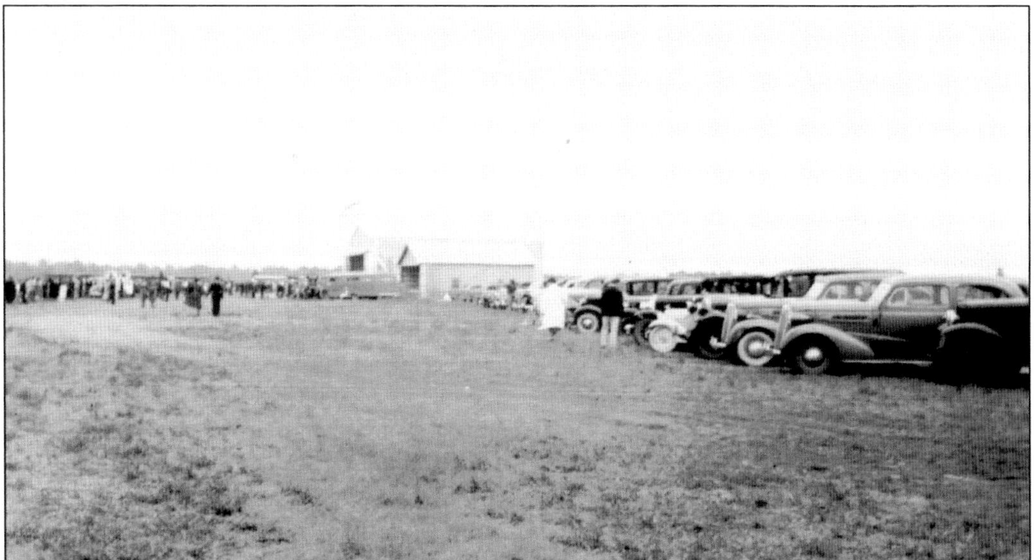

The year 1939 saw the grand opening of the DeLand Airport with an asphalt runway. The event was packed with citizens who marveled at the larger planes landing on the new surface. DeLand was "movin' along" as were most small towns in Florida. The Depression had come and gone, and although the threat of war loomed in DeLand as in the rest of America, the economy was on the rise, beginning to soar higher than it had during the height of the Florida Boom Days.

Seven

Readin', 'Ritin', and 'Rithmetic

From Henry DeLand's inspiration for DeLand becoming the "Athens of Florida," education was uppermost in his mind. Attending his first official town meeting in October 1876, DeLand offered, "Build a schoolhouse and use that for a place of worship as well as a school. If you wish to locate on land I have bought, I will give an acre...." He also donated funds to cover half the cost of construction.

By December news spread that a schoolhouse would be built. In a letter written by Henry Austin to his sister in Indiana, he boasted, "We will...have a good schoolhouse...in a few weeks." In March 1877 the schoolhouse was complete and ready for its pupils. Cosner and Bloomer designed the elaborate building, quite grand for such a small community. But then Henry's DeLand was to be an outstanding leader in education for the state of Florida. The construction of the one-room schoolhouse was frame with a large bell tower. For practical purposes the building faced south to take advantage of cross breezes from the Atlantic to the Gulf. Four tall six-paned windows were installed on each side to capture the east-to-west air flow.

On May 7, 1877 double-front doors opened to the laughter or trepidation of students entering for their first day of class as Miss Rowena Dean of New York, the school's first teacher, stood waiting. Inside the children were greeted with a sparsely furnished room, slate boards, chalk, a handful of books, and a hot four-month term before them.

The first social event held at the school occurred in July 1877 when the town's citizens decided to reduce the mortgage on the schoolhouse by planning an ice-cream fundraiser. Ten cents got a hungry participant inside but in order to obtain a delicious scoop of peach ice cream an additional sum was charged.

There was still no school board in 1879 so when a teacher was needed, a group of interested individuals got together to discuss the situation. And indeed there was a dilemma within days of the May opening for summer term. A young lady who had been hired to teach wrote from Kentucky to inform the town, "I have figured carefully and I do not see how I can possibly pay my fare down and back, and living expenses while there on a four-month's term at $21 per month."

But a solution was forthcoming as a few good men arranged for one of their friends to be teacher. Off headed Charlie Miller, a shopkeeper, to the town of Enterprise where he was tested by the county superintendent on reading comprehension and Bible scriptures. He passed and headed home to DeLand to become the school's next teacher.

In 1883 Henry DeLand moved his town toward a more progressive educational agenda by founding DeLand Academy, the second educational institution in the city. Little did Mr. DeLand suspect at the time that his initiative would one day lead to a nationally ranked university. Or did he?

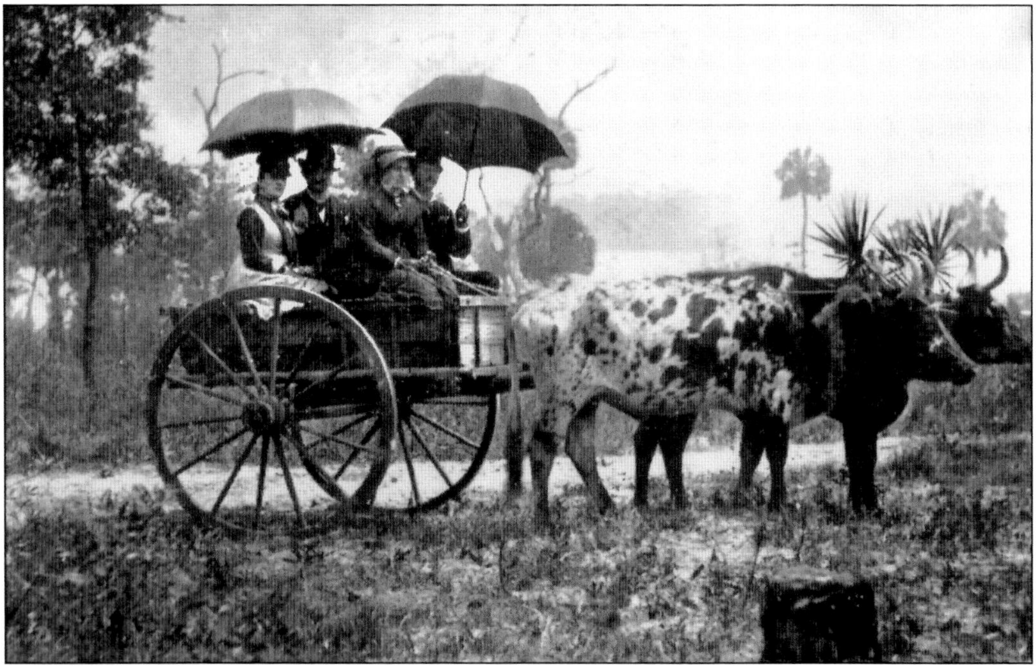

Miss Rowena Dean, DeLand's first school teacher, enjoyed a sightseeing tour around her new town with a few select friends. Not only was Miss Dean able to rein in her students, she seemed to be an expert at reining in her oxen, too.

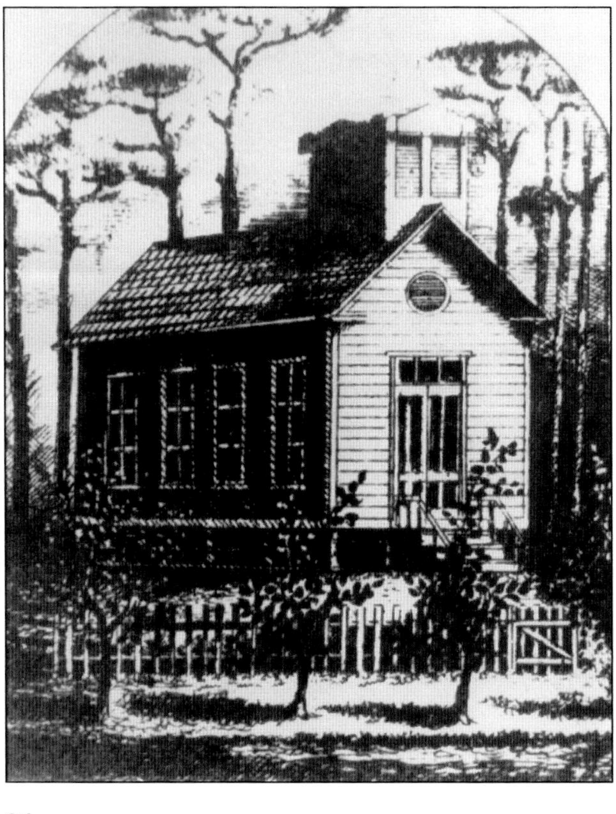

No expense was spared for the town's first schoolhouse; however, oddly enough, students supplied their own chairs and tables, often simple pine boxes. Located on the northeast corner of Indiana and the Boulevard, the building was constructed of wide pine planks, the roof wood shingled, and sat high off the ground to enhance cross ventilation. Citrus in the front, pine at the rear, and a picket fence completed a welcoming site. An 1884 map indicates only the Presbyterian Church used the building. Between 1886 and 1889 the building was moved to the north side of Indiana between Florida and the Boulevard and later used by the city's fire department. When the fire department required more up-to-date facilities, the historic structure that had given young DeLandites a proper education was demolished.

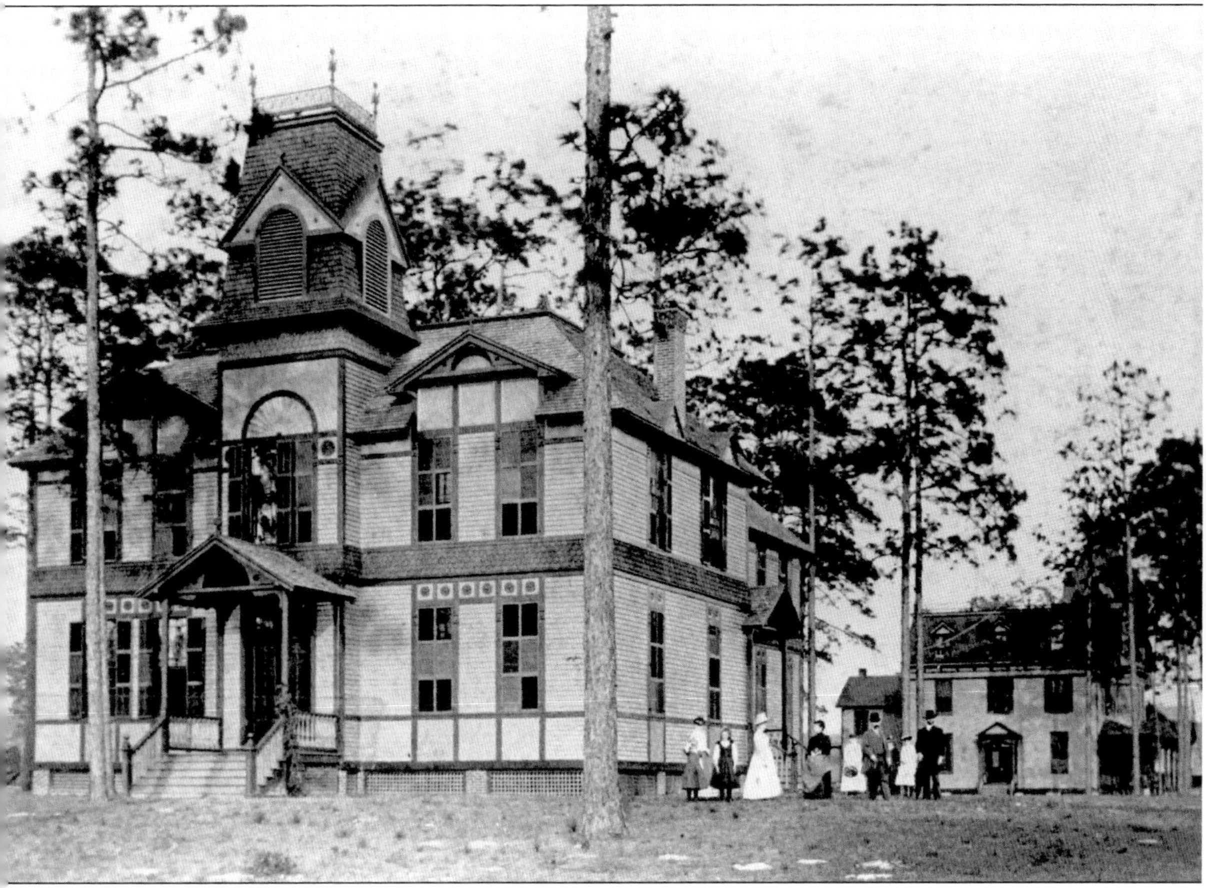

It takes wisdom to seek the advice of others, and in the case of Henry DeLand, he had both wisdom and vision. So off he went to Col. C.O. Codrington, editor of the *Florida Agriculturist*, to ask his advice as to how DeLand could be a more distinctive community. Codrington's sage comment was that the town should become an outstanding educational center. Since Florida had no four-year college, and according to a report presented in 1882 by the state superintendent of public instruction that there was strong interest for such an institution, in November 1883 Henry DeLand opened DeLand Academy to include advanced studies in preparation for college. Thirteen students met in classes in the First Baptist Church until Henry DeLand's two-story frame building was erected, for only $6,000, on four acres at the northeast corner of the Boulevard and Minnesota. Completed in 1884, DeLand Hall survives today and is listed on the National Register of Historic Places for holding the distinct honor of being the oldest continually operating building used for higher education in the state of Florida.

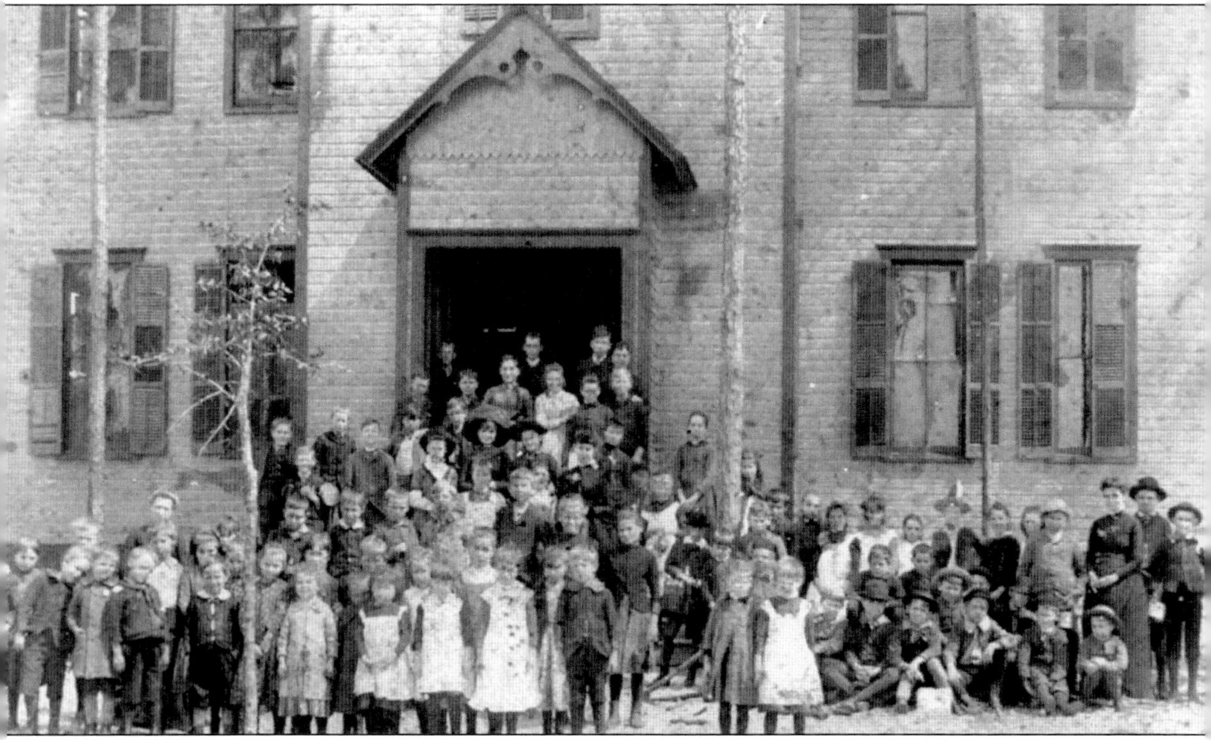

By October 1884 a total of 88 students ranging in ages from the very young to the teenage years attended the DeLand Academy. Classes for advanced students included history, geography, physics, and physiology. Of course the younger ones continued to study readin', 'ritin,' and 'rithmetic. Serendipitous as it seemed, just as Henry DeLand was preparing to construct his academy, the Florida Baptist Convention was attempting to establish a female college. The Convention promised that its college would be a place where "all forms of error, skepticism, and infidelity are to be met and refuted." While the Convention vacillated between Gainesville and Lake Weir as the location for the school, decisive Mr. DeLand stepped forward to offer his new academy building for the college. DeLand's generous offer of $6,000 in cash, $5,000 in land, and an additional $4,000 from the town's residents brought a unanimous acceptance by the Convention acknowledging the "generous offer of Brother DeLand" in 1885.

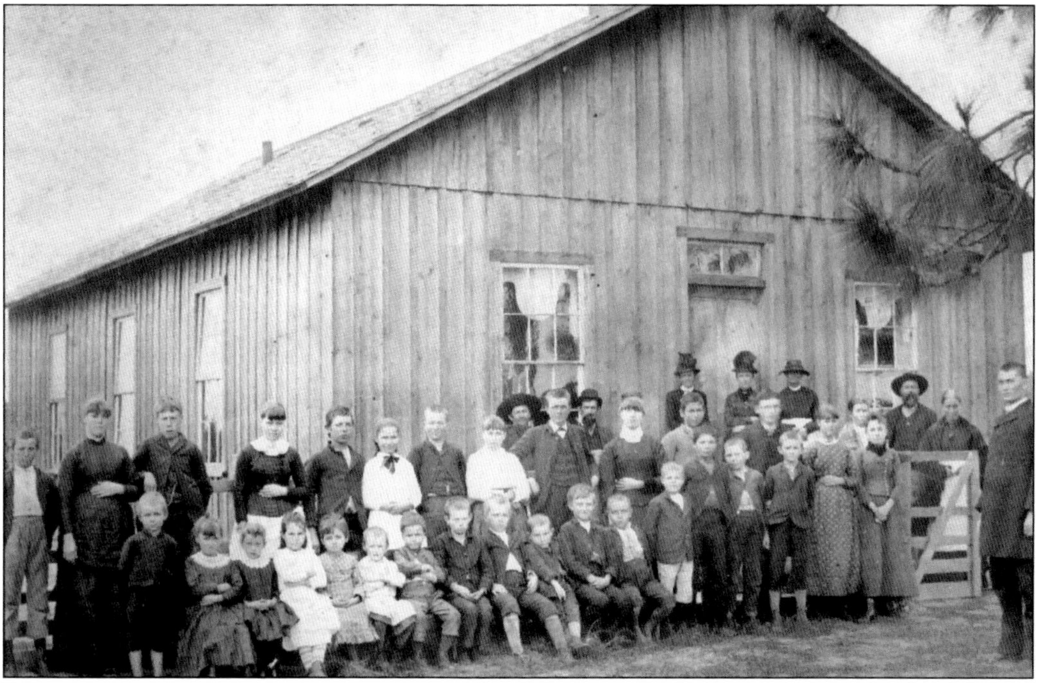

A new public grade school was constructed in 1884 on the northeast corner of Amelia Avenue and Church Street. Built using the frame board and batten style, it was one story and low to the ground. Its architecture was certainly not as grand as the first-grade school or the elegant DeLand Academy, but function over frills captured the essence of the times. This 1895 photograph suggests that all took a stern liking to learning or possibly the squat unadorned schoolhouse did not excite their curiosity.

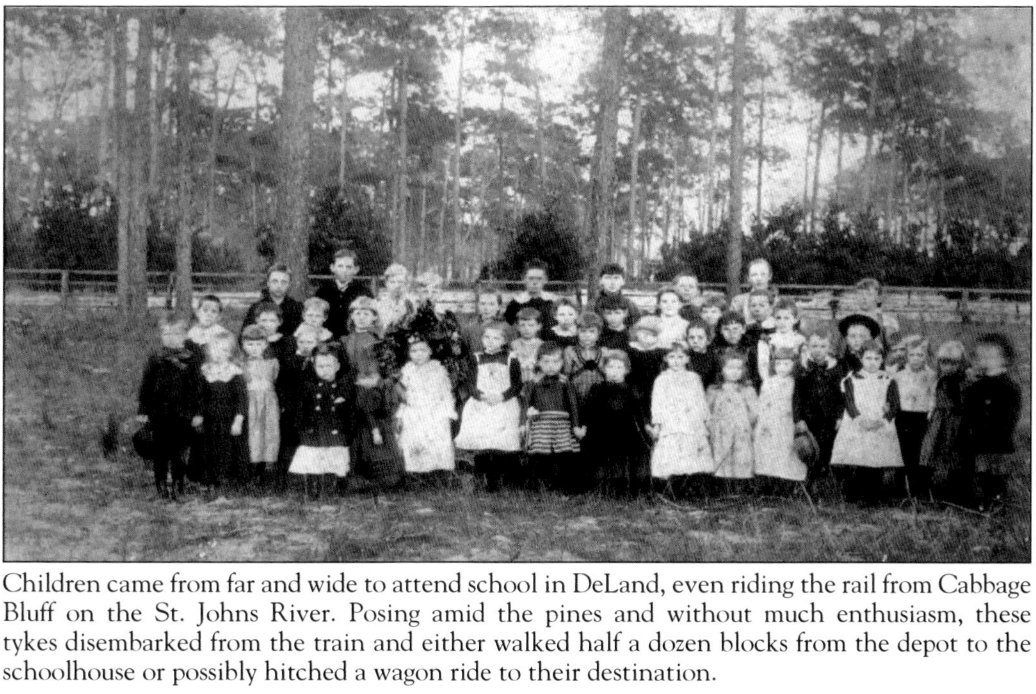

Children came from far and wide to attend school in DeLand, even riding the rail from Cabbage Bluff on the St. Johns River. Posing amid the pines and without much enthusiasm, these tykes disembarked from the train and either walked half a dozen blocks from the depot to the schoolhouse or possibly hitched a wagon ride to their destination.

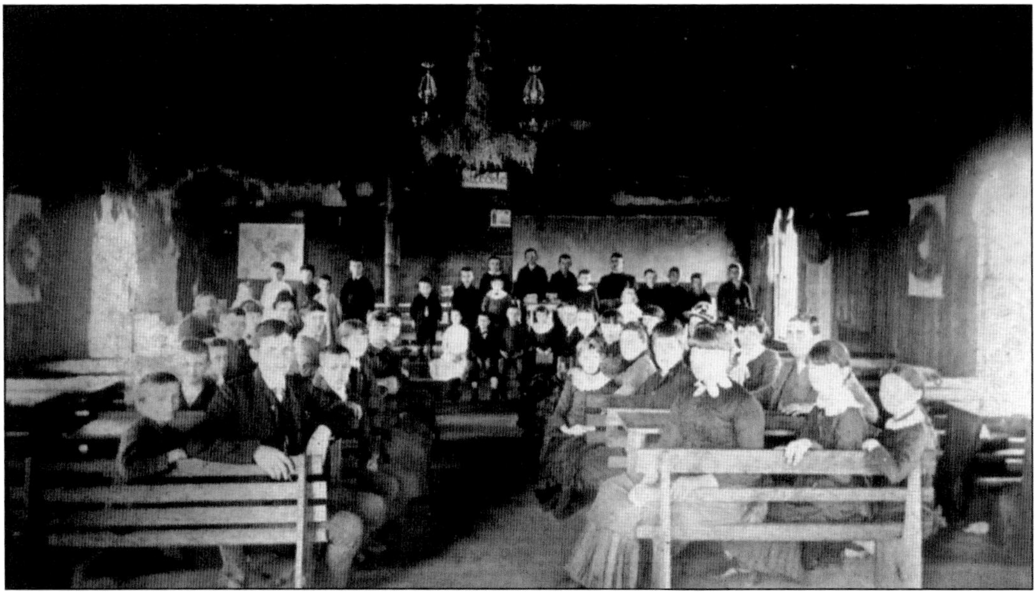

This interior shot of the plain little one-room schoolhouse depicts a classroom prepared for the Christmas season. Hard, long uniform desks and benches, formal attire, and a stiff demeanor mirrored the sentiments that education was no laughing matter.

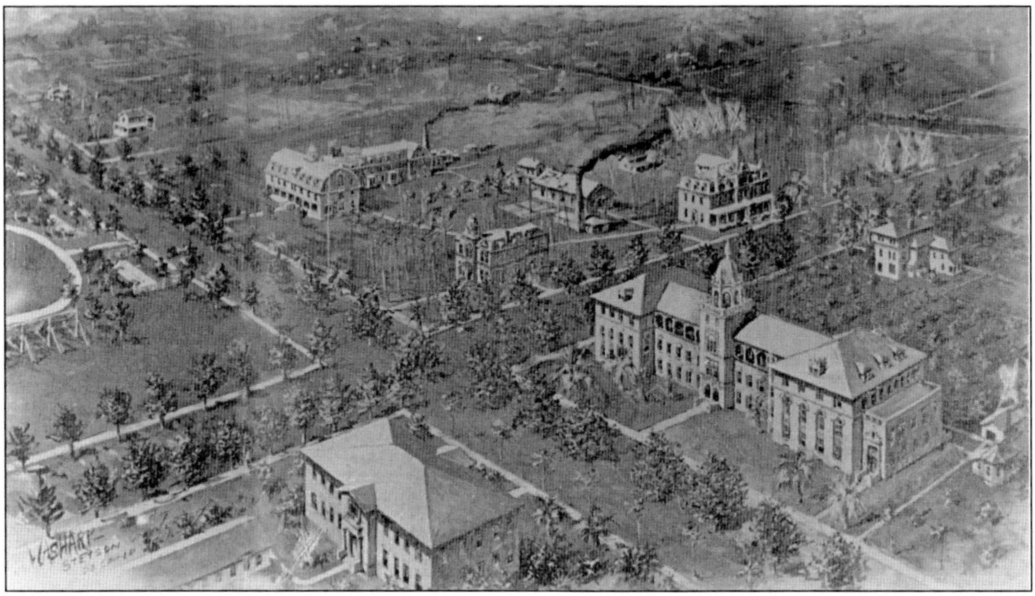

After the Florida Baptist Convention made its portentous 1885 decision to house a college in DeLand Academy, Henry DeLand's little academy was renamed DeLand Academy and College. In 1887 the school became DeLand College and University and in 1889 it was renamed John B. Stetson University to honor its new benefactor. At the time of Henry DeLand's death in 1908, his dream to make DeLand an educational center was fulfilled. The university had nine architecturally significant buildings, three of which were dormitories and a library, an enrollment of 233, and an income-producing endowment of over $225,000. This turn-of-the century lithograph shows Stetson's sprawling campus with Henry DeLand's oaks dividing the Boulevard.

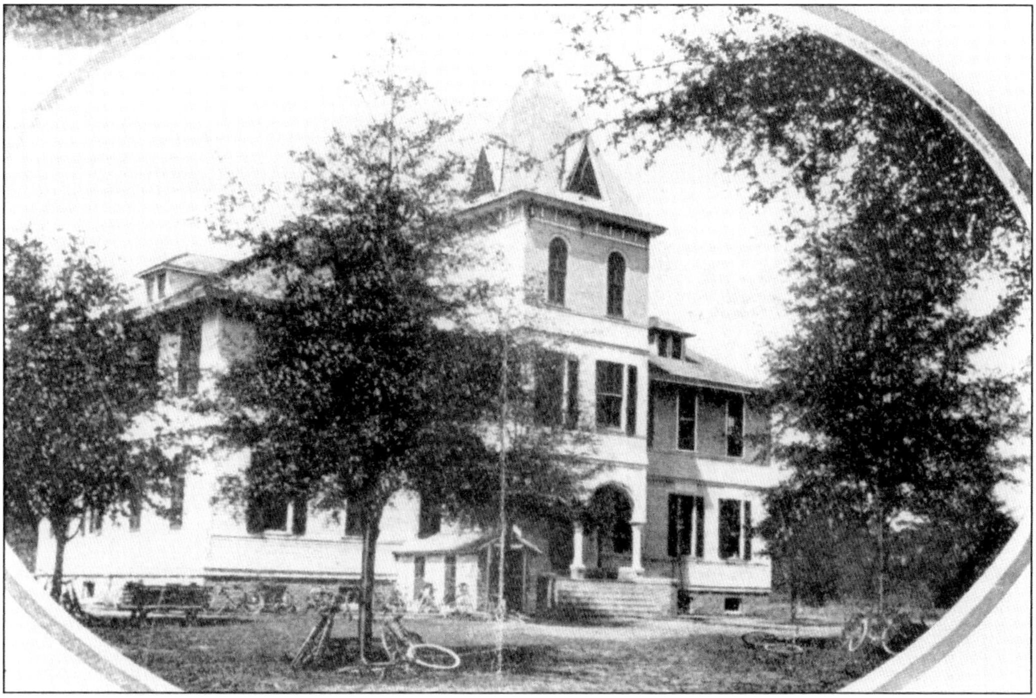

Once again architecture as art returned to DeLand with the 1899 construction of its third public school. This massive beauty, no longer extant, was located on the northwest corner of Clara and Rich. The cost of construction was $8,000, a large sum in those days. Students described the interior as "well-lighted, heated, and ventilated...beautifully furnished and appreciated." The school term had increased to eight months; there were 214 students in nine grades with six teachers on payroll. Segregation was an unquestioned fact-of-life through the early history of DeLand so when this stately building opened for white students only, as had been the case with all other schools, the blacks finally got to come in from the country and attend a city school—the 1884 squat schoolhouse on Amelia Avenue. Grades were one through eight, with an enrollment at 50. Records relate that when the new pupils took over, the building was "in good condition and contains four rooms, well furnished."

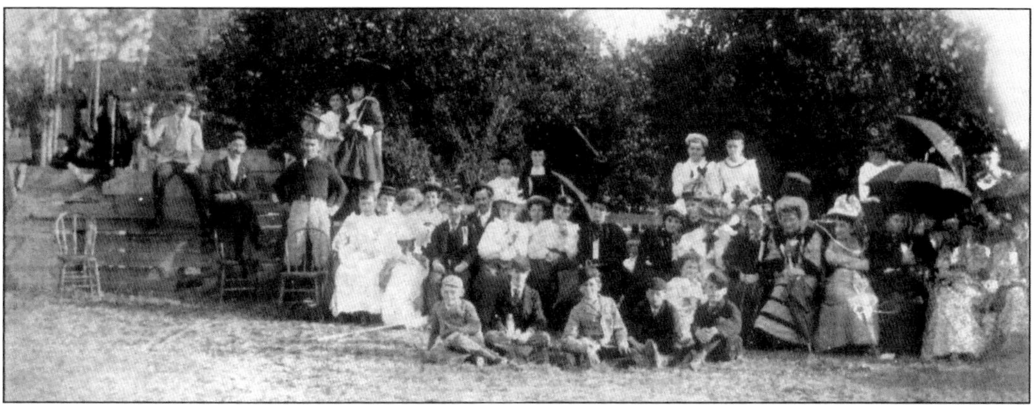

John B. Stetson University and its academy continued to grow with class offerings ranging from Greek and Latin to mathematics, history, literature, and the natural sciences. It even had a law school, the state's first. Surrounding the campus were orange groves as seen in this 1890s photo, some of which thrived into the 1980s.

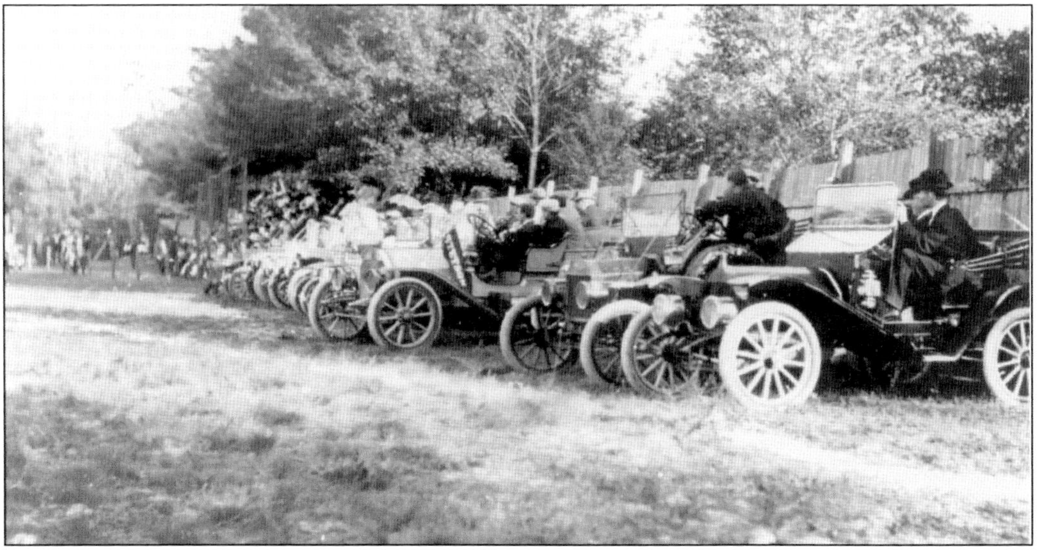

Stetson's football team brought out the crowds when the men played behind Cummings Gymnasium, constructed in 1920. The turf was mostly grass, weeds, and sand but no one cared. Bleachers were unheard of but no one cared. After all, Henry Ford's newest invention served quite nicely for a comfy seat to watch Stetson beat its rivals. The gym remains extant at its original site on the southwest corner of the Boulevard and University Avenue. After football was discontinued at Stetson, the hallowed sports field accommodated tennis courts and Stover Theatre, constructed in 1930 and originally named the Women's Assembly Hall.

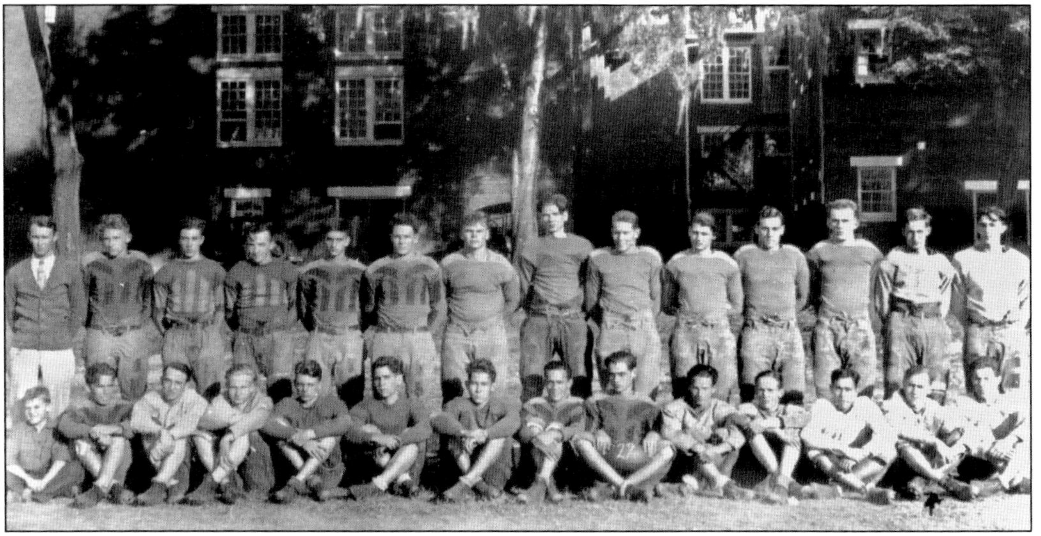

Stetson was not the only school that enjoyed football. DeLand High offered a rugged set of opponents for anyone in this 1929 shot. In the front row from left to right are Green, Carter, Rhode, Ramsey, Momberg, DeBella, Martin, Tatum, Thomas, Martin, Hayman, Michael, and unidentified. In the back row, from left to right, are Mackle, Cook, Bilderback, Hiers, Causey, Davis, Shadburn, Thursby, Tatum, Martin, and Whitman.

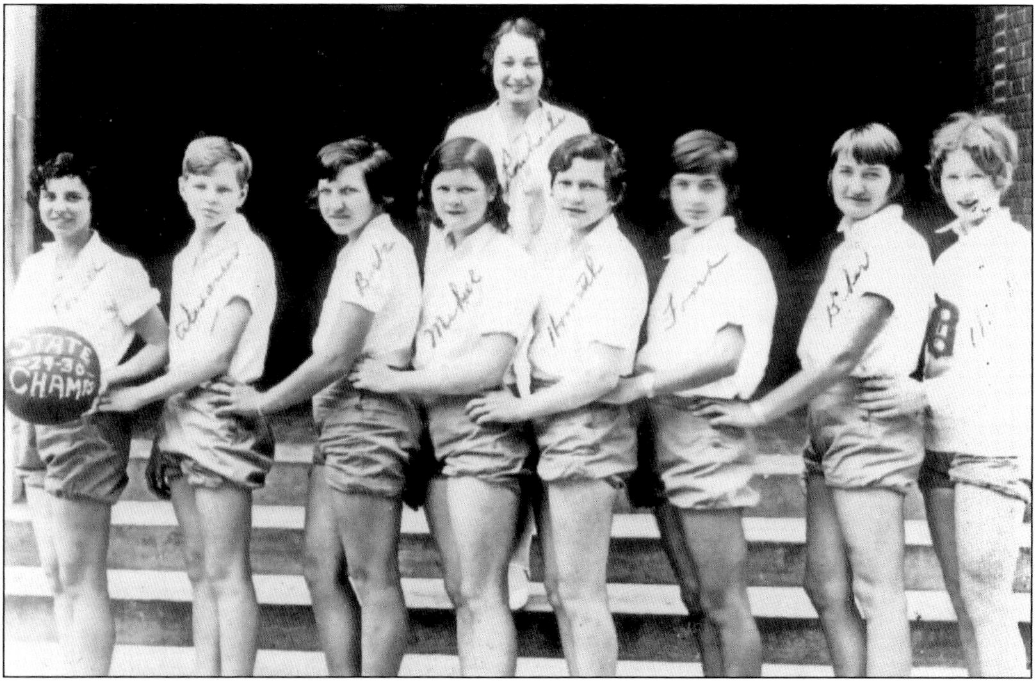

Even the girls had athletic fun as evidenced by the broad smiles on the faces of the DeLand High School basketball team after winning the 1929 State Championship. In the front row are Powell, Alexander, Barbe, Mikell, Howarth, Foard, Baber, and Harper. In the back row is Richards.

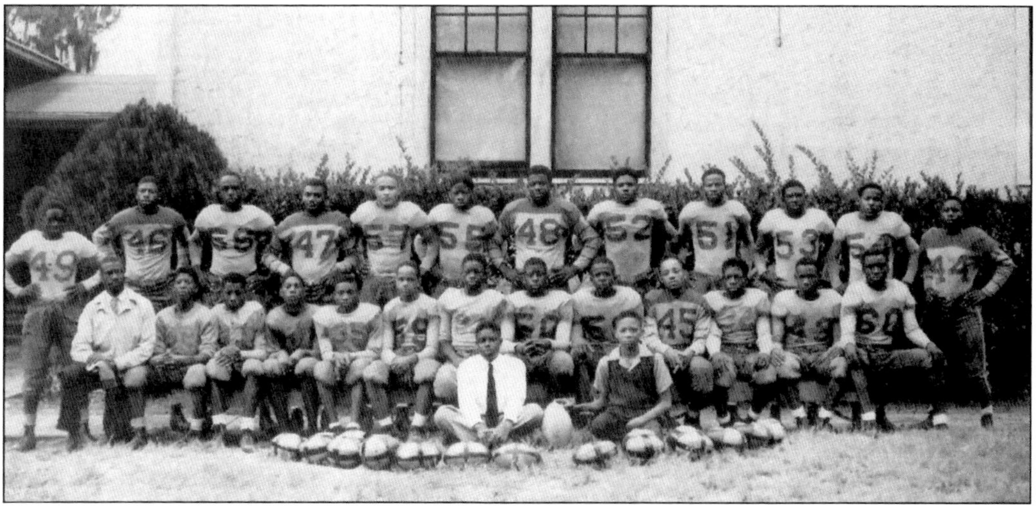

The Euclid High School Purple Tigers held scoreless all opponents for three consecutive years. Posing before their school in 1944 are the proud teammates. In the front row, from left to right, are Gentry Prather and Tracy Davis. Seated from left to right are Coach Jackson, Albert Davis, Henry Link, John Cook, Gomez Casminski, Carlton Culpepper, Willie Benjamin, Roosevelt Richardson, Bennie Colston, John Fisher, Henry Ford, James Hough, and Robert Golver. In the back row, from left to right, are Benjamin Howell Sr., James Bevel, James Johnson, Booker Marshall, Arthur Rosfford, James Jackson, Lester Witherspoon, Warren Brown, Willie Williams, Bill Brown, Alonzo Dixon, and James Livingston.

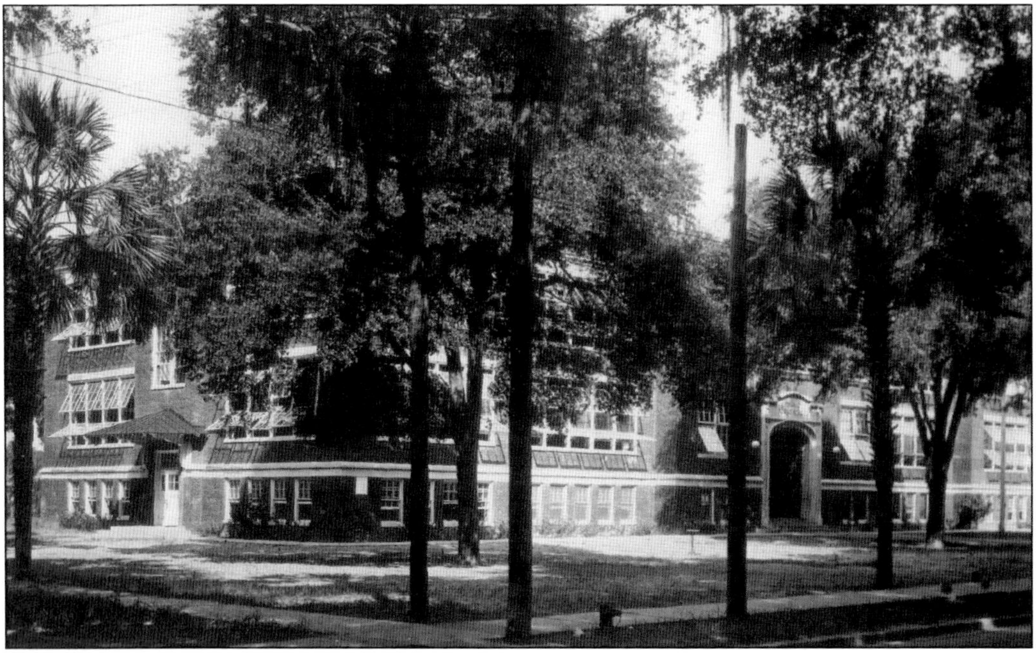

Education remained uppermost in the hearts and minds of DeLandites. Sturdier and grander new educational facilities replaced less substantial ones. In 1917 this building, located on the northwest corner of Clara and Rich, was constructed of brick, three-storied, and sprawled across a quarter of an acre. It was destroyed by fire in 1979.

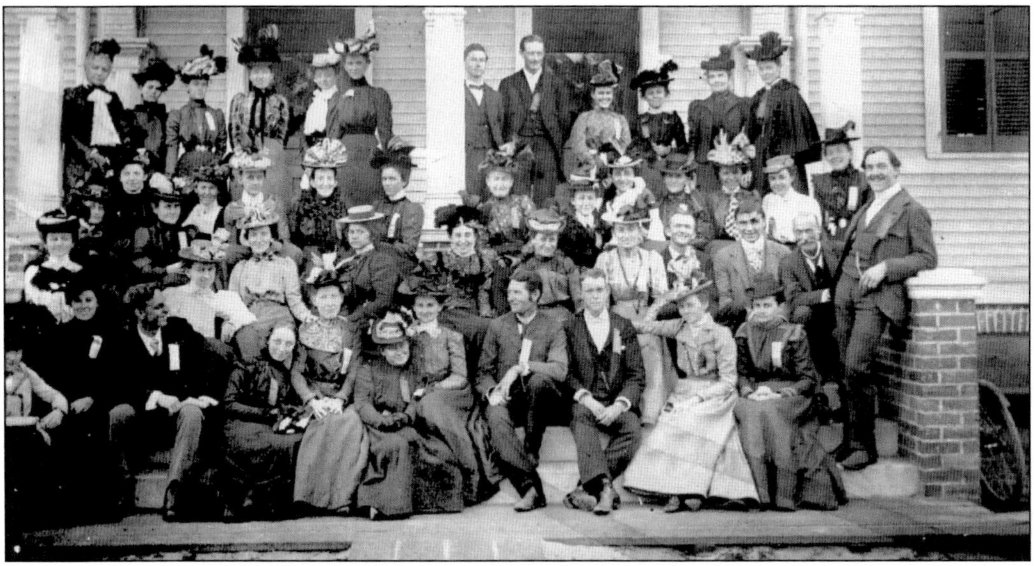

By 1902 teacher salaries had improved, however discriminatory. White teachers were paid between $35 and $120 per month, black teachers between $32 and $50. By the 1930s public schools were touted as "Accredited Schools of Superior Standardization" with John B. Stetson University acclaimed as "a national seat of learning…[having] fifteen departments, a student body of five hundred and a distinguished faculty...including a college of arts and sciences…and a college of law." Indeed, DeLand, "Athens of Florida," was meeting and moving beyond the educational expectations envisioned by Henry DeLand for his beloved Persimmon Hollow.

Eight

The Religious Experience

Religion has played a significant role in the culture of the world's civilizations. Even prior to the presumptuousness of Europeans in claiming the continent of America for themselves and their ultimate exploitation and domination of Native Americans, these early people had their gods. The conquering Europeans also brought with them their gods and their religions—Catholicism and Protestantism. And thus began the conflicts.

Proselytizing Native Americans by Catholic Friars during Spain's 400-year ownership of La Florida robbed the first inhabitants of present-day Volusia County, the Timucua Indians, of their indigenous beliefs and customs. So intent were the friars on saving the souls of these heathens that they published a Confessionario, *a booklet containing questions and guidance in Spanish and Timucua, written side by side, to assist friars listening to the confessions of the Timucua. And when the Timucua did not obey the strange rules of the friars, the friars often beat their parishioners into submission.*

History is riddled with gruesome accounts of religious fervor gone awry, of ridicule and rejection, punishment, torture, and even death at the hands of religious zealots—all in the name of their gods. But when the Constitution of the United States of America was penned and its first ten amendments ratified on December 15, 1791, the First Amendment stated with undeniable force: "Congress shall make no law respecting an establishment of religion, or prohibiting the free exercise thereof...." And with those profound words, freedom of religion in America was born, for all people, under one nation, without fear of persecution or reprisal, and regardless of color, race, or creed.

Belief in a Higher Being gives mankind a sense of hope, that the tragedies of the world will somehow be made right or at least explained to us at the end of time, that life does not end at an open grave, and that all the goodness that is bestowed upon us is a gift from Someone who knows us better than we know ourselves. Faith is the belief in something that we cannot see, that we cannot explain, and that we cannot comprehend. It is Faith in a Higher Being that causes us to congregate with similar kinds. Religious convictions cause us to build edifices to our gods so we can come together to join hands in a common spirit, to pray, to worship, and to show gratitude to our Creator.

And it is Faith in a Higher Being that ultimately prepares us for the final act of our life which we so gravely must face—our own mortality.

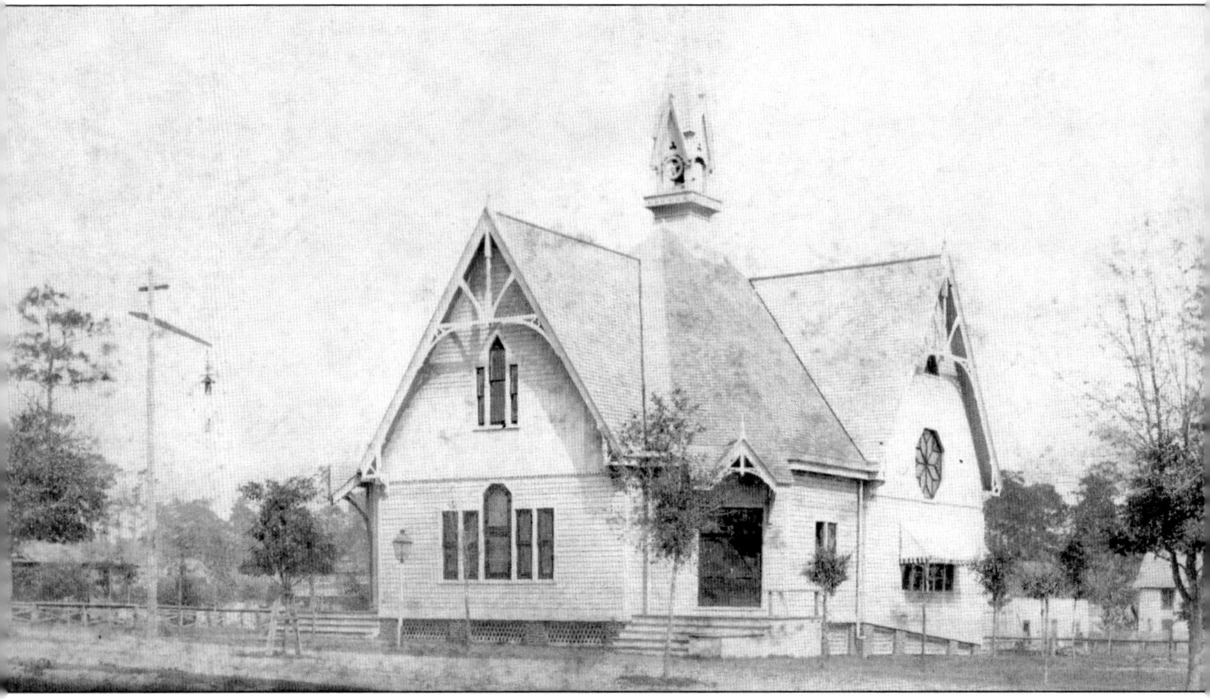

It was the search for a healthy climate that brought many to the area, not a search for religious freedom. But often accompanying those hardy pioneers was a strong sense of belief in a god. Early settlers, regardless of denomination, met in their log houses or beneath the shade trees to worship. The first documented mention of the need for a house of worship was in October 1876 when Henry DeLand called a meeting with the settlers of Persimmon Hollow. During that meeting Mrs. H.B. (Hettie) Austin announced that she was collecting money to build a church. Mr. DeLand, always sensible in his recommendations, suggested that one building be constructed to house both a much-needed school and a place to worship. All agreed and construction began within weeks. Mr. DeLand donated land and half the building funds required. (Photograph page 96). In a letter home to family members, Mrs. Parce, Henry DeLand's sister, proved that the community was willing to go to any expense or energy to promote religion by securing a house of worship. She boasted, "The ladies of the church gave an oyster supper last Thursday evening and after expenses, we find we have $86 left. Isn't that doing pretty well for a new country?" Originally the church was interdenominational but as the population grew, so did individual denominations and their need for individual space. The first to be organized was the Methodist Episcopal Church, in August 1880. Five-hundred dollars were raised for the construction while J.W. Howry donated a lot on the northeast corner of the Boulevard and Howry. The First Baptist Church, organized two months later, began with 13 members and beat the Methodists in building a church. In 1881 their building was constructed on the southeast corner of Church and the Boulevard with a majority of the money needed donated by Mr. DeLand, himself a Baptist. In the spirit of goodwill and ecumenicalism, the Baptists invited the Methodists to use the building until theirs was completed in 1883.

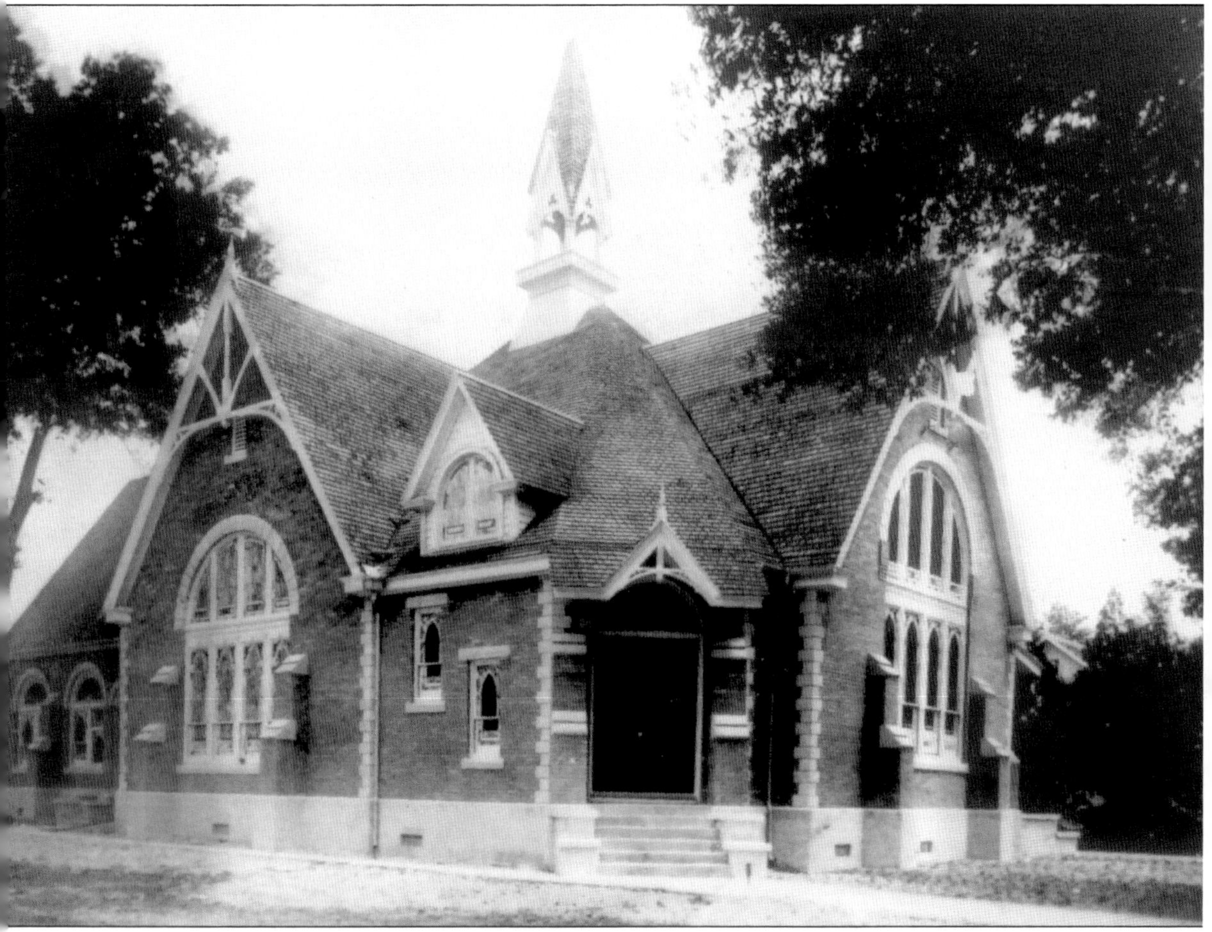

Trinity United Methodist Church acquired the pretty little Baptist Church and moved it half a block south to the 100 block of East Rich, *c.* 1896. Architectural changes occurred sometime after that including the addition of brick (*c.* 1914) and the redesigning of arched windows on the side, as seen in this 1925 view. The Methodists used the building until 1926 when their new church was completed on the southwest corner of Clara and Wisconsin. This stately creation was destroyed in 1929.

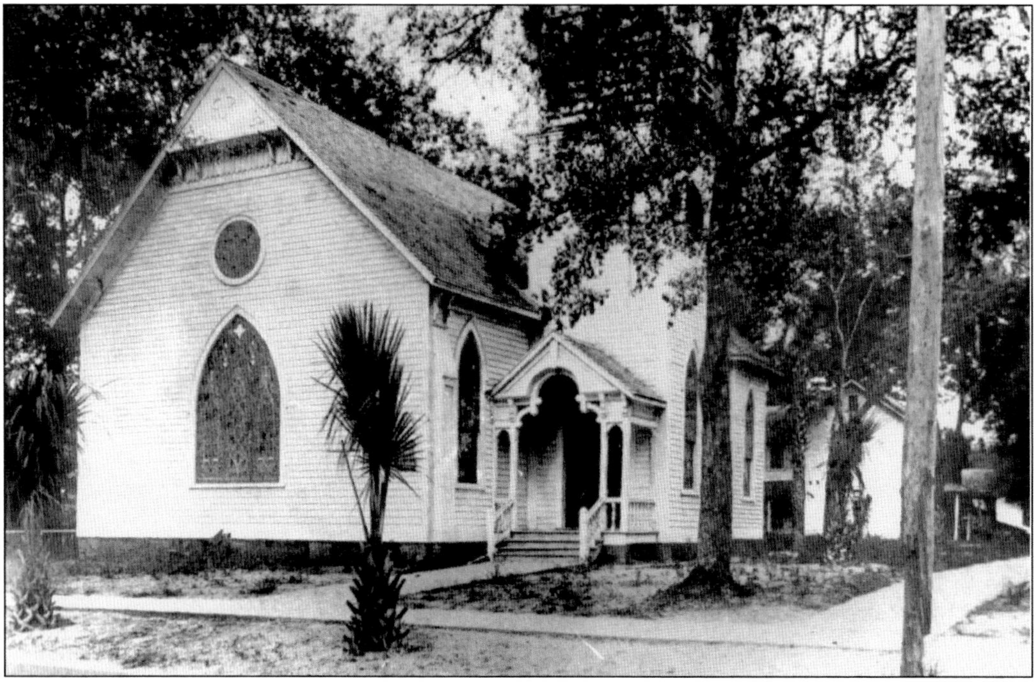

The frame First Methodist Church was completed in 1883 with a flair of Victorian detail. Stained-glass windows, a bell tower, gingerbread, and scrolls decorated the peaceful structure. Its attractive front entry was an invitation to both heathens and Christians alike. It was located on the northeast corner of Howry and the Boulevard and holds the distinction of being the second church built in DeLand.

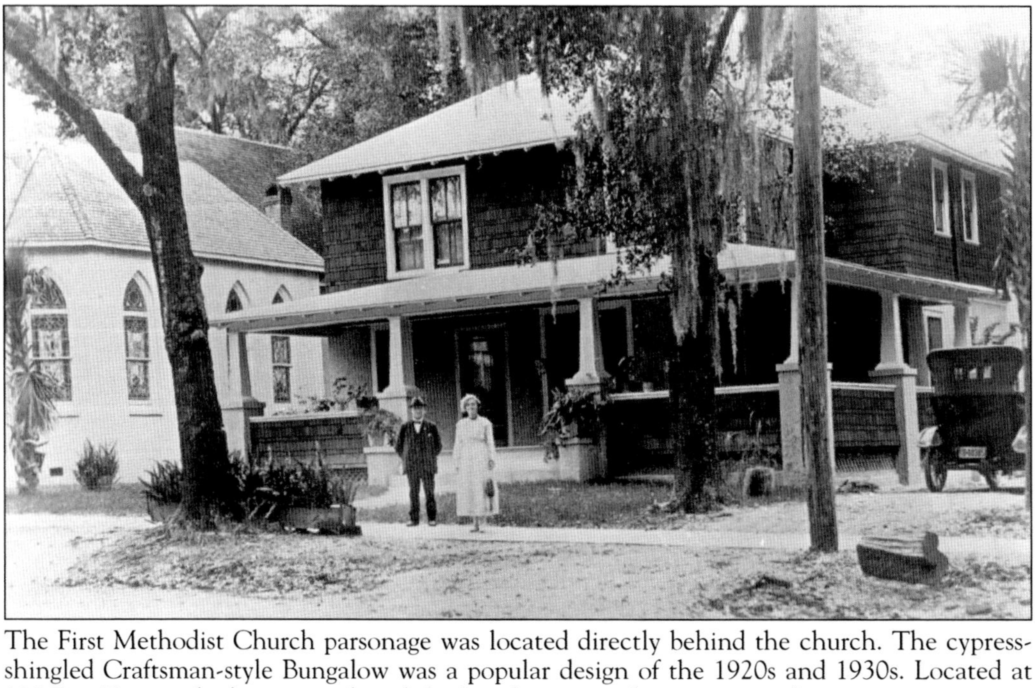

The First Methodist Church parsonage was located directly behind the church. The cypress-shingled Craftsman-style Bungalow was a popular design of the 1920s and 1930s. Located at 100 East Howry, the house was demolished in the name of expansion and progress.

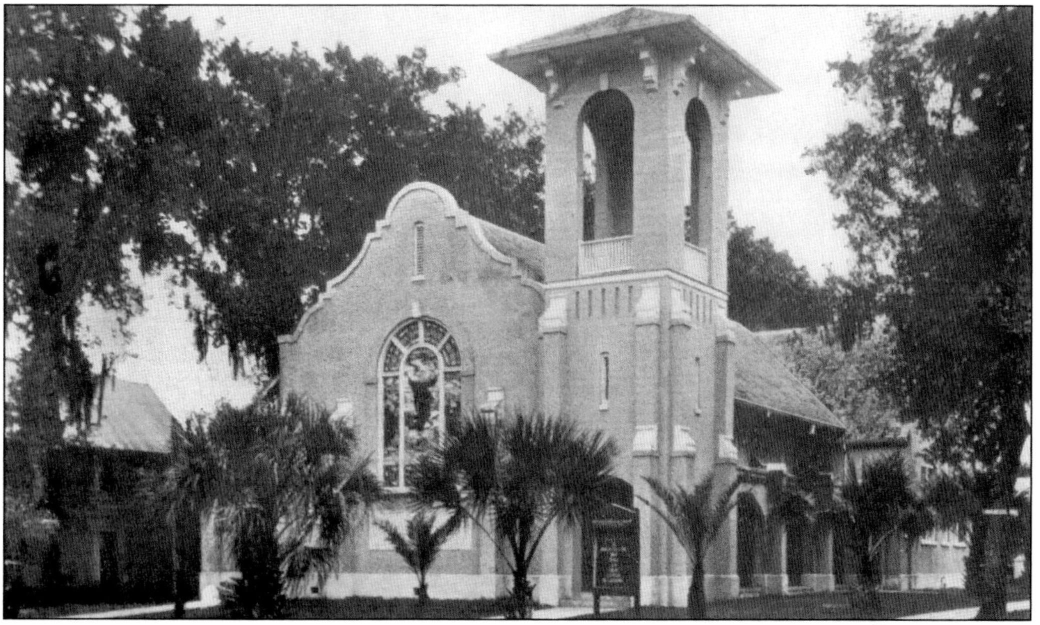

Rather than demolishing their house of worship and starting from the ground up, the Methodists modernized their building to match the vogue of the times. The Spanish Mission Style, popular during the 1920s Florida Land Boom, had crossed the continent from California and hit town. Construction of the walls was of hollow terra-cotta blocks covered with stucco. Leaded stained-glass windows adorned the front and sides of the building, shaped parapets were added, and the bell tower was rebuilt with hipped roof and brackets. The new look lent an air of sophistication to this Christian edifice.

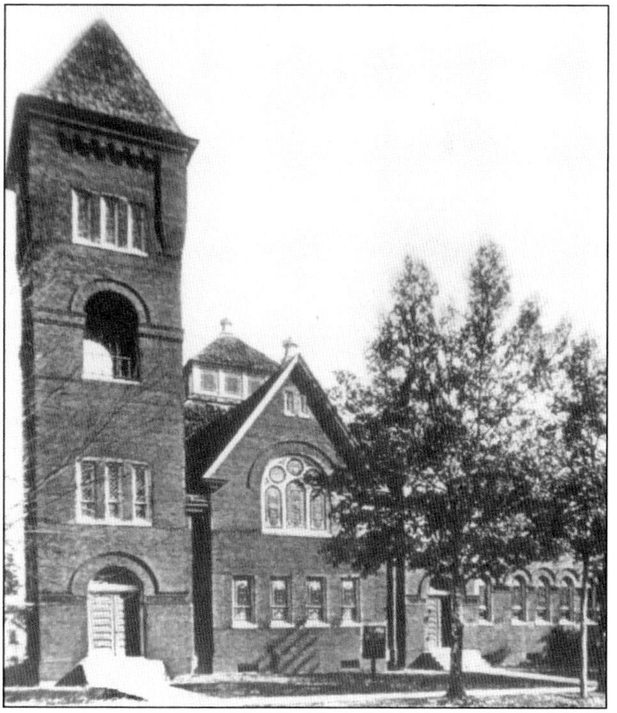

Whether for progress or the need for more space, numerous earlier worship houses were demolished to make way for the new. The Baptists sold its building to the Methodists and moved it 200 feet east of Woodland to the north side of Rich. Then with a generous donation from John B. Stetson, the First Baptist Church built this 1895 red-brick Romanesque-style structure on the southeast corner of Church and the Boulevard. It remained in use until 1960 when it met the fate of so many historic structures in downtown DeLand. And what replaced those magnificent religious works of art? Something as architecturally significant or pleasing to the eye?

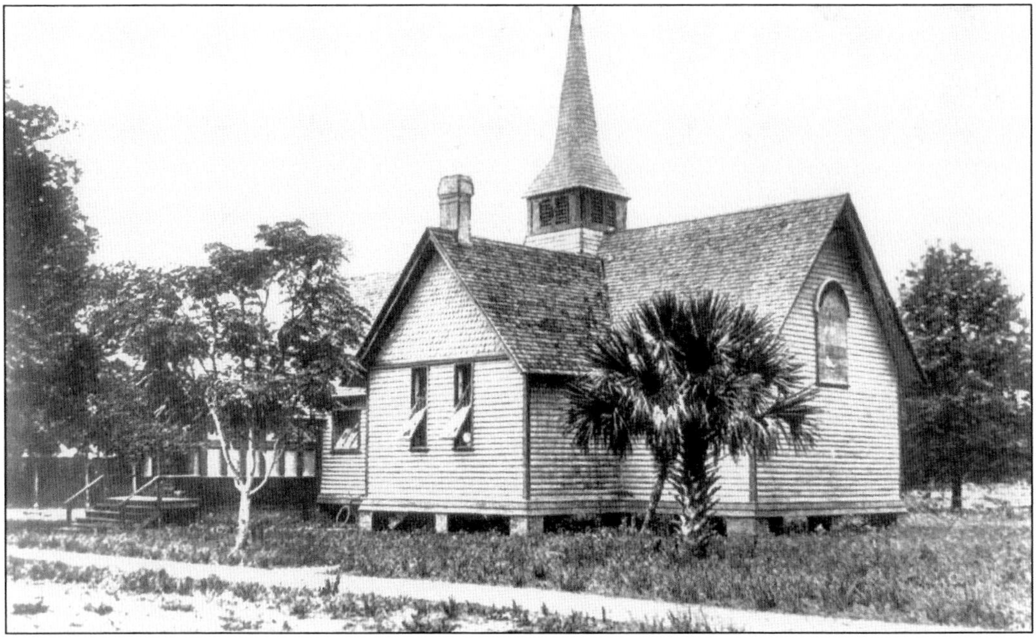

As early as 1880 Episcopalians had been holding services out-of-doors at the northwest corner of Wisconsin and Clara on land donated to the congregation by Capt. John Rich, DeLand's first resident. The church was officially organized September 1882 when Rev. Robert Wolseley called a meeting at the schoolhouse to establish St. Barnabas Mission Church. The building was modeled after an English parish church. Its cornerstone was laid in 1883 and the church dedicated Easter Sunday 1884.

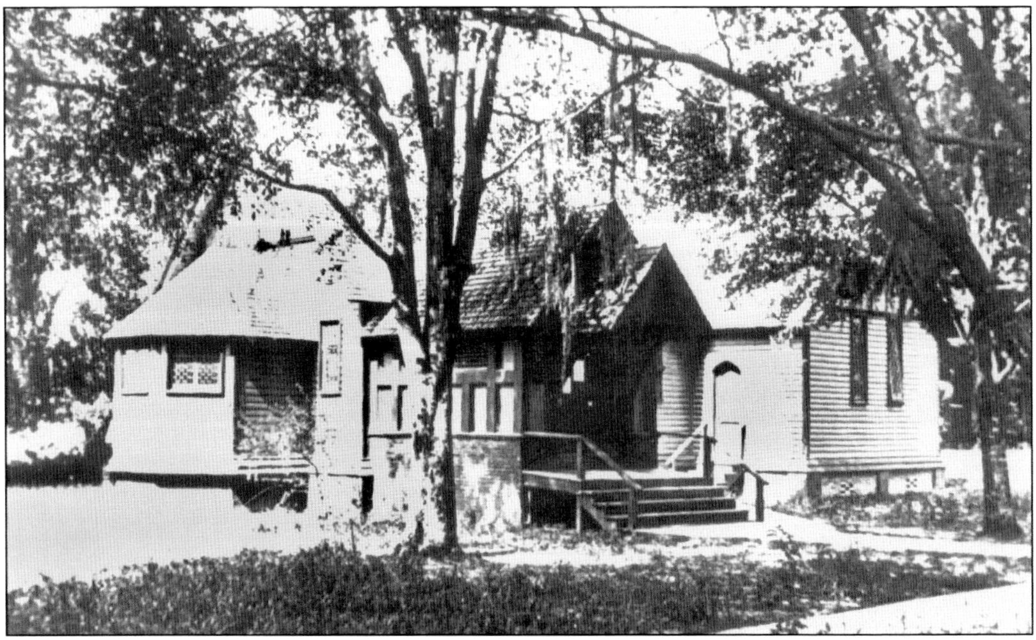

Over the years St. Barnabas has altered its building but allowed it to remain at its original location, reinforcing the notion that, after all, some things really never have to change. This 1919 view of the front documents its stylish character and additional enhancements.

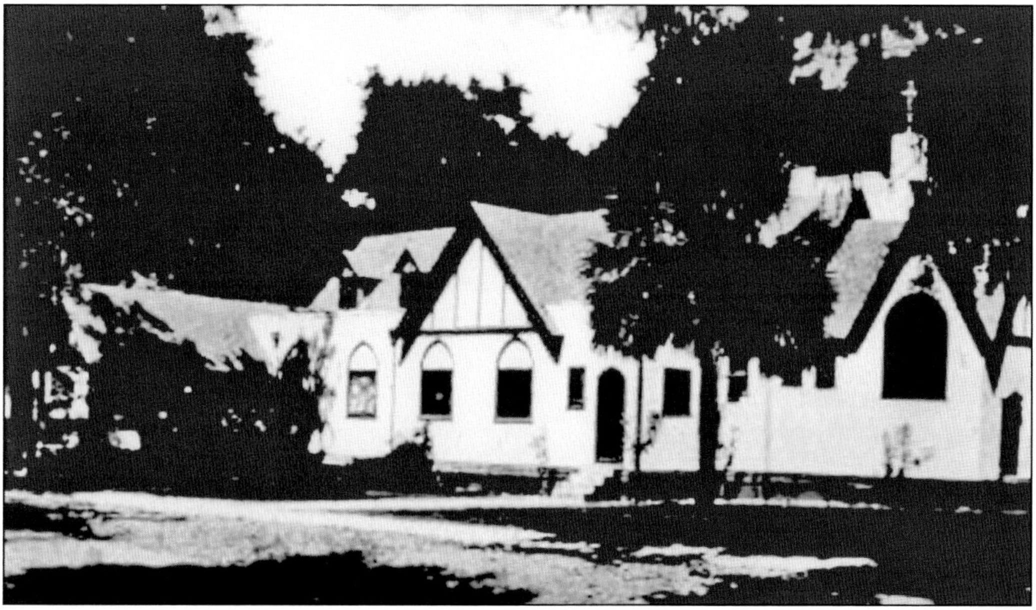

Although further remodeling occurred around 1923 and several times thereafter, the original charming architectural features basically have remained intact.

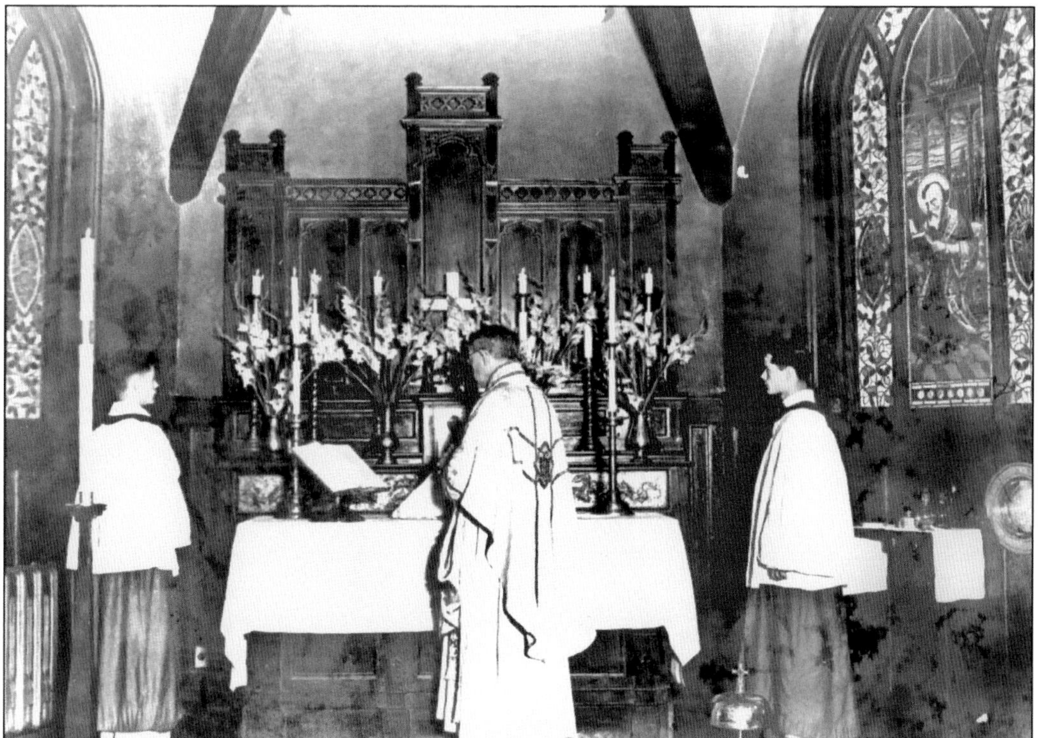

The altar in the eastern apse in 1937 depicts gothic elegance in quaint little St. Barnabas. When entering the sanctuary, its sacred influence quiets the harried soul and remains today a refuge for the weary.

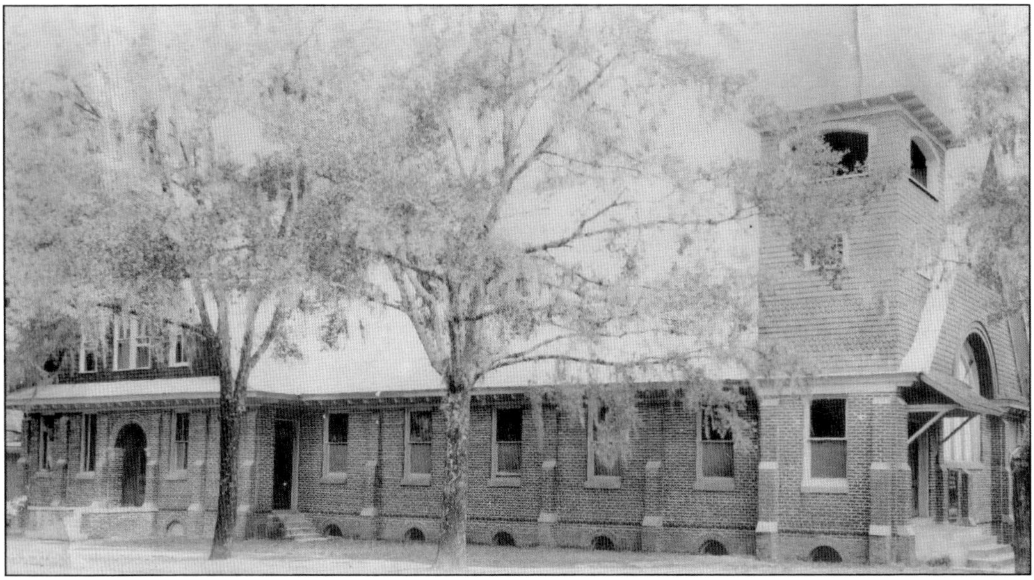

The First Christian Church, originally the Church of Christ, was founded in March 1883. Its first building was constructed in 1885 of heart-of-pine planks and located on the corner of West Voorhis and Florida. After it burned in 1891, $500 was raised to purchase a lot on the northwest corner of Wisconsin and the Boulevard. The new building was completed in 1894 and included electricity, heat, and comfortable oak pews. Red-bricked and a bell tower sheathed in cypress shingles, it remains today less grand, less surrounded by oaks, minus its tower, and no longer a house of worship. But it remains.

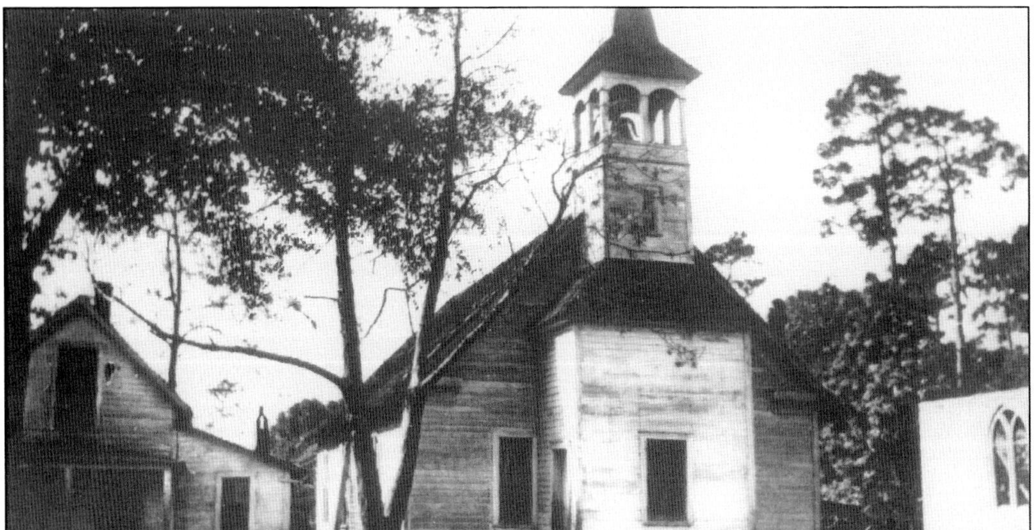

One block east of the new Methodist Church for the white folks at 100 East Howry in downtown DeLand, the African-American population built their own edifice. Framed with a bell tower to call their parishioners to worship, the American Methodist Episcopal began construction on its new building c. 1930, as seen in the right hand corner of this photograph. The church thrives today in DeLand's Garden District as a sign of its continuous religious commitment.

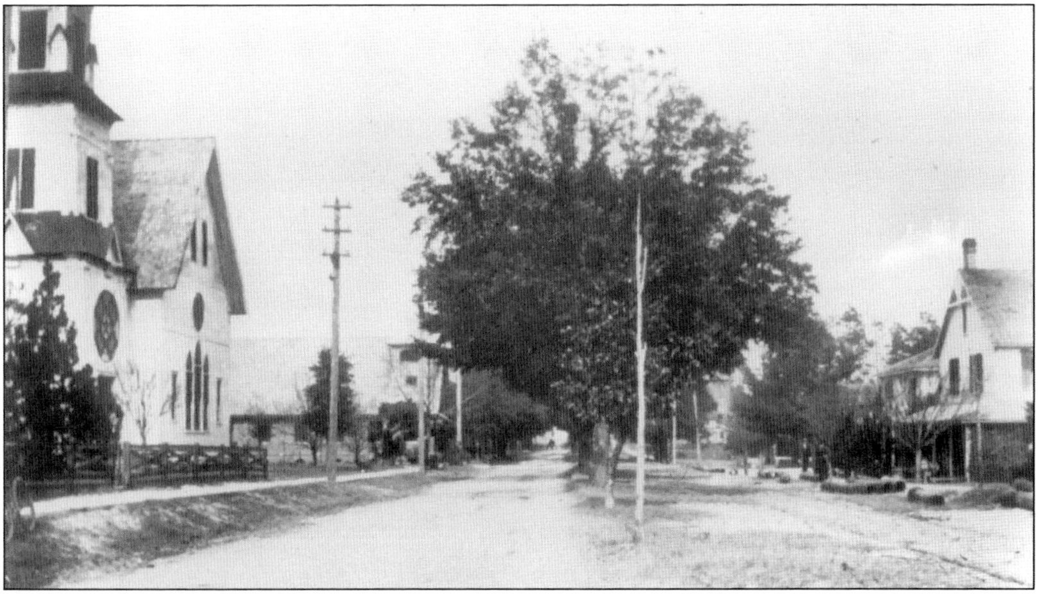

By 1884 the Presbyterians had inherited DeLand's first schoolhouse for its place of worship. Located on the northeast corner of Indiana and the Boulevard it was moved sometime between 1886 and 1889, one block west on Indiana to Florida. In 1888 parishioners constructed on the northwest corner of Wisconsin and the Boulevard a lovely frame edifice with a steeple, bell tower, and circular arched stained-glass windows. By the mid 1920s, as evidenced below, the building had undergone major renovations including removing the elegant steeple, lowering the bell tower, and bricking the exterior. It was demolished in the 1980s so Barnett Bank (now Bank of America) could build a modern complex. The Presbyterian Church built a larger edifice half a mile north on the Boulevard. As for the Boulevard's median with its spreading oaks? Also gone.

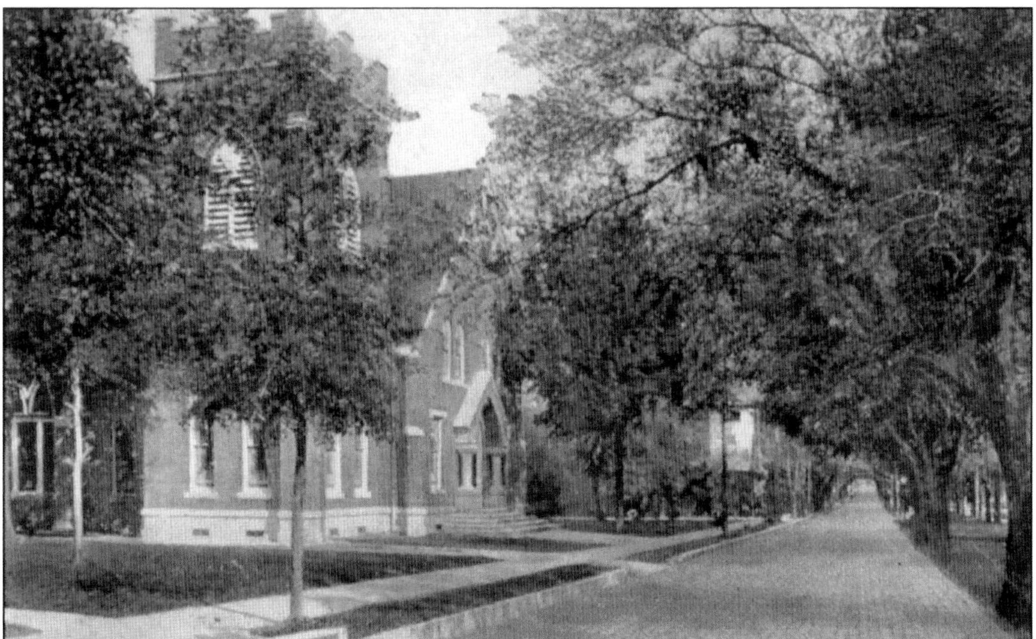

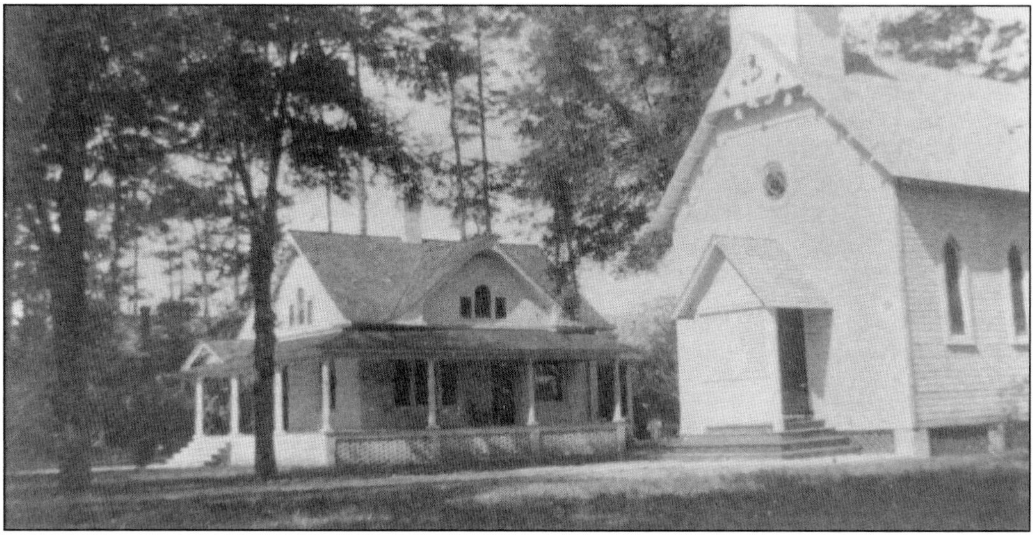

An April 1884 Mass was celebrated in St. Peter's Catholic Church. The rectory, built in 1906, sat to the left of the church. Within a few years of the church's founding, Bishop Moore of St. Augustine realized there was immediate need to organize a parish in the community. Bishop Moore purchased two acres from John and Clara Rich, which ran from West New York east to Delaware and north to Rich. Rich stipulated in the deed that if the property were ever used as a cemetery it would revert back to the Rich family or its heirs. Possibly Captain Rich did not want to take the chance that departed souls trapped in Purgatory might wander aimlessly across his land.

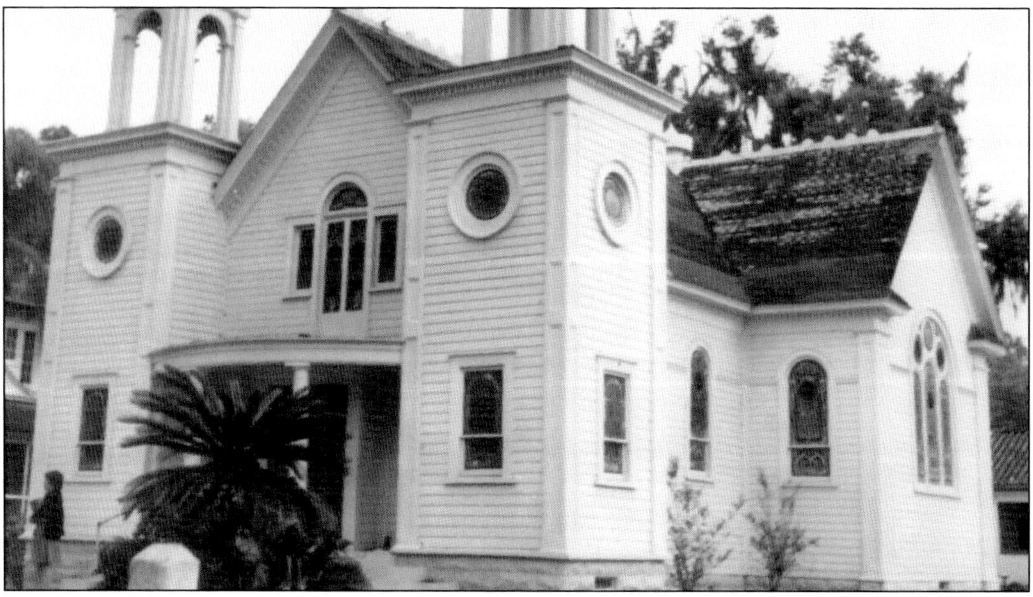

The first resident pastor of St. Peter's Catholic Church was Fr. Michael J. Curley from Ireland. When he arrived in DeLand in 1904 he held Mass at the Hotel College Arms at 6 a.m. and then at 10 a.m. in the little chapel to cover the spiritual needs of the growing number of parishioners. By 1910 Father Curley had set into motion plans for moving the church building to the northwest corner of Delaware and New York and enlarging it. The building was demolished in 1960 to expand the Catholic Complex to its present condition.

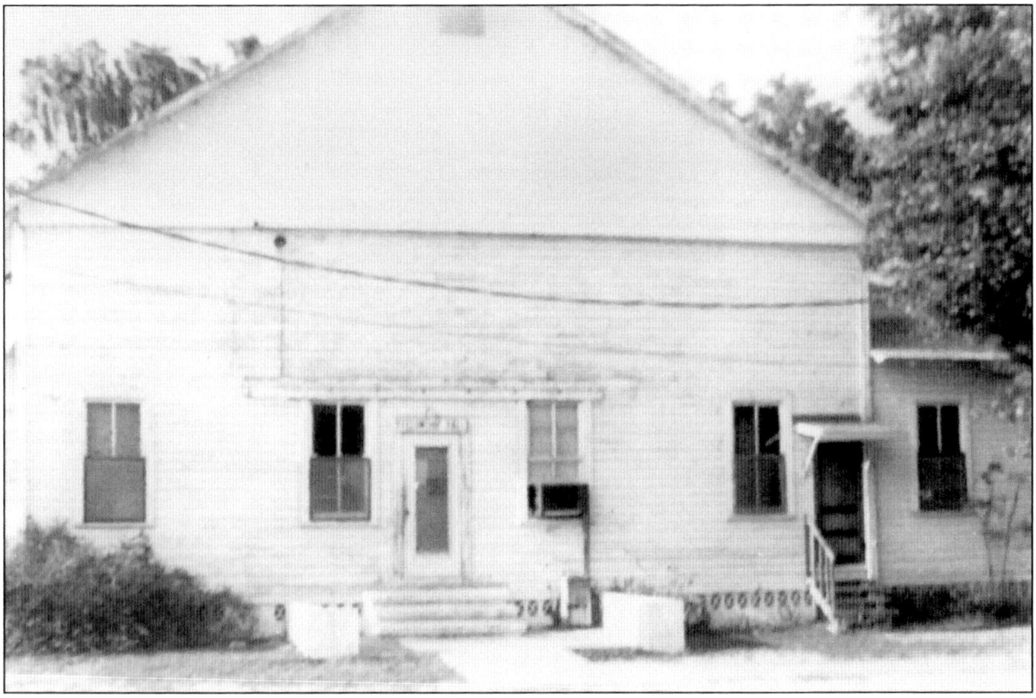

By 1911 the "Athens of Florida" boasted 15 pastors, 1 retired United States Chaplain, and 2 evangelists. Numerous denominations were represented with their small and their grand buildings. Church groups sponsored outings to the beach and Christian activities to encourage clean, responsible living. In 1928 three members of the First Baptist Church established a mission Sunday School that later became Stetson Baptist Church.

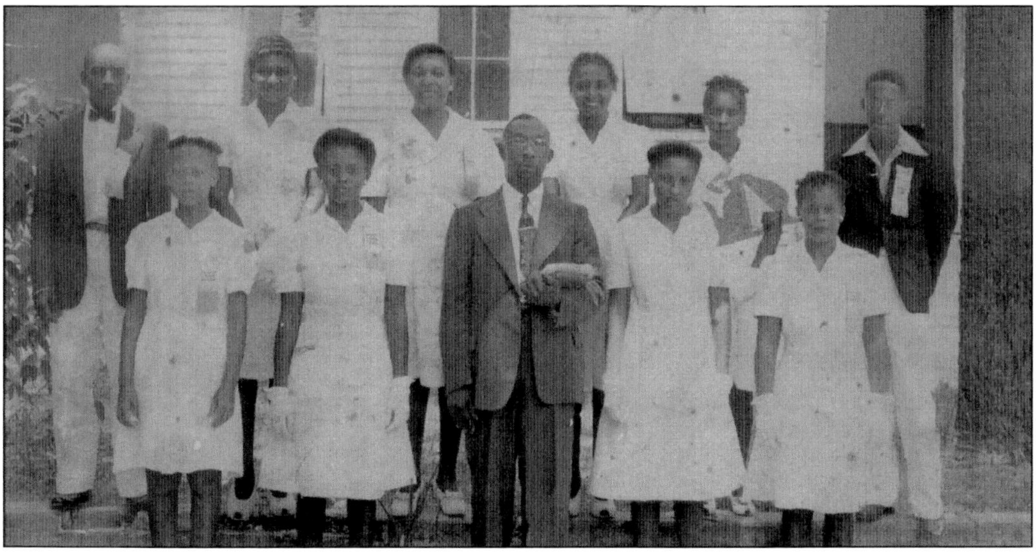

This 1945 photograph of the usher board of the Greater Union Baptist Church took pride in the fact that its church was a century old. In the front row, from left to right, are Dora Allen, Queen Jenkins, Reverend McQueen, Clarathe Jenkins, and Julia Hall. In the back row, from left to right, are Bill Carter, Rose Morris, Lila Johnson, Jeanette Morris, Lilly Prince, and Albert Smith.

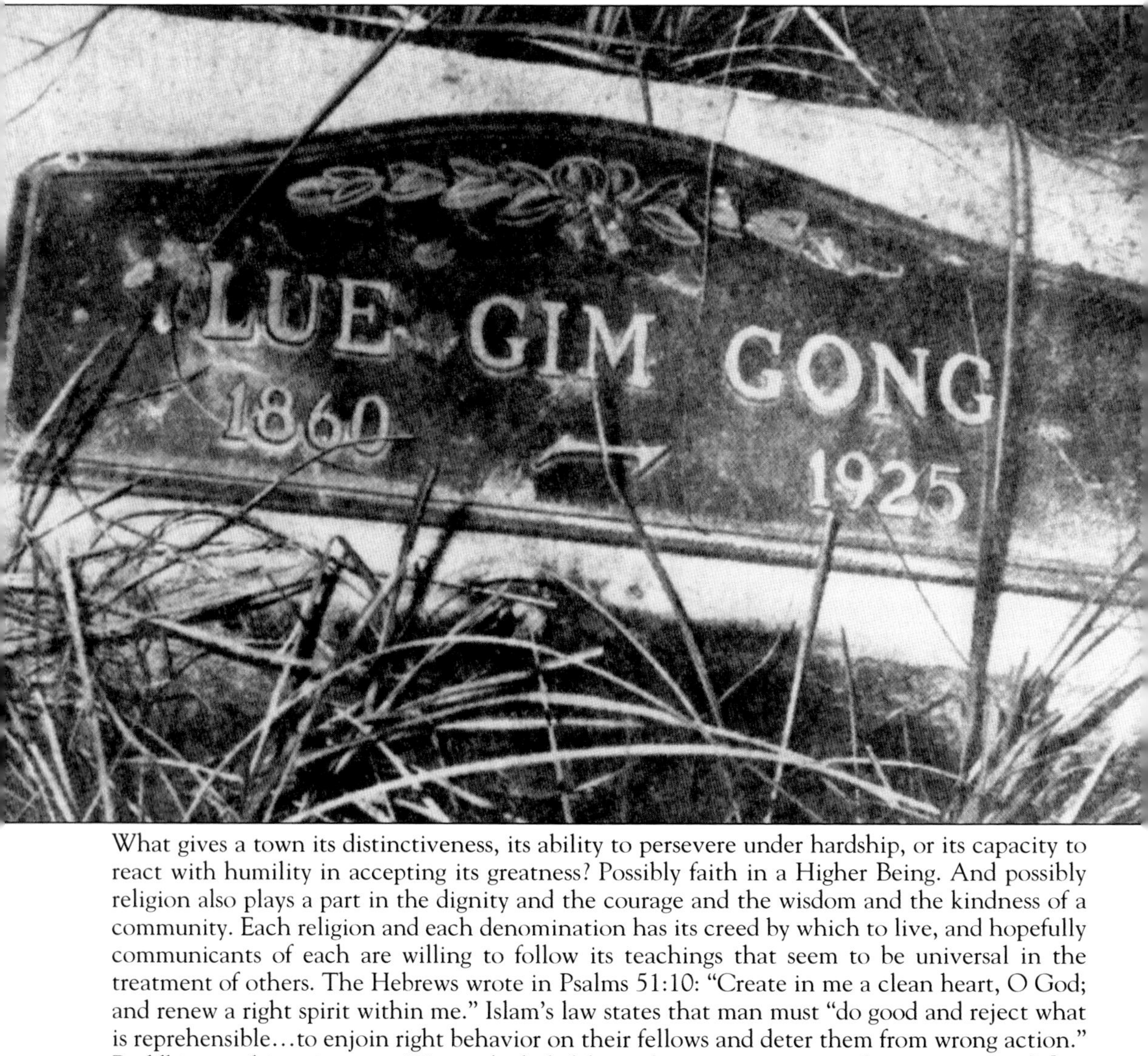

What gives a town its distinctiveness, its ability to persevere under hardship, or its capacity to react with humility in accepting its greatness? Possibly faith in a Higher Being. And possibly religion also plays a part in the dignity and the courage and the wisdom and the kindness of a community. Each religion and each denomination has its creed by which to live, and hopefully communicants of each are willing to follow its teachings that seem to be universal in the treatment of others. The Hebrews wrote in Psalms 51:10: "Create in me a clean heart, O God; and renew a right spirit within me." Islam's law states that man must "do good and reject what is reprehensible…to enjoin right behavior on their fellows and deter them from wrong action." Buddhist teachings instruct: "Not to be helpful to others, not to give to those in need….[is] to renounce the idea of a self." Hindus proclaim that "In darkness are they who worship only the world, but in greater darkness they who worship the infinite alone. He who accepts both saves himself from death by the knowledge of the former and attains immortality by the knowledge of the latter." The Native American Chief Sitting Bull proclaimed to his people that "Every seed is awakened and so has all animal life. It is through this mysterious power that we too have our being and we therefore yield to our neighbors, even our animal neighbors, the same right as ourselves, to inhabit this land." And of course a well-known statement from the Christian religion, paraphrased again and again, appears to be at the very core of all religions. From the King James Version of the Bible, St. Matthew 7:12 comes: "Therefore all things whatsoever ye would that men should do to you, do ye even so to them…." Is religion about the size and structure of houses of worship? Is it about the sum of money members give to their church? Or is religion about loving our fellow man, about attitude, about caring for our community, about generosity and acceptance, and ultimately, about how we prepare for what lies beyond?

Nine

Lost Designs and New Beginnings

As far back as 1876 when Henry Addison DeLand first rumbled into Persimmon Hollow on the hard seat of a wooden wagon, he had a vision of a community with panache. His exuberant ideas instilled in the early settlers of the Hollow a need for community commitment. Orange groves were cultivated, oaks and magnolias were planted, and pines felled to construct gracious structures. As the years passed, streets became canopied with majestic green towers while striking new homes enhanced the growing community.

Businesses, homes, and hotels sported front porches with inviting rocking chairs to encourage resting and visiting. Houses and shops were built close to the streets and sidewalks so passing DeLandites could wave and shout and speak to each other. There was the pervasive awareness that one did not live in isolation but was intrinsically connected to the city, its people, its buildings, and its natural environment. Back in the old days neighborhoods were downtown. Livelihoods were within walking distance of residences. And people congregated on street corners to discuss all they considered important.

Then things changed. Trees were cut down to widen roads. Uniquely designed homes and churches and commercial buildings were razed to make way for larger and more obtrusive structures of concrete and steel. The invention of air conditioning trapped people inside. The invention of television trapped people inside. There was no longer a need for front porches so they were either enclosed or forsaken as outdoor entertainment rooms. Newly constructed homes were built without front porches. The invention of cars caused pedestrianism all but to disappear from the cityscape. As the years passed most residents abandoned downtown living for the suburbs, causing urban sprawl to spread across rural America like a malignancy on the human soul.

But fortunately, there were some who remained faithful to the old ways and the endearing architecture that previous generations created. To view preservation efforts drive east and west on Minnesota, Michigan, Rich, Wisconsin, Church, University, and Pennsylvania; drive north and south on Clara, Adelle, San Souci, Florida—names given to city streets before present home owners were a twinkle in their parents' eyes. Wander those streets on bike or on foot to experience the impact of classic beauty and pride in workmanship of long departed builders and homeowners. Then shout praises to the rooftops for those whose hard work brought life back to so many once neglected treasures and to those in the process of establishing an historic district to protect these architectural gems.

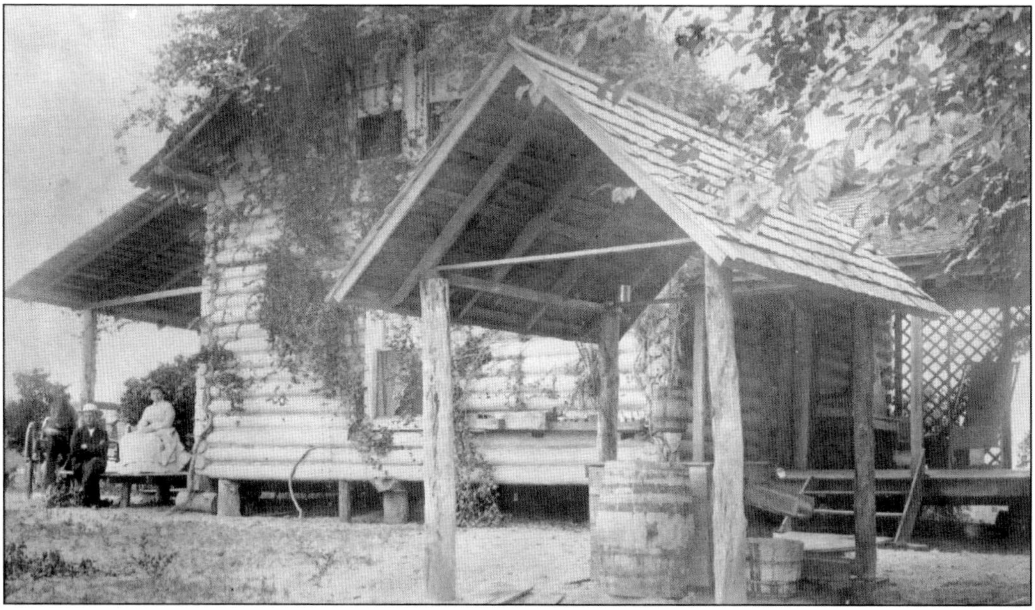

When Henry A. DeLand arrived in Persimmon Hollow March 1876, the house he stayed in that first night was the Rich cabin, built in 1875. It lasted for many years on the corner of Delaware and West New York but progress pushed it down as architecture evolved from log poles to board and batten to clapboard and then brick and stucco. The little community of DeLand began to build with flair.

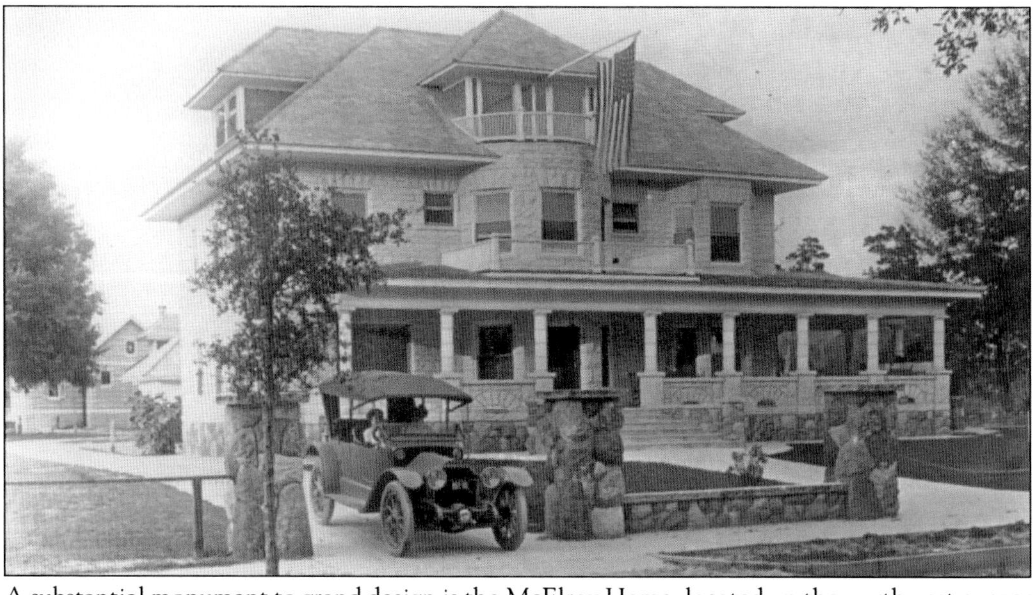

A substantial monument to grand design is the McElroy Home, located on the northwest corner of New York and Garfield. Over the years it went from a private residence to the DeLand Public Library to the DeLand Museum. At present its new beginning is that of a dentist office. The exterior is made of rough face cast block referred to as "art stone." While some of the material was made locally, most of it was produced in Jacksonville, Kissimmee, and Tampa. Many early 20th century homes in DeLand were built from "art stone." Rather than toss this gracious lady aside, she was adaptively rehabilitated to meet the needs of modernity.

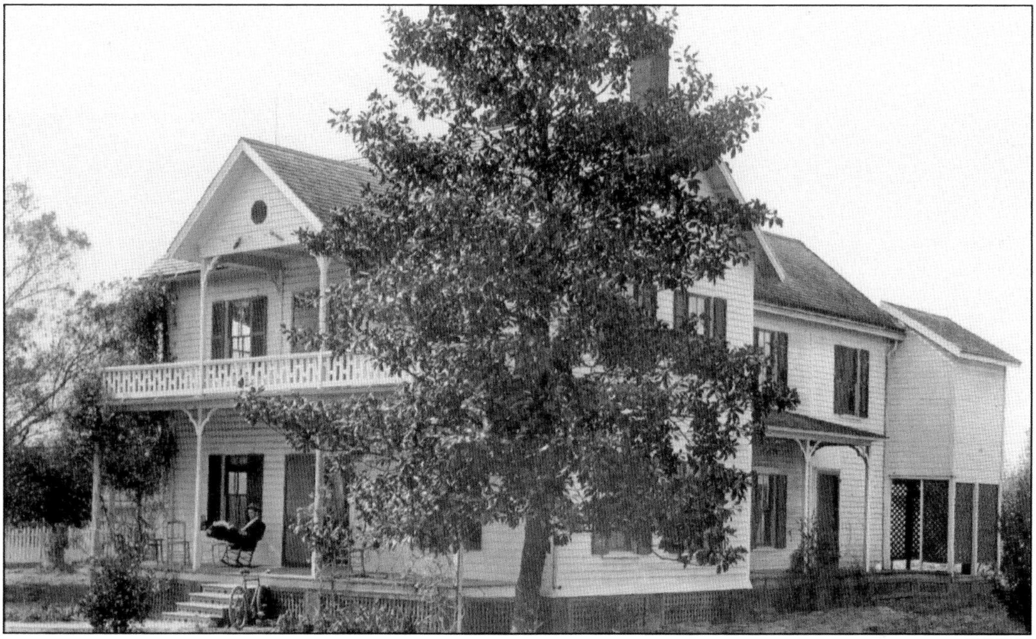

On the northwest corner of Michigan and the Boulevard once stood a Henry DeLand House. The frame two-story Victorian was later used as a men's dormitory for Stetson University. It was demolished in the 1960s for a parking lot. Past decisions caused the loss of many cherished assets but present-day sentiment now encourages restoration over destruction.

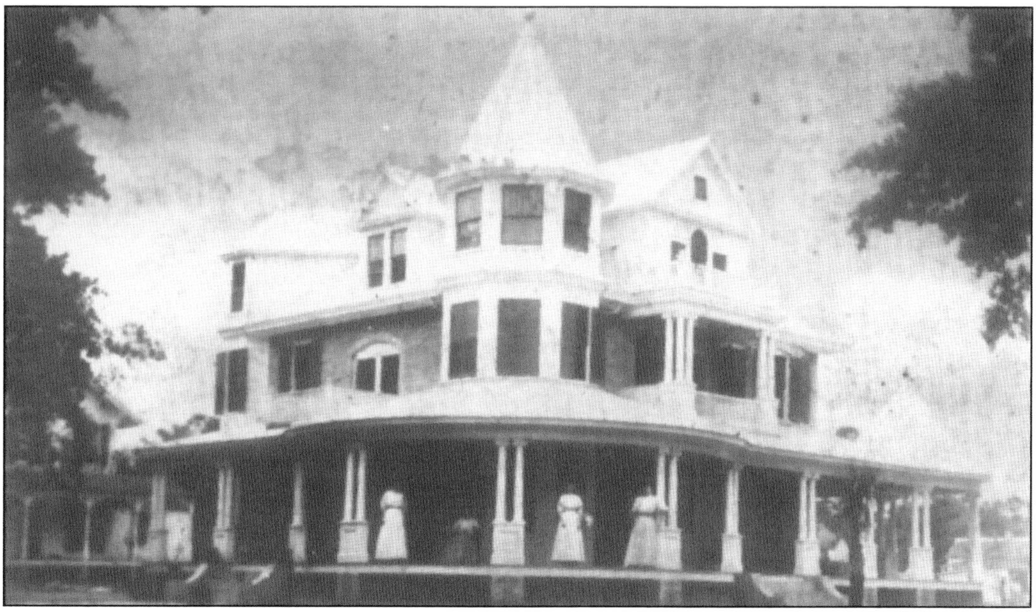

Now lost to time, the Warren C. Jackson Sr. House, built in 1902, was located on the northwest corner of Clara and West New York. The house featured a veranda that wrapped around three sides decorated with double unfluted Greek Revival porch supports and Ionic capitals. Mr. Jackson, in the timber and turpentine business, evidently did quite well. Past succumbed to progress with the destruction of such buildings that offered character and charisma to the community.

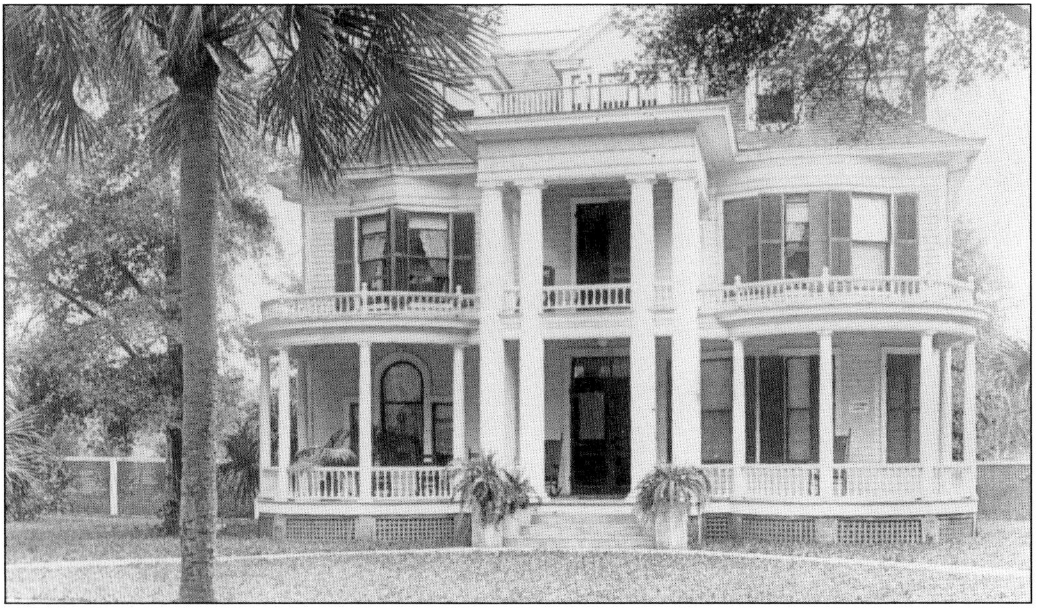

The Campbell Home, built *c.* 1910 in the 200 block of East New York, was an exceptional example of Early Classical Revival with its two-tiered entry porch featuring Tuscan columns. This three-story house used a variation on the typical flat façade by sporting circular projections on either side of the entryway. This grandiose style was typical for homes located on New York Avenue during this time. Partially demolished in 1950 and added on to, it found a new beginning as a funeral home.

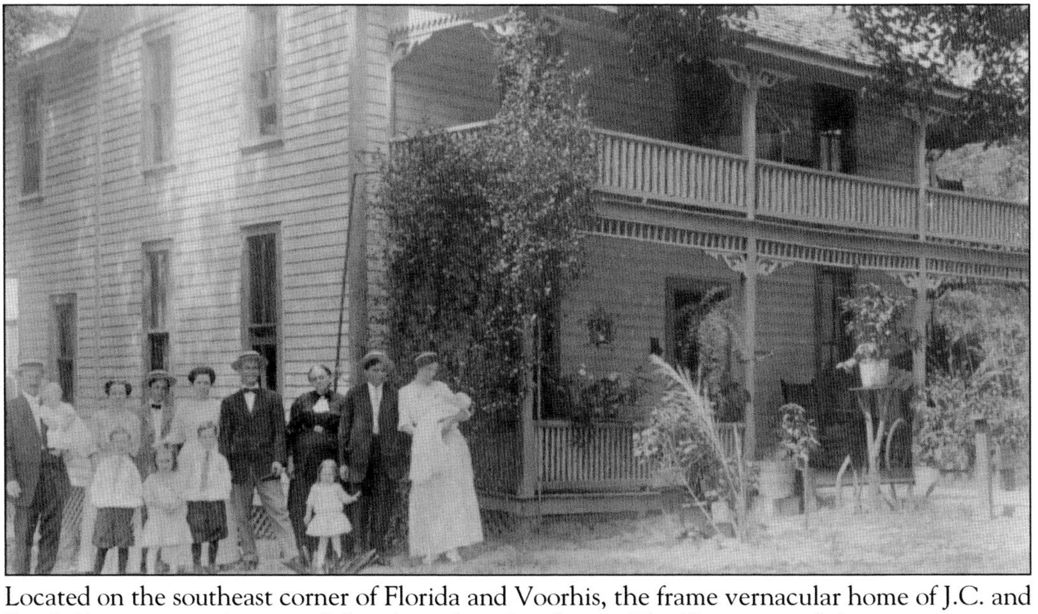

Located on the southeast corner of Florida and Voorhis, the frame vernacular home of J.C. and Sarah Yeargin, was, for several decades, a boarding house. The Yeargins and their paying guests posed beside this grand dame. This style of construction was immensely popular in DeLand during the late 19th and early 20th centuries. Like many Florida residents, the Yeargins allowed the lush native flora to coexist with their home. All that remains today is the image of faces, façade, and foliage.

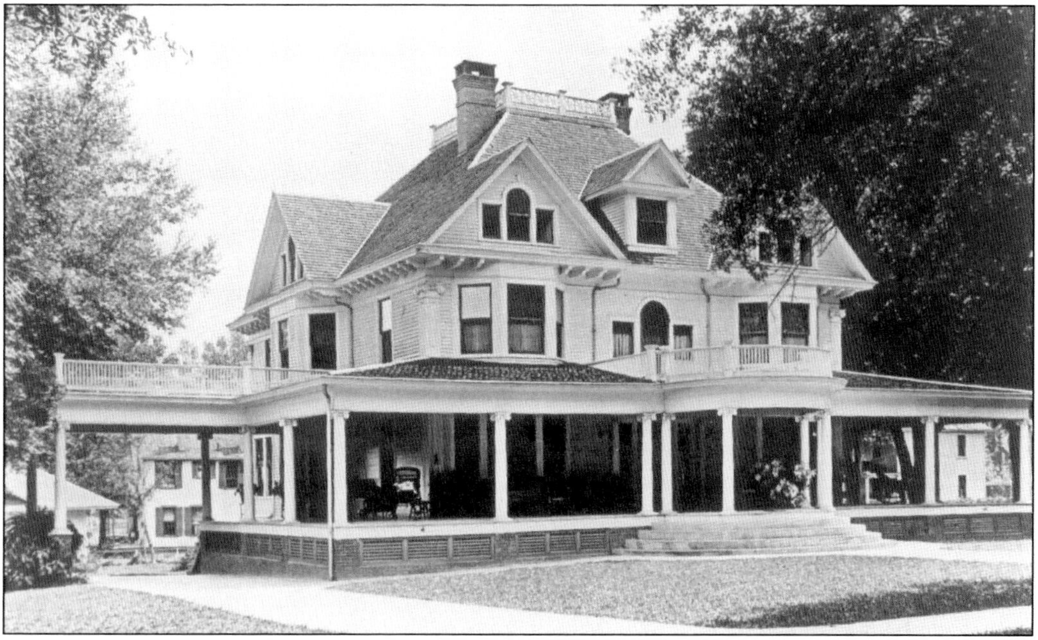

The Landis Home on the southeast corner of New York and Clara was built at the turn of the 20th century. This massive three-story house, designed in the Colonial Revival style, boasted a porch that wrapped around three sides. The porch was practical for the area as its shaded open space afforded those sitting outside the opportunity to catch a cool breeze. The beautiful home was demolished in 1965 to make room for a plain post office. It took losses like this finally to make people realize that preservation of historic properties not only beautifies a town but gives it credibility while enhancing the community's economic well-being.

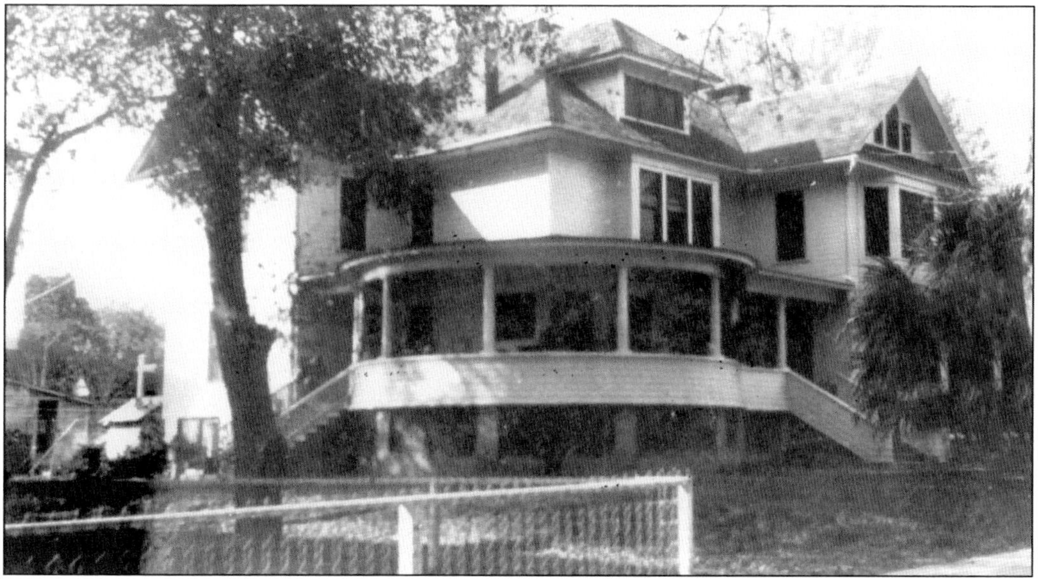

Verging Queen Anne and Colonial Revival, the Haynes Home, completed c. 1912, marked the transition between these two styles. Once located near the present-day DeLand Public Library on East Howry, the house, had it not been razed, would surely have been included among the numerous buildings recently rescued and restored in what is now DeLand's Garden District.

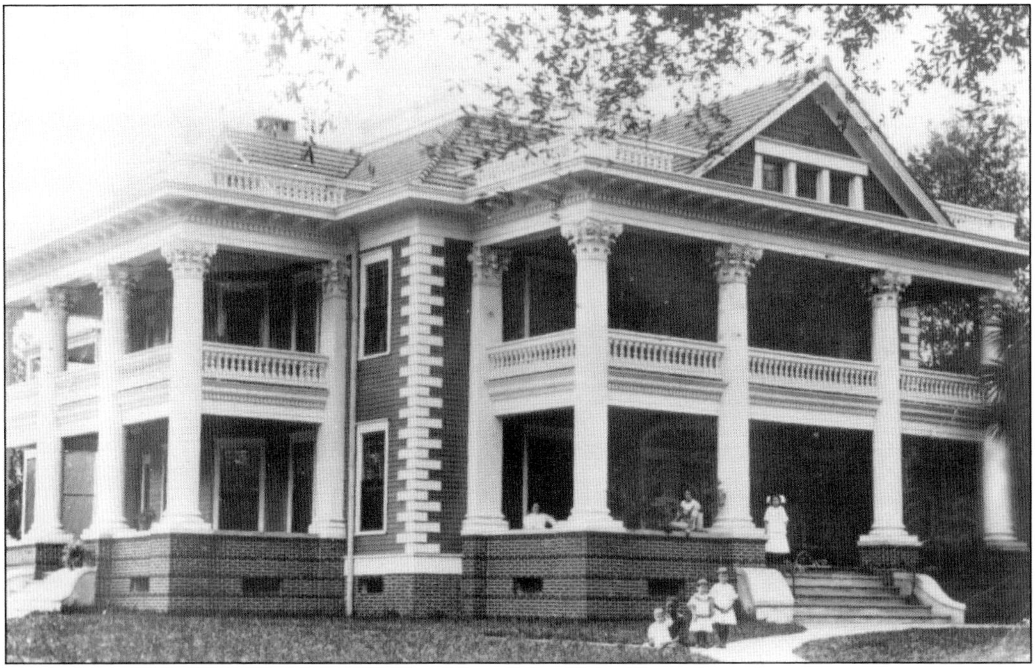

One of the largest Classical Revival buildings in Central Florida is located on West New York, the John Wesley Dutton House. It was completed in 1911 at a cost of $25,000 for its owner, a wealthy lumber magnate. Mr. Dutton spared no expense, as evidenced by the gargantuan composite Roman columns supporting the massive two-tiered porches and cornice-line balustrade that followed the roof line.

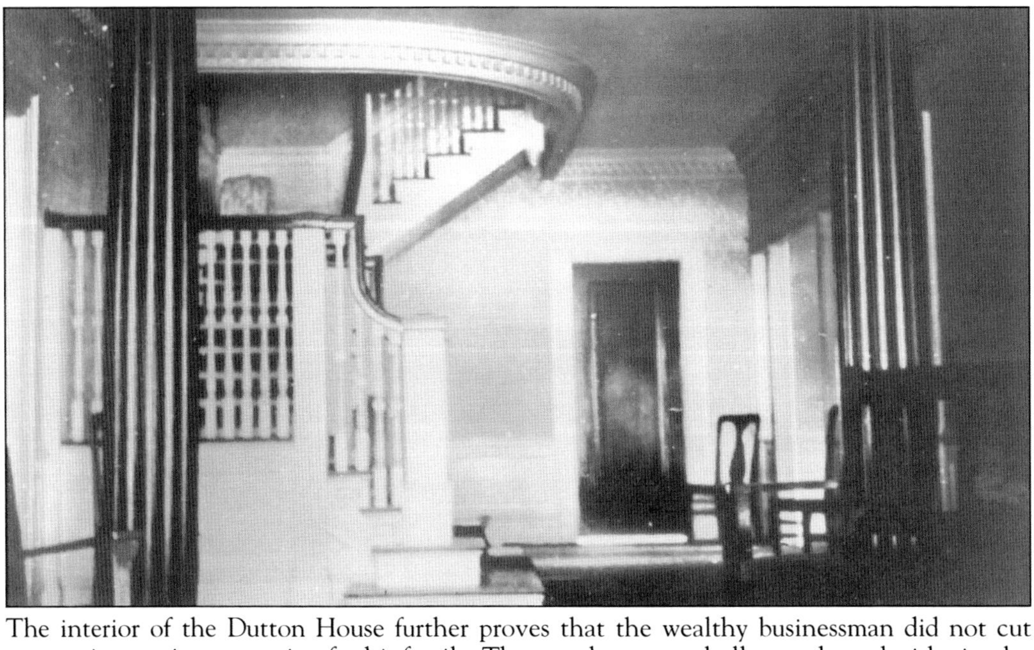

The interior of the Dutton House further proves that the wealthy businessman did not cut corners in creating a mansion for his family. The grand entrance hall was adorned with circular molding of dentils that emphasized the luxurious staircase. The tapered-round columns in the foreground were used throughout the house, signifying the extravagant nature of the place.

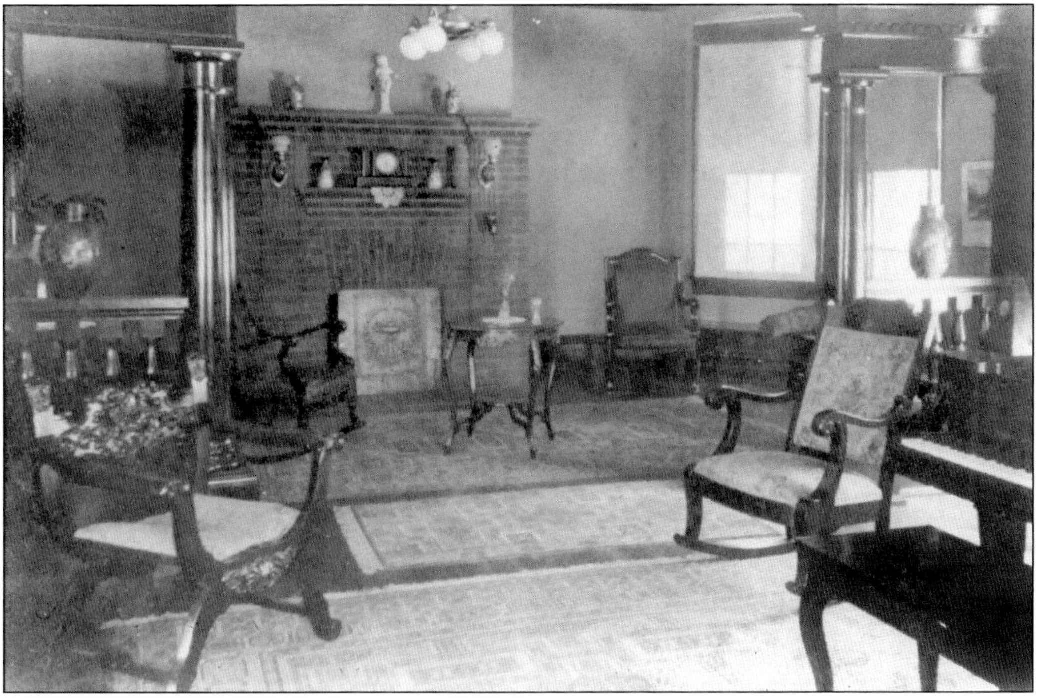

Another interior view of the Dutton House finds additional tapered-round columns and an elaborate fireplace with decorative wall sconces that hint at long-lost formal elegance. Over the decades the neglected house fell into extreme disrepair. Present-day restoration, thanks to a Florida Preservation Grant, promises to return this historic architectural gem back to its original splendor.

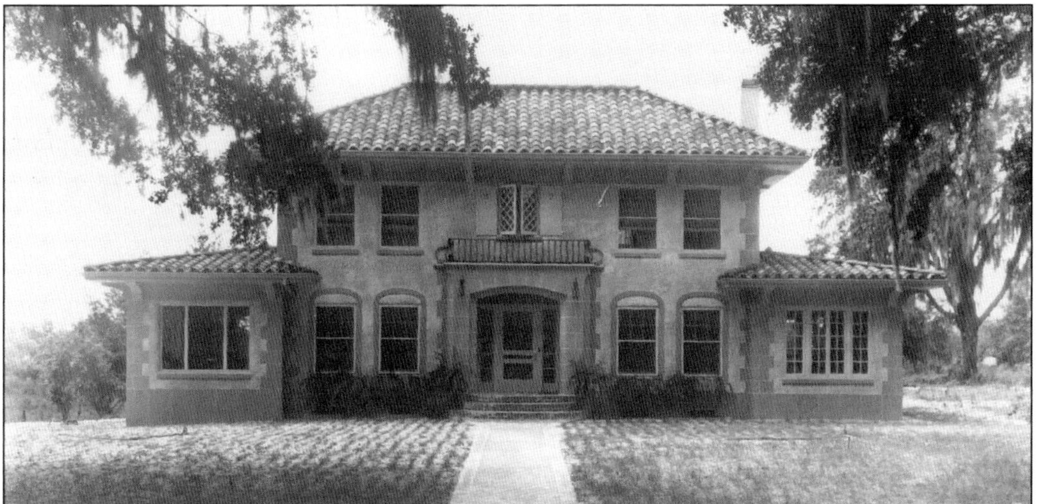

During Florida's "Boom Days" of the 1920s, local architect Charles Shawver designed and built several distinctive residences in DeLand. One was the Calvin Smith House, located at 518 East New York, and completed in 1925. Designed in the Italian Renaissance style at its peak popularity in the mid-1920s, the house has a tiled and hipped roof with projecting wings typical of the period. It remains today a testament to pride in design and ownership and the belief that the old is often far better than the new.

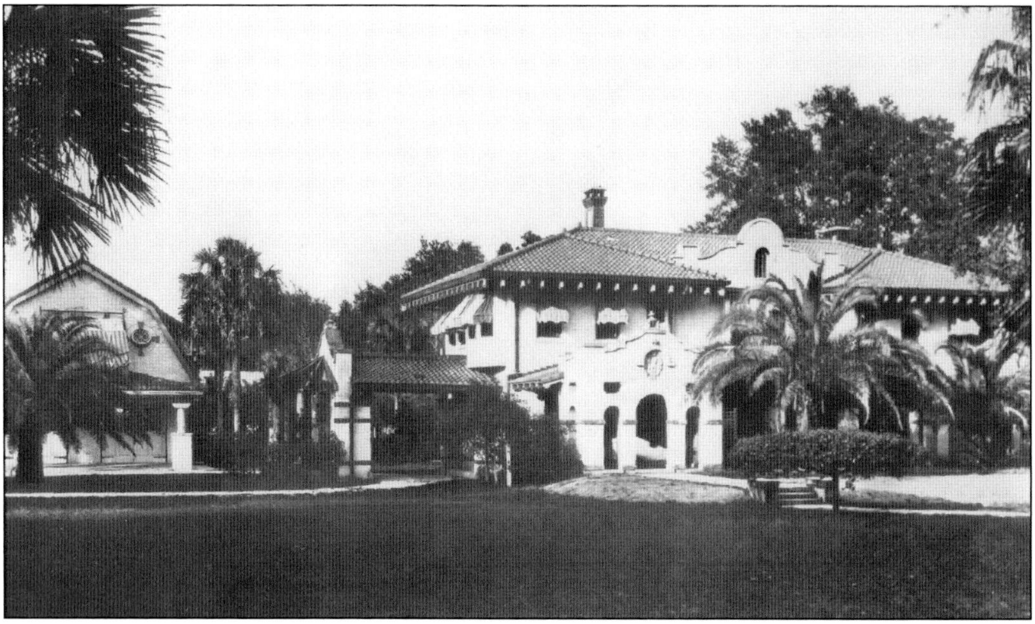

Another type of architecture popular during the 1920s was the Mission-style with its multi-leveled roof, widely overhanging eaves, stuccoed walls, and elegant parapets. Located on West New York, the owners of this home were the Bonds. This splendid building was demolished in order to enlarge the Catholic Church Complex. In retrospect, it would have added an historic dimension to the church's group of buildings.

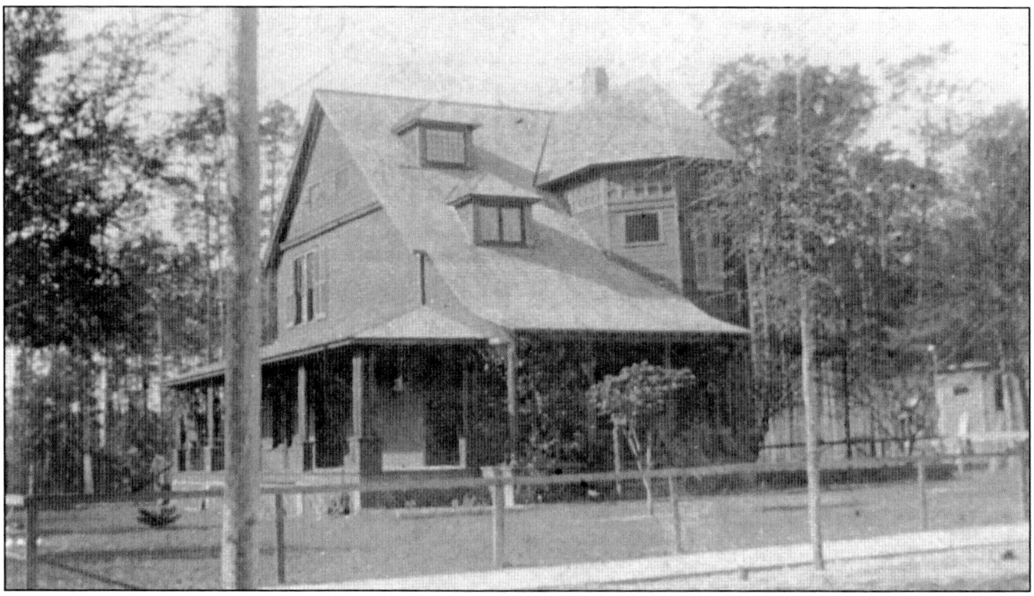

An excellent example of the Shingle design was found in the 1901 Anderson Home at 126 West Voorhis. This architectural style reached its highest expression in northeast seaside resort areas. The second owner was Hettie Austin, a DeLand pioneer and scribe for the Old Settler's Society until its dissolution in 1926. Her home has been tastefully restored even as her words live on through her loyal service and diligent journalist skills. Thanks to Hettie subsequent generations have a large portion of the history of DeLand preserved.

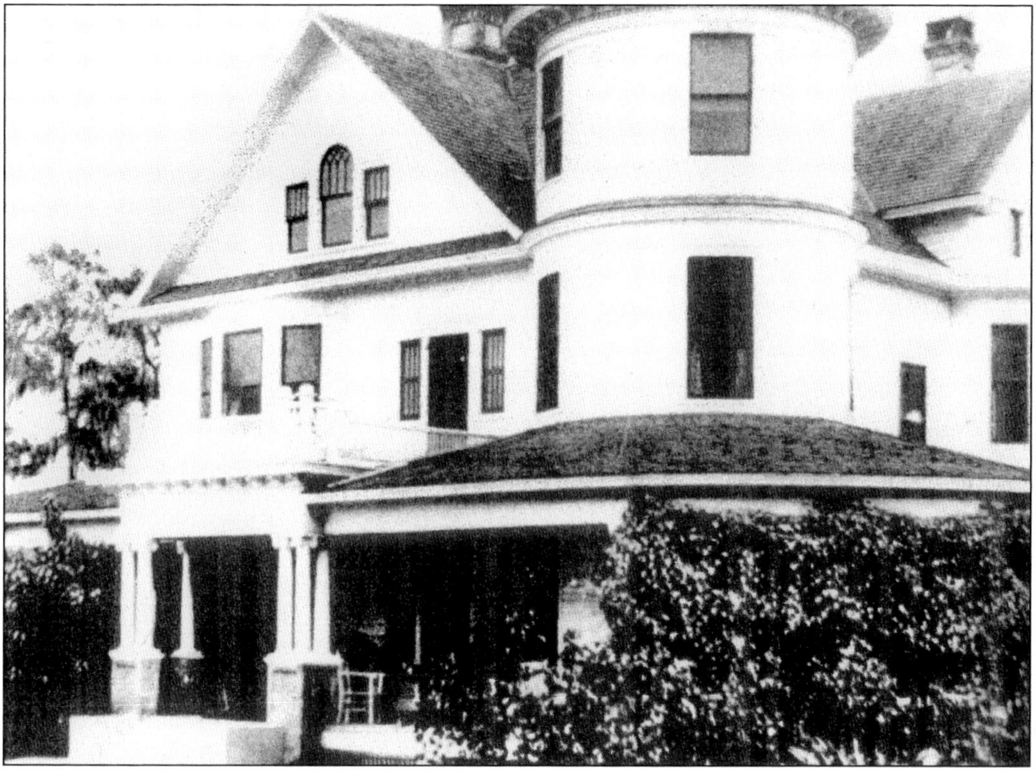

The H.W. Mercer House, c. 1910, was located on North Woodland Boulevard, standing majestic with its imposing tower. This elegant home was later purchased by Mr. Mercer c. 1920, a citrus and fern grower and owner of DeLand Hardware. The exterior of the house was of narrow clapboard and featured typical characteristics of the Queen Anne style. From the intricate pattern of brick texture on the chimneys to the pent roof that enclosed the gable and the second-story porch over the entryway, this home was a testimony to skilled craftsmanship. It, too, was demolished in the name of progress.

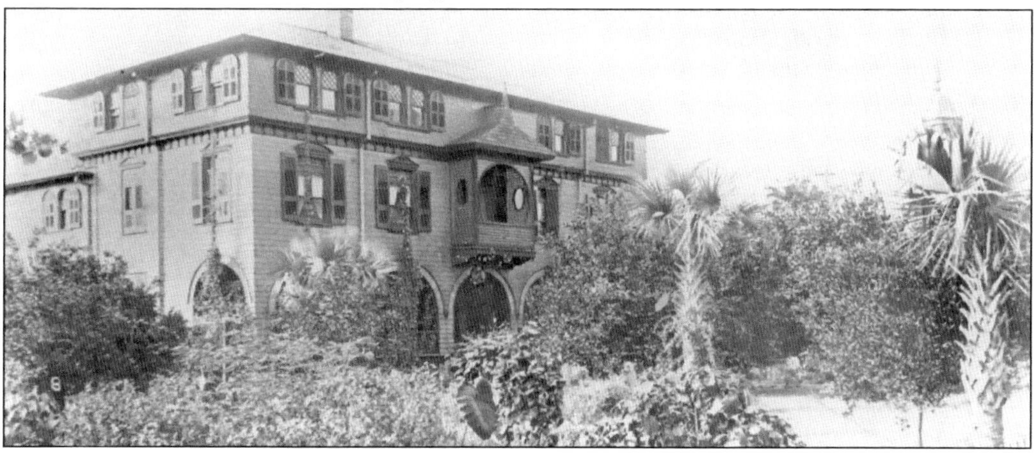

Another classic building lost to time was Holmes Hall, built in 1890 to house John B. Stetson University presidents. The architect was Mr. Clake who also remodeled the Hotel College Arms for Mr. Stetson. Holmes Hall was demolished in the early 1960s in order to construct the DuPont-Ball Library. Elizabeth Hall's cupola is seen at the far right.

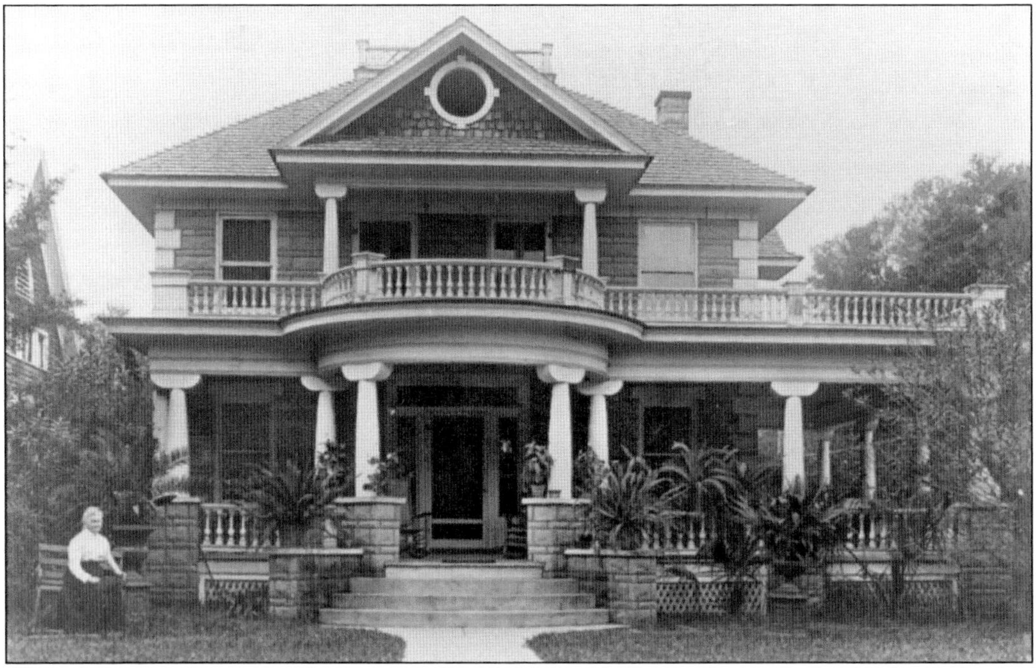

The Swift House, built c. 1915, was located where the Bank of America now sits. Massively constructed of the popular "art stone," this home was one of the focal points of downtown DeLand. Nestled amidst spiraling churches and business enterprises, the house and its occupants charmed all who passed by. One can just imagine the magnetism that drew neighbors and friends to its wide porch for a lively discussion or a glass of cool lemonade.

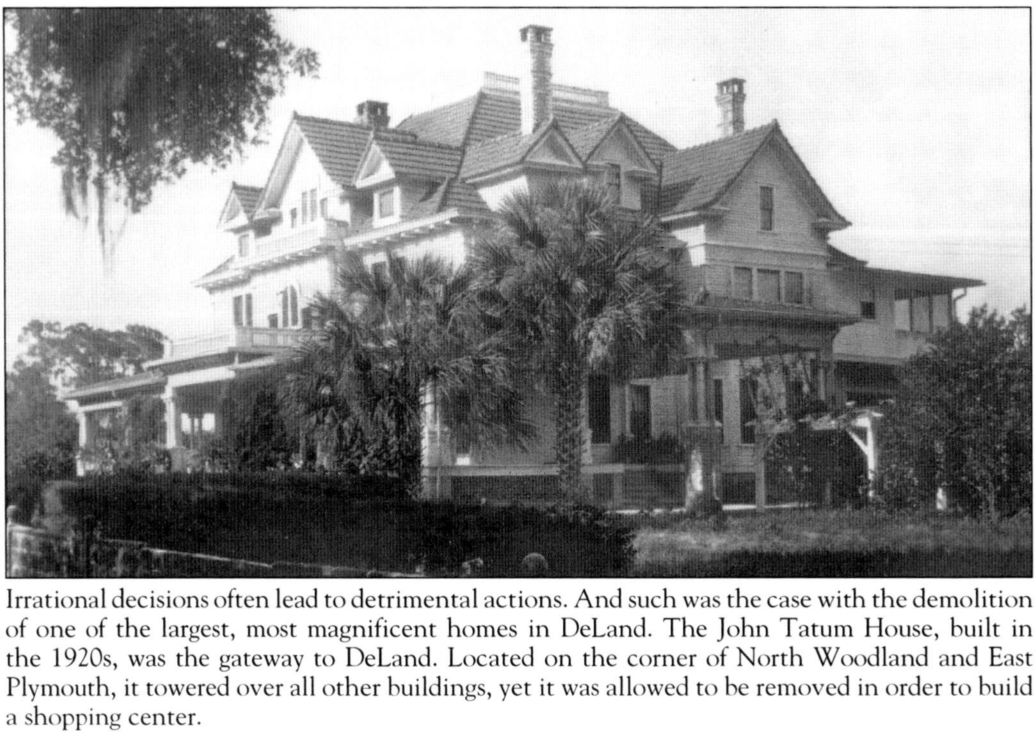

Irrational decisions often lead to detrimental actions. And such was the case with the demolition of one of the largest, most magnificent homes in DeLand. The John Tatum House, built in the 1920s, was the gateway to DeLand. Located on the corner of North Woodland and East Plymouth, it towered over all other buildings, yet it was allowed to be removed in order to build a shopping center.

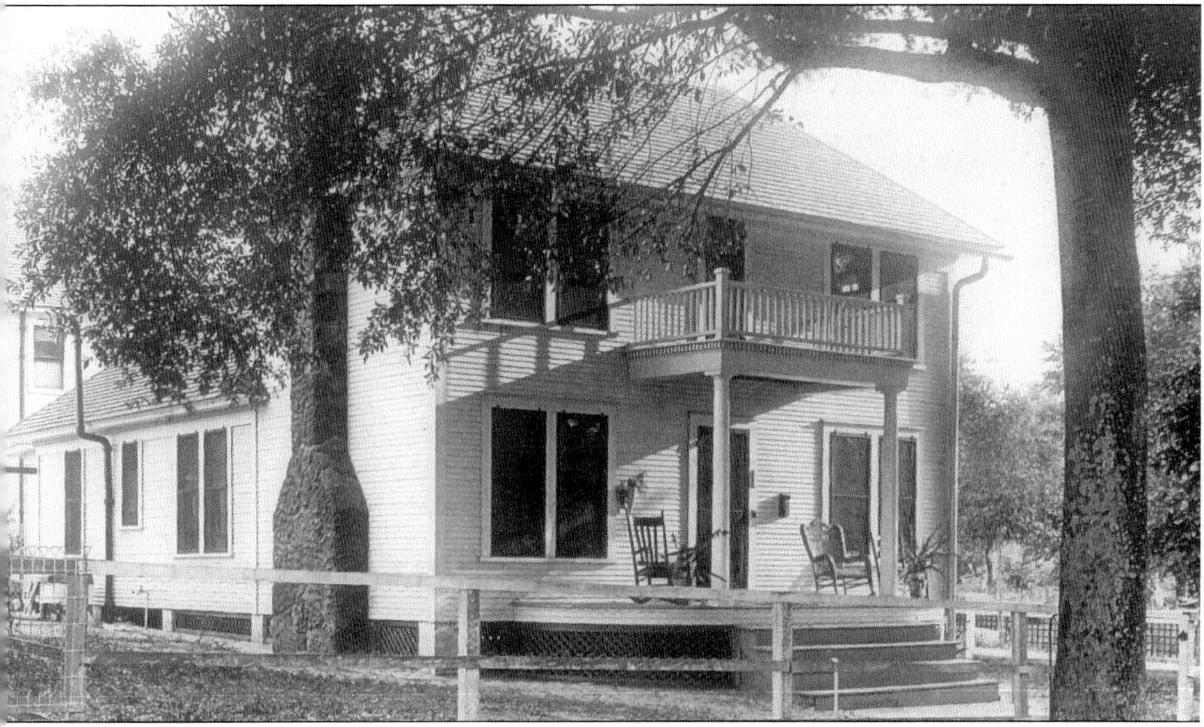

This 1910 clapboard jewel at 216 East Voorhis was, until the 1950s, in the heart of downtown residential living. There were a hundred such houses and small businesses surrounding it. Then things changed. Trees were felled, roads widened, and soon this little neighborhood became a drug-infested, crime-ridden, fearful spot, deserted by prosperous families. As time passed, it filled with the miseries of the living dead. Two blocks from town center this once thriving area festered with filth and neglect. Then things changed. In 2000 an urban renewal project was initiated by Maggi Hall, a preservationist and realtor. She encouraged property owners to let her sell their properties. When Hall advertised the project on the internet, Michael Arth, a California artist looking for a similar project, saw the advertisement and called. He wanted in. Working with Hall, Arth put in offers on nineteen buildings—no money down. The owners wanted out. The following summer Arth and wife, Maya, moved to "The Garden District," the name they chose for their new neighborhood. Christmas 2001, Sophia Arth became the first baby born in the Garden District in a former crack house on what had become one of the most notorious streets in town, "Crack Alley." Clean-up was contagious as the Garden District spread north, south, east, and west to encompass almost a hundred derelict buildings. Some, like Don Chase, improved their own homes. Arth brought in a partner, Dick McMahan. Hall sold properties to additional risk-taking visionaries: Rick and Jane Hutchinson, eight; Ron and Maggi Hall, five; Richard and Gena Swartz, Bill Mensinger, and Frank and Jane DuChaine, three; Janet Bollum, two; Howard and Renee Osterhouse, Charles Smith, John and Patti Murray, Thomas Creen, Richard and Heather Taracka, Pat Beuerlein, Justin and Erin Holder, Loren and Iris Seagert, and John Houser, one. Houser plans a bookstore. The Seagerts will open a coffee shop. Lisa Starks bought a vacant lot to build her law office. Rodney and Cheryl Floyd purchased land for a residence. The DeLand Police cleared the area of crime. The City replanted trees, repaired sidewalks, and plan an Intermodal Transportation System for bus, taxi, trolley, and parking. Alabama, intersecting the heart of the Garden District, connects Stetson University with DeLand's multi-million dollar recreational complex. The street will gain antique street lights, benches, a bike path, and a median planted with trees to shade future generations.

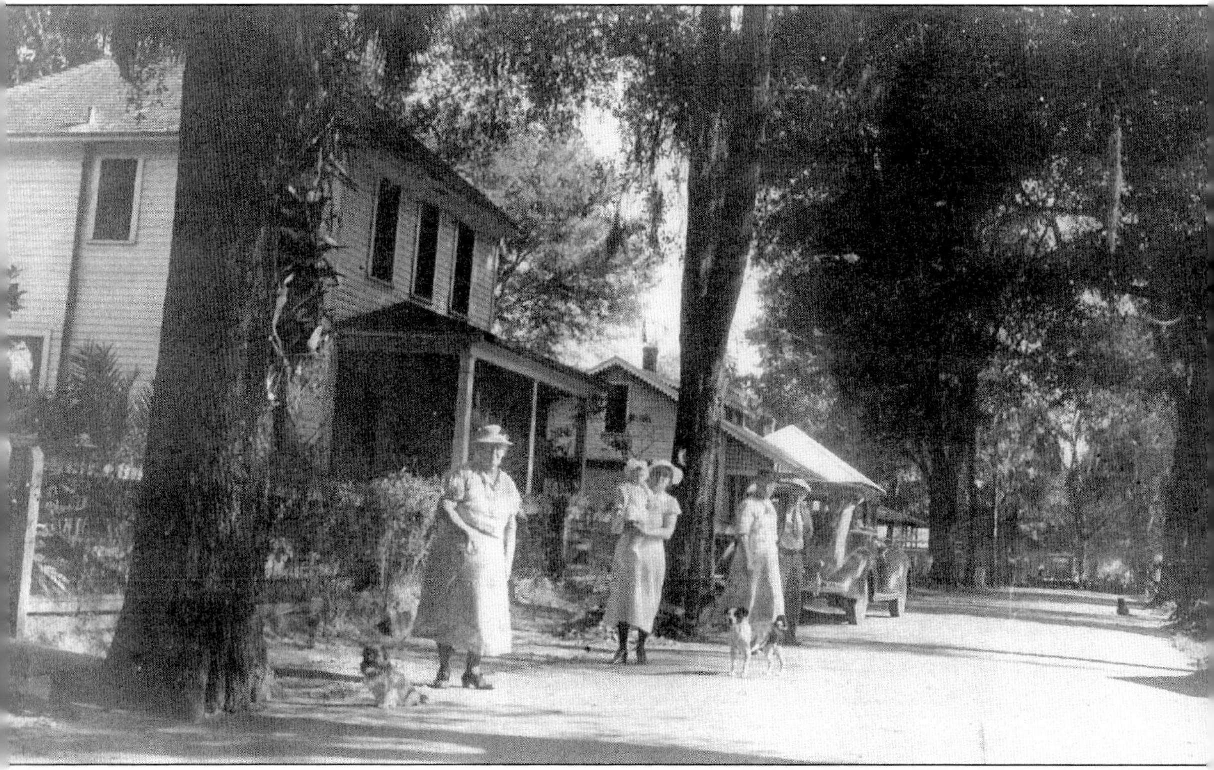

From the early 1900s until the 1950s, Hayden Avenue blossomed with families, pets, stylish homes, front porches, and trees. Forty years later the street is again blooming as part of DeLand's Garden District. Many of DeLand's architectural gems were lost due to negligence and greed. But gratefully somewhere along the way we finally halted the destruction of historic buildings as we came to realize that if we cannot save a building simply because it is beautiful, we can save it because it is economically feasible. Take time to stroll through Stetson University's campus and relish in the magnitude of architectural delights, a campus so unique that it is listed on the National Register of Historic Places. Visit Henry DeLand's 1883 Academy Building, completely restored, dazzling the center of campus. Then sing praises to University leaders who refused to follow the modern trend of removing rather than rehabilitating such gracious old buildings. And for the grand finale, head south to town center along Mr. DeLand's Boulevard, once again shaded by oaks. Gaze at building facades, appreciating the fact that most of what is there today was built a century ago. Stop in at one of the sidewalk cafes, pull a chair up to the table, order a cool drink, and contemplate the gifts that have been left for us to savor and to safeguard. Raise your glass to the Magnificent Seven—Dick Kelton, Mick Aleno, Steve Burley, John Gregory, Donna Lutz, Jim Stepp, and Jim West—whose diligent work created the MainStreet DeLand Association, and to Taver Cornett, who keeps this noteworthy organization on track as it steers preservation efforts. Take time also to toast the countless heroes who staunchly protect DeLand's downtown historic district—the merchants, the patrons, city officials, taxpayers, and tourists—even as insatiable expansion runs full throttle toward a collision with history. DeLand residents have proven that we can learn from lost designs and profit from new beginnings and in so doing protect our remaining architecturally significant buildings.

To those who chose the path of preservation over destruction, surely Henry Addison DeLand sends down his approval to each and every one.